Swoon

ALSO BY

BETSY PRIOLEAU

Seductress:

WOMEN WHO RAVISHED THE WORLD

AND THEIR LOST ART OF LOVE

Swoon

GREAT SEDUCERS

and

WHY WOMEN LOVE THEM

~

Betsy Prioleau

W. W. NORTON & COMPANY | NEW YORK LONDON

For information about permission to reproduce selections from this book,
write to Permissions, W. W. Norton & Company, Inc.,
500 Fifth Avenue, New York, NY 10110

For information about special discounts for bulk purchases, please contact
W. W. Norton Special Sales at specialsales@wwnorton.com or 800-233-4830

Manufacturing by Courier Westford
Book design by Barbara Bachman
Production manager: Louise Mattarelliano

Library of Congress Cataloging-in-Publication Data

Prioleau, Elizabeth Stevens, 1942–
Swoon : great seducers and why women love them / Betsy Prioleau. — First
Edition.
pages cm
Includes bibliographical references and index.
ISBN 978-0-393-06837-5 (hbk.)
1. Interpersonal communication in men. 2. Charisma (Personality trait) 3. Man–
woman relationships. 4. Men—Psychology. I. Title.
HQ1090.27.P75 2013
155.3'32—dc23
2012034643

W. W. Norton & Company, Inc.
500 Fifth Avenue, New York, N.Y. 10110
www.wwnorton.com

W. W. Norton & Company Ltd.
Castle House, 75/76 Wells Street, London W1T 3QT

1 2 3 4 5 6 7 8 9 0

To Philip

The Inspiration and The Man

Contents

—

Swoon

Great Seducers:

THE MEN, THE MYTHS

—

*A man without love's service is no better than
a wretched ear of corn.*
—PEIRE D'ALVERNHE, troubadour song

Almost all women have dreamed of "the great love."
—SIMONE DE BEAUVOIR, *The Second Sex*

Pembroke, a hamlet once known as Scuffletown (population 2,800), sits in the southeastern flatlands of North Carolina on Highway 711—home to the University of North Carolina Braves, the Lumbee Indians, the Berea Baptist Church, Dollar Tree, Papa Bill's Ribs, a nearby drag strip with wheelstanding contests, and one of today's hottest ladies' men. Jack Harris is a psychology professor at the university in his forties, with a buzz cut, Tidewater slur, and a vocation you don't see much anymore: women-charming. "As early as I can remember," he says over a beer, "there have always been women—in the attic, on Trailways, on Amtrak—who come on to me. What is it? Let me think . . . well, I kind of intuit what they need. I love them, I want to please them."

There are names for a man like Jack: roué, rake, ladykiller, Casanova, Don Juan, seducer, mack, babe magnet, and heart-fucker. In French he's called a *tombeur*; in Japanese, *ikemen*; in Russian, *krasavchik*; in Chinese, "color wolf"; in Spanish, *mujeriego*; in Portuguese, *mulherengo*; in German, a *Frauenjäger*. But he's a mystery man in any language, enveloped in a pall of myths, prejudices, and armchair theories. Who *is* this ladies' man, this sexy devil?

There's really no good name for him. A man who lights up women, adores them, and love-addles them for life defies all the familiar models: smooth players, hunks with big hoses, money lords, or any of the scientific/therapeutic versions of the alpha romancer. He baffles every ingrained image; he's the lover nobody knows.

Jack, for instance, fits no paradigm. "I've always found myself extremely average," he tells me. And it's true. He has a long, El Greco face and dresses in boondocks casual: short-sleeved shirt, no-brand jeans, rigger boots, and a gold crucifix around his neck. He's without rank, riches, power, resources, or the appeals of security and stability. (He left a tenured job in south Texas on a whim and admits he's pretty "volatile.")

As for seduction techniques: "I don't try to do it. I think it's instinctive. I'm just very comfortable around women. And," he drains his beer and crushes the can for emphasis, "I cannot make love to someone unless I have emotional feelings for them; I'm not the type to make a conquest and move on. I mean, the women who have broken my heart . . ."

This is the Mr. Irresistible of such renown? The man women chase down, covet, and can't forget decades later? Nothing computes. By all rights, Jack shouldn't be in the running, much less reeling in women right and left and fending off coeds with mash notes in their trembling hands.

For centuries, ladies' men like Jack have been locked in a stereotype, distorted and stigmatized beyond recognition. But feelings about them are deeply divided; they're both denounced and admired, censored and secretly cherished. They're walking projections of the forbidden—an amalgam of envy, suppressed wishes, and stifled passions.

They've also been silenced. If we let them have their say, though, we'll see a different man altogether—a complex, out-of-box charmer who smashes the "seducer" templates and redefines male allure. Despite the concept of an individual "love map," a unique Jack for every Jill, a few men have garnered the majority of women throughout history. In a 2004 cross-cultural DNA study, Dr. Michael Hammer and his colleagues at the University of Arizona found that certain males passed on the bulk of genes to the next generation. Women, he concluded, seem to have similar tastes; some men are consistently chosen over others—they're sexier, more fascinating, more *something*. A recent critic proclaimed that "there's no more to be said about [Don Juan]." But we've just begun.

What, for example, is that *something*? Where do such men get that voltage, that touch with women? How do they manufacture the magic—the spells to enamor and keep enamored whomever they fancy, whenever, wherever? Who are these enigmatic characters? For starters, we need to scrape off the accumulated layers of cultural debris from the canvas—the inherited superstitions, the mildewed myths and caricatures, the "scientific" biases and iffy theories—and see the real picture.

Ladykillers, be advised, come with a PG warning. They're not moral guardians, straight arrows, or docile house cats. They take us into X-rated territory and the dark corners of our psyche, and they aren't always politically correct. But they're a select fraternity who love women and enchant them. And they have some valuable wisdom; they're not only insanely attractive, charismatic, and forever lovable, they know one of the most fire-powered secrets: what women *really* want and how to deliver it.

First, let's cut through the myths.

The Satanic Seducer

Forbear, foul ravisher! Libidinous swine!
—BEN JONSON, *Volpone*

The evil ladykiller is the most familiar face of the seducer. With his sinister leer and lethal charm, he stalks through endless novels, poems, plays, and films, bringing ruin to the female sex. He is the prototype, writes critic Juliet Mitchell, for the most "unspeakable type of masculinity." A cold, calculating sexual profiteer whose goal is conquest and digits.

He's John Malkovich with his malefic drawl, the wicked lord who despoils hapless victims in French hotels and disappears into the night. He's the continental lover named Carlo your mother warned you about, a reptilian smoothie with dark designs and sadistic ploys. He comes in three colors: black, blacker, and blackest.

Historian Denis de Rougemont thinks there is something demonic about the ladies' man, an idea that goes back millennia. In 2400 BC Sumer, the seducer took the form of "Lilu," a night hellion who preyed on women in their beds and left them pregnant. He's the ancestor of the incubus, a nocturnal spirit of Western folklore, fond of sleeping beauties and neglected wives. Dante put the seducer in the eighth circle of hell, and John Milton portrayed him as Satan incarnate in *Paradise Lost*, snaking his way into Eden, ravishing Eve, and damning her to eternity.

The malevolent Don Juan has remained a fixture in the cultural imagination. From Lothario of the eighteenth-century play *The Fair Penitent*, who defiles the pure Calista, to the Romantic "fatal man," to Jacqueline Susann's *Love Machine* and television's Don Draper of *Mad Men*, this scourge of the female sex is everywhere. In Francesca Stanfill's modern novel *Shadows and Light*, a sophisticated socialite-artist is undone by a roué's perfidious machinations. Rap star 50 Cent is a recent spawn-of-Satan impersonator: "I'm into having sex, I ain't into making love /," he sings, " . . . the hoes they wanna fuck / But homie" won't be held down.

These reprobates pursue their calling for a host of warped purposes: power, domination, thwarted military ambition, lechery, and most of all, sheer misogyny. They loathe their female prey. Lovelace, the dissolute cavalier of Samuel Richardson's *Clarissa*, takes his hatred of women to the logical extreme and savagely rapes the heroine. Incapable of love, the licentious fiends view their "kills" as ciphers, nonpersons, and interchangeable objects in an endless carousel of partners.

Women don't stand a chance against the satanic rake. Sucked in by his stealth arts of deceit and trickery, they come to tragic ends. Their psyches shred and they spiral into illness, madness, and catatonia. Usually they go to an untimely grave or wind up, like Anna Karenina, in the path of an advancing train.

The Real Satanic Seducer

Undoubtedly there *are* heartless philanderers and cold-plotting rogues, but they aren't real ladies' men. An authentic woman-charmer doesn't despise his conquests or seek their destruction. "The professional seducer is an abominable man," Giacomo

Casanova insisted, "a true criminal who if he has the qualities required to seduce, renders himself unworthy of them by abusing them to make a woman wretched."

He himself is proof against the blackguard stereotype he has come to personify. An eighteenth-century Venetian adventurer and man of accomplishments—author, entrepreneur, violinist, scholar, diplomat, and bon vivant—Casanova was one of the world's greatest lovers. He admired and respected women and made their happiness his life's work. He treated them "as if they were his equals," writes a biographer, "and undress[ed] them as if they were his superiors."

Eager to please, he specialized in female pleasure, once delivering fourteen orgasms in a single session. Women were usually the aggressors, and none were abandoned and ruined; partings were by mutual consent. Instead of broken and suicidal, his partners were often better off afterward, materially and psychologically. He didn't keep score, cheat, or rack up huge numbers by today's standards (approximately 120 lovers over a lifetime), and he remembered his inamoratas with affection.

If anything, he was a fool for love. During the period of his grand amour, he nearly lost his mind and life. At twenty-four, he met the mysterious "Henriette," a Frenchwoman traveling incognito to escape her family, and fell "helplessly" in love with her. She was a wit, scholar, and accomplished musician, and they spent three idyllic months together without "a moment of ill-humour," or a "yawn." When her relatives finally caught up with her, she wrote on the windowpane of their Swiss hotel with the point of a diamond: "You will forget Henriette." But he could not, even as an old man.

After she left, he fled to a remote inn, refused to eat, and would have died if a stranger hadn't broken into his room and saved him. Sixteen years later he was near death once more when he next heard from "Henriette." Traveling through Aix, he became gravely ill. He found a nurse in his room each day for four months, compliments of his old love, now a marquise in a nearby chateau. She still loved him, she wrote, but refused to see him again, due to her changed appearance. She called him the "most honorable man I have known in this world." A far cry from the brutal rake of historical renown.

Casanova had his vices—gambling, petty cons, and vanity—but on balance he was a man of character and sensibility who was centuries ahead of his time. His mistake was being "born for the [opposite] sex," being too good at it, and incurring envy at every turn.

Ladykillers aren't pillars of virtue by any stretch, but they tend to fit the Casanova pattern. Rather than hackneyed, mustache-twirling stage villains, they're a mixed breed—men like French philosopher Albert Camus—who endear and magnetize women. As Camus noted, *he* was the pursued: "I don't seduce," he wrote in his journal. "I surrender." Nor do they coldly shuck conquests. They love deeply, can be faithful, and treat mistresses with respect, courtesy, and erotic genius. Rarely are women torn asunder and destroyed; they often come out ahead, and continue to love these ladies' men. With genuine "seducers," we're beyond the stock ravishers-of-women, in uncharted, complicated territory.

The Pathologic Woman-Pleaser

[The ladies' man represents a] clinical picture of
the perverse character.

—GAIL S. REED, *Psychoanalytic Quarterly*

With modernism, the seducer acquired another demonic persona. In this rendition, the ladies' man is more than just an amoral womanizer and sexual gangster, he is disturbed. Wired or raised wrong or both, he's fixated on women through an array of mental maladies. Although Freud (oddly enough) had nothing to say about the seducer, his successors wasted no time putting Casanova on the analyst's couch.

A Spanish doctor in 1927 labeled the ladykiller a male hysteric, while psychiatrist Otto Rank diagnosed him with a "mother complex" on an eternally thwarted quest for maternal possession. A later generation of psychologists targeted his narcissism, an abnormal self-absorption that prevented normal empathy and attachment. Jules Feiffer's antihero in *Harry, the Rat with Women* is a classic case, a "love monster" who panels his apartment with mirrors and answers a girlfriend's question, "What are you thinking about?" with "Myself."

The diagnoses get worse. The problem with ladies' men, contends Gregory Pacana in the *Philadelphia Mental Health Examiner*, is a "Casanova disorder," a subset of borderline personality disorder, which includes eleven symptoms ranging from social anxiety to mania. One twentieth-century psychiatrist described "Don Juanism" as "eroticism deformed into delirium." Today this goes by the name of sexual addiction and leads malefactors down "the Gentle Path" to a twelve-step program of enforced sexual abstinence, public penance, and group therapy.

An even graver psychiatric profile is the seducer as socio-path. These are romantic con men devoid of conscience who are masters of seduction and out for thrills and sexual pillage. At the criminal end of the spectrum, they are psychopaths—scary imposters, like thirty-six-year-old Michael Murphy. An inmate serving twenty-six years in a Montana jail, Murphy put his seductive talents to such effective use that he persuaded at least five female prison employees to have sex with him and grant other contraband favors. His therapist, who found herself kissing him in her office (and more), said, "I couldn't say no to him." And two guards sent him letters, one of which read, "I'm in love with you." The other is unprintable.

The Real Woman-Pleaser

Mental health, of course, is relative and exists on a continuum. Rare is the person who can withstand life's heavy weather with perfect poise. The ladies' men are no exception. They have their share of hang-ups and unhinged moments. Romantic poet and love idol Alfred de Musset suffered occasional nervous seizures, Casanova once contemplated suicide, and Richard Burton and Kingsley Amis were alcoholics. But as a group, they challenge the disease model of the seducer. Not infrequently, they belong to another category: the supernormal men of positive psychology. Most share some or all of the qualities of the actualized "healthy human specimen"—ego strength, vitality, resilience, authenticity, creativity, autonomy, nonconformity, personal growth, and the capacity to love.

In her revisionist study, psychoanalyst Lydia Flem puts Casanova in this class. He was sincerely infatuated by each of his lovers, sought in-depth relationships with them, and never ditched anyone. A striver and thriver, he lived with effervescence and "complete harmony between the mind and senses." He became a polymath and social adept befriended by Voltaire, Catherine the Great, and other leading lights.

Among these friends was a ladies' man of nearly the same caliber who has slipped into relative obscurity: Lorenzo Da Ponte. An *home du monde* and librettist of twenty-eight operas, including three of Mozart's, Da Ponte had an ability to charm that seemed "near-magical." Woman after woman succumbed to his fascinations, from two married Venetians to an Austrian innkeeper (who wrote "*Ich liebe Sie*" on a napkin at their first meeting), to "la Bella Inglesina," Nancy Grahl, who became his wife of forty years. At the time of his marriage to Grahl, he was broke, toothless, jobless, and twenty years her senior.

Like Casanova, a confrere of his youth, Da Ponte was a psychological high achiever, a man of stature who sparkled with élan and self-belief. He surpassed simple sanity; he was able to create, love deeply, evolve, and bounce back from adversity. Born Emmanuele Conegliano in 1749 in a Venetian Jewish ghetto, he came up the hard way. He was poor, motherless since age five, unlettered (his classmates called him the "Idiot"), and forced to convert to Christianity and change his name when his father married a young Christian girl. Pushed into the seminary, he became an ordained Catholic priest.

Da Ponte, however, beat the odds. He taught himself to write poetry and at age twenty-four fled the cloister for Venice, where he tutored and wrote sonnets on demand. He was magnetic and handsome—with an elegant aquiline nose, strong jaw, and flashing iridescent eyes. Women took notice. For four years he returned the compliment and played the cicisbeo to several signoras before being exiled by the Inquisitors for loose morals and seditious poems.

In Vienna he charmed Emperor Joseph II into appointing him poet to the court theater. There he collaborated with the greats, Mozart in particular, and became a celebrated librettist. As before, women descended. A "serial romantic," he was often in love, although he never said "'I love you' to a woman," he insisted, unless he meant it. He had a regular "sweetheart" for ten years who bore his son, and a "Calliope" who brought him "coffee, cakes, and kisses" whenever he rang a bell while he was writing *Don Giovanni*.

One inamorata rejected a surgeon's proposal too fervently for her lover's good; not only was the doctor ugly, she said, but she adored Da Ponte. The surgeon retaliated by prescribing nitric acid to Da Ponte for an abscess, so that all his teeth would fall out. Still women found him delectable. Always a fancier of strong mistresses, he had a last fling with a feisty diva, "La Ferrarese," until disaster struck; his patron, the emperor, died and enemies drove him from Vienna.

Soon after, he met and married the twenty-two-year-old linguist Nancy Grahl and moved to London without a shilling. He made shift as a bookseller and left for America with his wife in 1805—bankrupt and unconnected. A veritable "Phoenix," he reinvented himself in Pennsylvania and New York, tried a number of professions (including grocery-store owner), and lived to become a distinguished member of Manhattan society. He wrote his memoirs, helped found an Italian opera house, and finally taught Italian at Columbia University. In his late sixties, his fifty-eight schoolgirls "sighed for him in secret."

Admittedly, Da Ponte had issues; he was vain, quick to take offense, and overanxious to be liked. But a Casanova with a complex he was not. More than symptom-free, he thrived amid hardship and took the high road to a replete, creative identity. He is of a piece with many great lovers—men like Denis

Diderot, Prince Grigory Potemkin, and Benjamin Franklin—
adored precisely for their expansive selfhood, ability to rebound
from tragedy, and raging life spirits.

The Darwinian Alpha Male

Displays of power and abundant resources work
in any epoch.

—REUBEN BOLLING "Tom the Dancing Bug," *Salon*

"Surely," say the mating biologists, "no one has seriously
doubted that women desire wealthy, high-status men." This
image of the ladies' man comes to us courtesy of evolutionary
psychology. Since it carries the imprimatur of science, the
Darwinian beau ideal has become an established dogma in
relationship circles.

Surprisingly, though, the whole alpha male theory is based
on a thought experiment of dubious validity. Projecting into the
deeps of prehistory, psychobiologists speculate that the earliest
women—vulnerable and beleaguered—sought power males to
protect them from the elements, support progeny, and provide
superior genes. Over eons, these scientists argue, the preference
for such men became soldered into the female libido, creating a
permanent sexual "fix." As a result, women instinctively gravi-
tate to the guy who supplies the best survival benefits and DNA.
His qualities vary among scientists, but nearly all agree on the
big four. Evolutionary psychologist David Buss sums them up:
1) money and status; 2) stability and fidelity; 3) kindness and
compatibility; and 4) physical superiority.

The first premise of male sex appeal, wealth and prestige,
has the widest cultural currency. A ladykiller without rank and

riches is practically an oxymoron. Almost every mating authority, from Dr. Helen Fisher to Dr. Phil, subscribes to it. "A high-status male," writes biobehaviorist Donald Symons, "is both the best choice for a husband and for a sex partner." Propelled by the sugar-daddy dictate, men battle their way up the social ladder and flash credit cards the way lightning bugs flash photons. It's "basic": swells get the babes; they have the adaptive edge—resources and top-of-the-line sperm.

Security is another article of faith. Women, say neo-Darwinians, want "dependable" men—faithful, committed, and "emotionally stable." Their dream man, declares Richard Dawkins in *The Selfish Gene*, is a "good, loyal domestic type." With infants under foot and saber-toothed tigers at the door, our female ancestors didn't need mercurial mates and gadabouts on the premises. By Darwinian logic, a woman would be crazy not to put her heart in the service of a homebody, a protector who can be counted on to hold down the fort and stick around.

Compatibility and decency are equally seductive. In unsettled times—tribal warfare, treks over ice scarps, and the struggle for provisions—the dark stranger signaled potential danger and difficulty. Hence the female preference for a nice man from the same tribe, someone with similar views, customs, tastes, and opinions. Commonality, claim scientists, confers an evolutionary payoff: domestic cooperation, less strife, and longer relationships, all of which accounts for the guy-next-door allure.

Then there is beauty and brawn, the quintessence of male sex appeal. From an evolutionary perspective, women are predestined to go for taut beefcakes who telegraph protection and beautiful babies. Sociobiologist Bruce Ellis belabors the point: "For women the world over, male attractiveness," he writes, "is bound up with strength . . . and prowess." Ladykillers, by selective right, are tall, buff, and handsome with biceps like Smithfield hams and bulging crotches.

The Real Alpha Male

Science popularizers never tire of saying that "from a biological standpoint we're still prehistoric." If so, ladies' men hail from another prehistory. The kind of men who consistently enrapt women call the whole Darwinian alpha model into question.

Gabriele D'Annunzio is typical. One of the most compelling figures of the fin de siècle Europe, he was a noted Italian poet, novelist, politician, war hero, and ladykiller. "The woman who had not slept with him," said a Parisian *salonnière*, "became a laughing stock." Women found him devastating. They trailed him around Europe like frenzied maenads, pouring out passionate declarations, abandoning families, and twice offering a fortune for his favors. The international stage diva "La Duse" never got over her "Apollo."

With D'Annunzio, Apollo doesn't come immediately to mind. Proof against evolutionary progress, he was a sad physical specimen—short, bald, and "ugly," with "unhealthy" teeth, fat legs, wide hips, hooded eyes, pallid lips, and thick mottled skin.

Nor did he radiate "strong provider" appeal. He was nearly always in debt and went spectacularly bankrupt midcareer, losing all his possessions, including his thirty greyhounds, in a ten-day auction. When he first arrived in Rome, he was a nonentity without pedigree, reputation, money, or connections. Men of his sort weren't "received." Yet due to his impact on women, he breached high society and bore off the daughter of a duchess—three months pregnant. Despite his mistreatment of his aristocratic wife, she loved him to the end and came to look after him in his old age.

Instability was his middle name. Chronically unfaithful and forever in transit, he lived from caprice to caprice. Women, however, were undeterred. Not only did Eleonora Duse endure his affairs, but she once dispatched him into the arms of a rival. "Look, look, since you love him," she declaimed to a houseguest, "there he is!" and discreetly closed the door. Another rival refused to go quietly. A Russian marchesa confronted La Duse after a tryst with D'Annunzio, drew a gun, and tossed it "from hand to hand" until the diva packed her bags and left. La Duse tried "in vain to forget her great love" for the rest of her life.

D'Annunzio was also impulsive and labile, subject to rash moves and buying binges. After one of his sprees, he rhapsodized, "I have a need for the superfluous . . . divans, precious fabrics, Persian carpets, Japanese china, bronzes, ivories, trinkets, all those useless and beautiful things." Ever undependable in a crisis, he fled from women when illness and tempests struck.

He was not the brotherly type. D'Annunzio was a man of enigma and exotic otherness with bizarre habits (quill pens and clerical robes), mysterious haunts (a baroque monastic hideaway), and a penchant for remarks such as "green mouths of the sirens suck my voluptuous blood." Instead of a guy next door, he was the guy from the next galaxy, a self-described "sorcerer."

Sorcerers aren't known for fair play, and D'Annunzio disported above bourgeois morality. Although gentle and generous when he chose, he could misbehave. But no one could beguile, spoil, and transport women like D'Annunzio. He was "the most remarkable lover of [his] time," "a ladies' man before whose exploits the most dashing Don Juan must bow his head in admiration."

Like D'Annunzio, few ladykillers fit the neo-Darwinian bill. There *are*, of course, rich, handsome, famous, kind, and stable ladies' men. But something else accounts for their erotic firepower. Starving artists and working-class nobodies fill the ranks of great lovers. Stolid guardians of the hearth and wholesome, known-forever men also belong but don't predominate—far from it. Casanovas aren't always pinups either. A guy can have belt overhang, bat ears, mini-genitals, dewlaps, and bad skin and still be the most desirable man on the planet. It takes more, much more than evolutionary psychology imagines, to enthrall women.

The Player Seducer

Women aren't attracted to wussies.

—DAVID DE ANGELO, *Double Your Dating*

Dating coach and radio host Payton Kane has a promise for all the lonely men out there: his "Makeover Team can turn ANY regular guy into a Ladies Man within 4 hours!" The ladykiller who emerges from this transfiguration is one of the most pervasive versions of the nouveau Casanova. He's the gamer, the player, the pickup artist—the PUA. Popularized by Neil Strauss in his 2005 bestseller, *The Game*, and dozens of online dating gurus, he's a lowbrow incarnation of neo-Darwinian machismo. The operating premise is that a master lover is a top gun who takes down women with a repertoire of paramilitary maneuvers: bravado, flak, and precision strikes. By Casanovan standards, the goal is modest: not to get loved (another league) but to get laid.

The heart of the player system is the dominance display. Unless you're a "tribal leader," you won't get the girl, exhorts high-priest "Mystery," a goth-boy figure in a shag-carpet hat and black nails. Swagger into a bar, he instructs, act like "the prize," and let the ladies know who's boss. This entails a broadside of wisecracks and sarcastic "negs" such as "How do you rate in bed?" followed by "You're now downgraded from booty call # 1 to # 10."

Closing the deal is as scrupulously plotted as Operation Overlord. Often with the help of a "wingman," a "seductionist" softens the target with "trance words" (sensual triggers like "blow" and "job" and "pleasure") and an onslaught of praise and scorn. It's as effective, claims Mystery, as a sharp snap of a dog leash.

When the mark tosses her hair and smiles, the time comes for "kinos," strategic touches on the thigh, waist, and breasts. Finally, a "Venusian Artist" isolates the girl, kisses her, gets her number, and leaves as though he has better things to do. Later, he calls with a "sex location" in mind, and goes in for the kill. Boasts "Extramask" in a field report: I "slammed her hard."

Throughout this seduce-and-conquer campaign, the ladies' man keeps his counsel and shuts down emotionally. A PUA learns "to eliminate desire" (as the womanizer Dex advises in the film *The Tao of Steve*) and to conceal feelings if they do intrude. Seducers stay cool, deflect the L-word, and realize in a pinch "there's always another woman." In their case, there *is*; the "hits" they describe are interchangeable numbers (graded 6 to 10). They are usually a desperate lot—strippers, bored housewives, model wannabees, and stray singletons who haunt dance clubs.

Gamer convert Neil Strauss says he studied with pickup artists for two years to "become what every woman wants—not what she says she wants, but what she really wants." But he went to the wrong school. Real-world enchanters provide a different message as well as a different grade of woman from Strauss's sad assortment of teenage waitresses, exotic dancers, and ladies with "porn star" skills.

The Real Seducer

Prince Aly Khan would be the envy of any gamer. Known as the "Golden Prince," Khan was a marquee name in the 1950s: international playboy, decorated soldier, sportsman, philanthropist, UN vice president, spiritual leader of twenty million Ismaili Muslims, and lover of the *crème de la crème*. Said one: "You weren't in the swim and you were really *déclassé, démondé*, nothing, you hardly counted if you'd not been to bed with Aly." He famously seduced "Love Goddess" Rita Hayworth away from her husband, and married her at a gala wedding with the swimming pool filled with two hundred gallons of eau de cologne.

Khan, though, repudiated the player credo. He "threw away the rule book and played the game by instinct." Instead of cool and cocky, he was gallantry personified and put himself out to please women. He was modest and discreet about his conquests, which outstripped a PUA's wildest dreams. Unspectacular in dress and looks (a sallow complexion and receding hairline), he radiated "sweetness," "softness," and "disarming humility."

When he wanted a woman, he disdained battle plans, dominance displays, and feigned indifference. He came on strong. Lovers said he singled them out of the crowd at parties and made a beeline for them. Once at Ascot, he turned his back on the horserace and stared at his soon-to-be mistress in the bleachers the whole time. On another occasion, he said to a dinner partner he had just met, "Darling, will you marry me?" The Honorable Joan Guinness, wife of the brewer mogul, promptly divorced her husband and did.

Laconic put-downs weren't his style. French chanteuse and film star Juliette Gréco believed flattery was Khan's forte. On their first date, she recalled, he ego-massaged her in a "charming, very special way." He focused exclusively on her, her interests and career, never glancing at the parade of glamour girls who walked past their table. He made her feel like a "queen." To take a woman down a peg would have struck Khan as gauche and puerile; he invested in the aphrodisiac of applause—compliments, undivided attention, and strokes.

Although his liaisons were many, Khan was always "madly, deeply" in love—however briefly—and wore his heart on his sleeve. Rather than masking his feelings, he made a pageant of them. As soon as he saw Rita Hayworth, he gasped, "My God! Who is that?" and launched a siege on her affections. He hired a new chef, overhauled his chateau (even down to new table linens), and called her around the clock until she agreed to come for lunch.

Afterward he sent her three-dozen red roses from Cannes every day. The phone calls accelerated with solicitous inquiries: How did she feel? Did she need anything? Eventually she needed *him*, and soon they were a couple, off to romantic holidays in Paris, London, and Spain. His hotel rooms, though, weren't "C3 locations," as gamers call them; Khan was a sexual artist, intent first and foremost on a woman's satisfaction. "He made women feel marvelous."

Every fascinator worth his women, from antiquity to the present, refutes the player model; he works it another way. Even Jack Nicholson, the mascot of cool, is a "sentimental guy" who courts women with ga-ga flattery, exuberance, and open lust and vulnerability. Great lovers handle women with a velvet touch, not a war manual.

The Therapy Heartthrob

Just What the Love Dr. Ordered.

—VERONICA HARLEY, "Best Relationship Books," AOL

Another distortion of the ladies' man persona is the "Mr. Wonderful" of couples' therapy—the flip side of the player. Instead of a tough hombre with Machiavellian schemes, this epitome of male sex appeal has been sensitized, civilized, and customized for a postfeminist generation. He's an Identi-Kit creation, a composite of the therapeutic ideal. Liberated and omni-competent, he's empathic, housebroken, companionable, mature, and well behaved. And with sufficient counseling, he can be mass-produced.

On paper, he sounds like every woman's fantasy. Women, he realizes, are frazzled and overworked and crave sustenance. A one-man support system, he supplies whatever is required: groceries, tile regrouts, car inspections, and shiatsu massage. He ministers to the inner woman as well. At Dr. John Gottman's "love laboratory" in Seattle, men learn to communicate, express feelings, listen, and validate.

This love-coached ladies' man also learns to be a fair fighter. When the fat hits the fire, he is the soul of compassion and calm. Through careful self-monitoring, he avoids "flooding" and responds nondefensively in order to defuse the argument. Rephrase her complaints, counsels Gottman, compromise, conciliate, and never stonewall; "choose to be polite." As Dr. Phil advises, he works hard, "like you would on any project."

In the boudoir he is equally conscientious. Couples' guides supply copious help with horizontal skills, how-tos as detailed as flight manuals that itemize mechanics from A to Z. Foreplay looms large, beginning with careful preparation of mood—music (playlists included), bubble baths, and candles—followed by at least "twenty-one minutes or more of foreplay." Sex itself should be minutely choreographed—toys on hand, positions mastered, and a rolling inventory of mattress moves.

The Real Heartthrob

The counselors' Casanova has a lot of things going for him; he checks every box. A woman could do worse than have such a to-spec lover in her life, a hassle-free mate who gets it right and lends a hand. His creators mean well. The only drawback is desire. The therapists' ladykiller has been built by rational design, without regard for eros, the unruly life force. The men who inspire and keep grand passions aren't practical, paint-by-the-numbers products from a relationship lab.

Lord Byron, the British nineteenth-century poet, patriot, and romantic icon, would have been a love coach's nightmare. Irreverent, moody, and hot-tempered, he violated nearly all the therapy sanctities. Yet he was "quite simply, irresistible." More than a rock-star poet who caused a tsunami of female fans—a Byronmania—he won the undying adoration of innumerable women throughout his life.

Hardly helpmate material, Byron trailed an aura of wanderlust and foreign adventures, decked out in a wardrobe of Albanian turbans and Turkish pantaloons. And he looked only half-civilized. "Once seen" and never "forgotten," Byron had the chiseled face of an antique Bacchus, with "wild" blue eyes, a full sensuous underlip, and a high forehead strewn with dark, flyaway curls.

His club foot and chronic limp played on female sympathies, and women nurtured *him* instead of the other way around. They copied his poems, lent money, monitored his health, and coddled him like a maharajah. The role of male caretaker left him cold. Three months into his marriage, he informed his wife, "What on earth does your mother mean," he announced, "by telling me to take care of you? I suppose you can take care of yourself."

Communication—couples' therapy style—wasn't his strong suit. Although in touch with his feelings (he wept easily) and capable of long intimate talks with beloved women, he had a mixed record as an amorous communicator. He toggled between endearments and sarcasms with his mistress Lady Caroline Lamb, and treated his new wife to a crossfire of tender confidences and cruel outbursts.

Conversation was another matter. When he chose to, he could be adorable. Talking in a mellow baritone with a lisp, he entranced women with his gay, playful badinage and verbal pyrotechnics. "His laugh is musical," gushed Lady Blessington in her memoirs, and his manner of speaking "very fascinating."

A fight with Byron, though, was a bad idea. There was no hearing the other side, no dousing the flames with the balm of understanding and sober restraint. He once handled a spat with his wife by hurling a clock to the floor and smashing it to bits with a poker. Lady Caroline Lamb was driven to such desperation by his silent treatment in a quarrel that she threatened him with a dinner knife at a London ball, then stabbed her hand and dashed bleeding from the room.

He may not have always been a sexual standout either. Stories abound of his exploits and of the women unable to stay out of his bed, like Mary Shelley's stepsister, Claire Clairmont, who begged to spend the night with him, succeeded, and followed him to Italy for more. But he treated his wife on occasion with a lack of finesse—deflowering her without ceremony on the sofa before the wedding and taking her *a tergo* by surprise one night. Despite all this—his therapeutically incorrect behavior and complex, uncooperative nature—Byron was a "loveable man," swamped by women and cherished by them. His wife rolled hysterically on the floor in an "agony of regret" when they parted; Caroline Lamb never fully recovered and grew ill after he died at thirty-six. His last mistress of five years, Countess Teresa Guiccioli, made a pilgrimage to pray at his grave, and as a Parisian hostess in her fifties she placed a portrait of Byron in her salon before which she said to anyone who would listen, "How beautiful he was! Heavens, how beautiful!"

Ladies' men rarely meet relationship doctors' standards. They are off the therapeutic drawing board. Modernist painter Willem de Kooning, for example, was uncommunicative and wrapped up in himself and his work—a "little boy" who required a succession of female nurturers. Yet he was a sex-meteor of the art scene, a delicious lover who "let women come to him."

Many Casanovas flunk the fight test too. Frank Sinatra had a short fuse and an anger-management problem. He raved, broke the furniture, and once in a fury, fired a gun into the mattress. But nothing stopped the female stampede. Said Ava Gardner, his second wife, "I wanted to punch him, but forgave him in about twenty-five seconds."

Nor are great seducers by the book in bed. Casanova tailored each tryst to the lady's taste and brought raw, unscripted lust to the bedroom. The "amazing lover" Jack Nicholson focused less on technique than creative whoopee in the rack: whole-hog fun, nude gambols in the kitchen, and dedication to a woman's "total pleasure."

Relationship counselors concede that they can't manufacture passion. Their goal is companionate accord, grown-up, workable, peaceful coupledom. Their ladies' man is a careful-what-you-wish-for artifact—a sexless android programmed for a stressed, overtaxed female population. The therapy model has also been constructed in the absence of evidence—actual Casanovas, the real hot hands with women.

Counterfeit Ladies' Men

Besides the overt stereotypes—the satanic seducer, Darwinian stud, player, and couples' therapy heartthrob—there is a subtler, more ubiquitous distortion of the ladies' man: the media-spun love god so often mistaken for the genuine article. *People* magazine's annual "Sexiest Man Alive" issue with its cover men and breathless captions ("Star Leaves Women Saying 'Oh . . . My . . . God!'") may be good public relations, but it's an unreliable guide to ladykillers. Who knows if George Clooney or Matthew McConaughey is a great lover? Both are sleekly packaged products of the studio system, mirage men designed to sell movies and TV series. In fact, Valentino was a dud as a lover, and Cary Grant, who lived for years with Randolph Scott, was probably gay. John F. Kennedy, on inspection, bombed in bed, objectified women, and preferred the company of men.

Some so-called ladies' men, like matinee idol Errol Flynn, were twisted beyond romantic redemption. His epic dissipations effectively canceled out his beauty, sexual prowess, and allure.

He not only had dark dealings with Nazi criminals and the New Guinea slave trade, he treated women (and boys) like "bog paper," preyed on underage girls, and engaged in such pranks as masturbating into an omelet he was preparing for guests.

Other famed "seducers" of history fail the grade for the same reason. The boorish seventeenth-century Lord Rochester died at thirty-three of drink, debauch, and syphilis; the marquis de Sade glutted his jaded appetite with near-death flagellations of destitute *poules*; and painter Modigliani battered and abused women, tearing a lover's dress apart in public, throwing another through a closed window, and boasting to the concierge that he was just "beating [his] mistress like a gentleman."

Real Ladies' Men

With so many false images of the ladies' man obscuring the picture, it's no wonder we can't see him straight. Once we clear away the accumulated myths and cultural baggage, we can get a truer look at this great seducer. Women love him for a reason: he adores them and their society and knows what they yearn for and rarely get. Although hardly an Eagle Scout, he's not close to his stereotypes, negative or otherwise. He transcends easy generalizations and defeats categories—the angel/devil, wuss/ he-man polarities—and personifies complexity.

Ladykillers run the gamut. They include every conceivable breed and condition of man. Spanning the social spectrum, they range from blue-collar Romeos with pinkie rings to polo-playing plutocrats. In personality they can be flamboyant extroverts like twentieth-century conductor Leopold Stokowski or bookish introverts like Aldous Huxley. Age has little bearing: Casanova and pianist Franz Liszt were as devastating to the female sex at age sixty as they were at sixteen. And no profession, from diplomats, generals, and financiers to freelancers of all stripes—artists, actors, cab drivers, and *flâneurs*—is exempt.

Heartbreakers encircle the globe and extend throughout history. They go back at least as far as King Gilgamesh of Sumer in 4000 BC (so ravishing, the sex goddess tried to bribe him into bed), and continue until the present. Seemingly a universal archetype, they turn up everywhere: east, west, on the steppes of Russia, and in the south side of Chicago.

Preferences *do* fluctuate. The Romantic era, for example, favored melodrama in its ladies' men—tears, duels, operatic declarations, and histrionics—while the 1990s fancied irony and sophistication. A woman's proclivities may change too over a lifetime, with a penchant for authority and experience in youth and all-stops-out frolics later on.

Yet despite these fluctuations of erotic taste and the wide variety of men, Casanovas share an unusual cluster of similarities, both in personality and amorous artistry. Again and again, the same qualities resurface, whether at the court of Louis XV or a twenty-first-century singles' bar. They're not bulleted in any ladykiller literature; they're one of the best-kept secrets among men who bewitch women.

With a few tools and clues, we can try to crack these secrets. We'll find some specimens—ladies' men past and present—and subject them to scrutiny. We'll anatomize the man, his charisma and character. What exactly *is* his seemingly innate *shazam*, and those acquired traits women find so irresistible? In the second part we'll home in on the way it's done, how the great lovers heart-hook women, from the charms of the senses to the more sophisticated arts of perpetual passion. Here we're in unfamiliar territory, beyond conventional love manuals into little-known erotic artistry of an advanced order.

At the end, we'll take stock, survey the contemporary culture, and see where and if ladies' men fit in. A roundtable of today's savviest women will join the debate. What would a Casanova of tomorrow look like? To begin, though, we have to restore the original. It's just a question of scouring off the detritus of fallacies, canards, and caricatures. Let's bring him into the light, and feast our eyes.

—

PART ONE

Anatomy

OF THE

Great Seducers

CHAPTER I

Charisma:

LIGHTNING IN A BOTTLE

—

He had like a halo around his head of stars.

—MISS MARYLAND ABOUT FRANK SINATRA,
Vancouver Sun

Father "Jake" was a priest without borders. He had seen and done it all: served prisoners and gangsters, worked in slums, heard confessions in bars, run a nonprofit restaurant, and counseled Kennedys, royalty, and superstars. If anyone knew men, he did. But he was at a loss about Rick the fire captain. "I don't know . . . ," he told me on the phone. "Rick has something. What? I have no idea. I mean, we used to have coffee at this little place on MacDougal Street, and the women! They sort of appeared and were all over him."

A month later, Rick arrives at my door and *boom-ting*: there's that certain "something." He's perhaps in his late sixties, with a square cartoon-cop's face, and eyes that sparkle like black mica. He's a powerful presence, a man who gives off licks of electricity. Over a glass of port (his present), I finally ask, What *is* it about him that sets off women?

He's not much help. He leans back, cracks a smile, and

reminisces. Years ago, he recalls, he got lost in a maze of back streets in Dublin when a young blonde approached and asked if she could help. He invited her to lunch, and two hours later they were in his hotel room and "naked in three minutes." "But here's the thing," he says, "every time I go to Dublin to this day, I see her. She's just a lovely person."

Maybe he knows and isn't telling, or maybe he's just as baffled as everybody else about charisma, that *je ne sais quoi* some people radiate. Within seconds, we feel it; we're fascinated and strangely elated. Normally associated with politicians and media personalities, charisma has been studied, lab-tested, and reduced to a familiar formula: self-confidence, an aura of authority, and communicative brilliance.

Many experts, however, caution that the spell cast by people is "a very complex one," especially in charismatic ladies' men. As psychoanalyst Irvine Schiffer observes, sexual spellbinders are a subtle species—less cocksure than diffident, unassured, and enigmatic. Yale professor Joseph Roach thinks contradiction is at the core of "It," a play of opposite personality traits that transfixes us. Mythologists stress the impact of early deities and the primordial shaman, "the charismatic figure par excellence." These priest-magicians who engineered ecstasy and channeled cosmic sexual energy, they claim, still have a powerful hold on the collective unconscious.

There is no agreement on any front. Charisma, notes *The Social Science Encyclopedia* with studied understatement, is "one of the more contentious" issues. But you can't mistake men with that *wow* factor. They crackle, they phosphoresce, they create a whirlpool of sexual allure that sucks up every woman in sight. Why, we may never know for sure. We can, though, mine the available knowledge on the subject and gain some hints. We can analyze the ladies' men's allure and zero in on the mystery—the tidal pull to *that* man across a crowded room.

Élan

If you can't live with gusto, find another guy.

—ADAGE

The man was poor, semi-employed, and lived in the seediest part of Venice Beach. Patti Stanger of *The Millionaire Matchmaker* would have kicked him to the curb. By all rights, Marisa Belger wouldn't have looked at him either; she was a bookish freelance writer and international traveler from a world of privilege. But Paul blew her away with his surging élan and "firecracker sense of humor." He boogied like James Brown, played guitar, and made her laugh so hard she ached. She had never met a family like his, a large Irish clan who whooped, made music, and danced on tabletops. The most alive man in the room, Paul infected everyone with his vitality. When he asked her to marry him, she said, "*Yes, yes, yes. I would be honored and humbled to spend my life with you.*"

Joie de vivre packs huge sexual charisma. As Mae West quipped, "It's not the men in my life; it's the life in my men." German nineteenth-century sociologist Max Weber identified charisma with the life force, "the thrust of the sap of the tree and the blood in the veins." Exuberance and eros are cross-wired in our brains. When we're passionately in love, we're flooded with euphoria; it's like an adrenaline hit, say scientists, that induces a giddy, near-manic high. Philosopher José Ortega y Gasset even defines love as a "splendid triggering of human vitality."

As an aphrodisiac, gusto can't be beat. "Exuberance is seductive," claims Nobel laureate Carleton Gajdusek, and can "engender devotion and love." Mythology may account for part of this élan allure. If we're turned on by a seducer's brio, say cultural anthropologists, we have only to look at the fertility gods. These charismatic deities, which flourished throughout culture, personified phallic energy, the generative force of existence. The Greek Dionysus, a Western prototype of the ladykiller, incarnated *zöe*, the spirit of "infinite life." A gorgeous heartthrob, he wandered the earth distributing enjoyment, followed by a band of besotted women. His names were "the exultant god" and "the joyful one."

Dionysus cast the mold for fictional ladies' men to come. "In no love story," remarks Roland Barthes, "is a character ever tired." Chaucer's Wife of Bath ranks Solomon as history's supreme lover because "he was so much alive," and women are bewitched against their will in Mozart's opera by Don Giovanni's "exuberant joy of life." Effi Briest, the heroine of Theodor Fontane's German version of *Madame Bovary*, betrays a perfect husband for an "animated and high-spirited" roué. Heroes of women's popular romances (a window onto female fantasies) come prepackaged with vim and masculine vigor.

Real ladies' men pulse with ebullience. Nineteenth-century French Romantic poet Alfred de Musset won the hearts of half of the Parisian female population with his "delicious verve." A vivacious dandy, he bounded into drawing rooms in tight sky-blue trousers, bubbling over with *bon mots*. The actress Rachel doted on him, and a duchess, princess, and leading belle rushed to his bedside when he fell ill. His greatest coup, though, was his conquest of literary celebrity George Sand. Deploying an élan assault, he paraded his vitality before her like a "peacock before a demure, quiet little peahen." Victorian Prime Minister Lord Palmerston, aka "Lord Cupid," put his "puckish high spirits" to the same erotic ends, as did such master lovers as twentieth-century David Niven and Kingsley Amis.

American composer George Gershwin was as effervescent as his music—foot-tapping classics like "I Got Rhythm," "Things Are Looking Up," and "'S Wonderful." He was "exactly like his work," said a girlfriend; he took "a joyous delight" in everything he did. What he did, besides produce some of the nation's finest music, from songbook standards to *Porgy and Bess*, was enthrall women. He was a stellar ladies' man, adored by a cast of hundreds.

Gershwin lacked the requisite matinee-idol looks. Of medium height and dark complexion, he had a broad hook nose, thinning black hair, and a prognathic chin. But when he walked into a room, women sat up. Each mentioned the same aphrodisiac: "his exuberant vitality," "gaiety," and "many-sided zest for life."

The ladies in his life were legion. A fancier of smart, attractive women, he romanced the glitterati of the social, show business, and musical worlds. His more serious amours included French actress Simone Simon and Hollywood star Ginger Rogers, who told reporters, "I *was* crazy about George Gershwin," and "so was everyone who knew him."

Kitty Carlisle, then a rising ingénue in film, recalled how seductively he flirted; he would sing at the piano at parties and insert her name in love songs. He never married, but he sustained a ten-year relationship with musician Kay Swift, his collaborator, muse, and "utterly devoted factotum."

Biographers have long speculated that he found *the* woman in his life in 1936, the just-married actress Paulette Goddard. He wrote the ballad "They Can't Take That Away from Me" for her, and urged her to leave her spouse, Charlie Chaplin, for him. But Gershwin died a year later, at thirty-eight, of a brain tumor.

The loss to music was incalculable. But the greater loss, said those who knew and loved him, was his ebullience. "He loved every aspect of life, and made every aspect of life loveable," said lovers and friends. "People thought they would never sense that special joy again." It's no coincidence that *charisma* is related to the Greek *chaírein*, "to rejoice."

Intensity

All love begins with an impact.
—ANDRÉ MAUROIS, "The Art of Loving"

If you see Vance behind the counter of his Manhattan gourmet store, you may get the wrong idea. Dressed in khaki pants and docksiders, he looks like a midlife version of Charles Lindbergh from a staid suburban enclave. But in two minutes, you feel that *ʒoop!*, that sexual voltage. When I ask about his reputation as a ladies' man about town (before his conversion to monogamy), his cobalt-blue eyes blaze.

"Believe me," he says, over a glass of 2005 Margaux in his office, "it was a wonderful time. And very easy. I must say, I was sought after. Oh, there must have been dozens." "Why?" he reflects. "In simple terms: passion within, passion, *passion*." A man of keen interests who raced cars and gambled, he was never laid back with women. Once, he tells me, he saw a stunning blonde on the sidewalk, swung a U-turn, knocked on office doors until he found her, and said, "Let's get out of here." "I'm very aggressive, firm, but sincere," he explains. "I loved that gal. I'd fly to LA just to have dinner with her."

Ladies' men aren't slow-pulsed, impassive islands of calm and Zen indifference. They fire on all cylinders. "Emotional intensity," exceptional personal force, is one of the hallmarks of charisma. It also defines erotic passion. Casanova credited his conquests to his sheer ardor: "I turned the heads of some hundreds of women," he wrote, "because I was neither tender nor gallant nor pathetic. I was passionate." Romantic love is one of the most extreme human experiences. As philosophers say, love is "strong stuff." Under a functional magnetic resonance imaging scan, passionate love looks like a lightning strike; centers deep in the midbrain flare up and release a torrent of dopamine and norepinephrine. It's so close to what happens when we're angry or afraid that psychologists believe any intense feeling, in a "spillover effect," can ignite desire.

A woman at the end of a double-shift day doesn't always want an exciting partner. But as a rule, women like their lovers, real and imaginary, charged up. Sometimes that includes a spritz of danger. After all, Dionysus was a two-sided god, like eros itself, with a potential for discord and violence. His appearances were awesome, "disquieting" events; he revealed himself with a numinous bang, often masked and swathed in ivy.

Fantasy erotic heroes are impassioned creatures who seethe, like Heathcliff in *Wuthering Heights*, with teeth-gritting desire. Balzac's ingénue in *The Memoirs of Two Brides* has her pick of the Parisian beau monde, but she chooses an ugly, mono-browed Spaniard because of his ferocity. Which is why Colette's heroine of *The Other One* junks her husband; he's lost his fire. "God, how slow he is!" she rails; at the least, he should show "passionate violence." To qualify for the romance leagues, the hero must be "deeply intense," a model of coiled manhood, whether a count or a carpenter.

A number of ladies' men are high-strung powerhouses. Nineteenth-century pianist Franz Liszt was "demoniac" in his fervor. Tightly wound and "aggressively ardent," Liszt targeted women with one of his fiery looks, and they went down like sacks of sand. A century later, conductor Leopold Stokowski was an equally *fortissimo* phenomenon, as were Frank Lloyd Wright and Frank Sinatra.

No one, though, surpassed the fifth-century BC Alcibiades for charismatic intensity. A renowned Athenian politician and general in the Peloponnesian War, he was a byword for sex appeal. "His personal magnetism," wrote Plutarch, "was such that no disposition could wholly resist it."

In a culture that enshrined moderation, Alcibiades was an emotional extremist, "man of many strong passions," who riveted men and women alike when he stepped into the agora. Aptly, his shield depicted Eros armed with a thunderbolt. Handsome and showy, he dressed in fancy sandals and long purple cloaks instead of demure white togas. He drove chariots too fast, caroused with flute girls, and was so intense in his affections that he frightened his friend Socrates. Women, his wife included, worshipped him in spite of his excesses and infidelities.

This "second Dionysus," however, imitated his patron deity once too often. On the night before he was to lead a Sicilian expedition against Sparta, he defaced the sacred phallic totems, a crime punishable by death. He fled to the enemy and lived in Sparta for two and a half years, where he enchanted the populace with his "rare and incomparable presence." The king's wife numbered among them and was so unrepentant about their affair that she called their son "Alcibiades" in public.

Driven to flight a second time, he took refuge in Persia, only to be recalled, then exiled once more from Athens after he lost a key sea battle. Finally, his enemies hunted him down. They found him on the frontier in Thrace in the arms of a courtesan and felled him with javelins. Afterward, the heartbroken courtesan wrote a poem to commemorate her lover—a charismatic dynamo whose name became synonymous with the seducer for millennia.

Sex Drive

The subject of this treatise does not concern men who lack a sexual temperament.

—*Kāma Sūtra*

Women in Trenton, New Jersey, prowled the streets and committed crimes in hopes of meeting this man. Joe Morelli, the strapping cop in Janet Evanovich's Stephanie Plum mystery series, is a smoking ladykiller with a string of conquests and a one-track mind. Whenever he greets Stephanie, he hooks a finger inside her tank top, and it's off to big O's in the bedroom or the shower, where he does her favorite thing. On "fierceromance blogspot" readers put Joe at the top, not just for his sexy wisecracks and rescue instincts, but for his "hot Italian libido."

Sexual energy is the heartbeat of sexual charisma. As sexologists point out, sex drive lies on a continuum from take-it-or-leave-it to can't-get-enough. Ladies' men occupy the lusty end of the spectrum. According to Søren Keirkegaard, that's the essence of their magnetism—pure "sensuality" and carnal appetite.

Primeval religion and myth may help explain this magnetism. Throughout deep history, ancient peoples worshipped the virile principle and fashioned penis-shaped relics capable of miracle cures and spells. At Dionysian festivals men filed through the streets brandishing huge phalluses to celebrate the divine force of male sex-energy. This is sexual charisma at its most primal; the root meaning of *fascinating* is "*fascinum*," Latin for "phallus."

Women's dream lovers are more sexed up than usually believed. These fantasy studs are so stoked they get hard at the sight of the heroine's hand and singe the sheets. The "walking orgasm" in one novella is up and at 'em minutes after a cupboard-rattling session on a kitchen counter. "It's bath time," he announces. "Watch me." Vadinho, the Brazilian satyr of *Dona Flor and Her Two Husbands*, dies at Carnival waving a cassava tuber, but he returns to life, like the deathless phallic principle, to sexually satisfy his wife again.

Nineteenth- and early-twentieth-century authorities claimed women cared little for such gross satisfactions; they didn't like sex as much as men, preferring soul unions and evenings *à deux* with a good book. Two great lovers of the 1950s proved them wrong. Aly Khan and Porfirio Rubirosa won their romantic renown on the strength of their prodigious sex drives.

"Don Juan Khan," as Aly Khan was known, had "charm in neon lights." The last of the post–World War II playboys, he transcended the breed. More than a jaded womanizer, he combined old-world courtliness, fondness for his lovers, and skill with a strong libido. Trained as a boy in the esoteric techniques of the Middle East, he was endowed with a sensitive touch and such "physical fortitude" that he could bed and sate three women in a day.

Like Aly Khan, Porfirio Rubirosa stood above the crowd. A Dominican diplomat, sportsman, and cosmopolite, he had an illustrious career as a lover and cocksman, with the emphasis on cock. (Large pepper grinders have been named for him.) He married five times, most famously to heiresses Doris Duke and Barbara Hutton, and was embroiled with Zsa Zsa Gabor in a tabloid romance for years. But he added supreme "class" and romance to his high sexual gear, not to mention expert swordsmanship. Said a blissed-out girlfriend, "Rubi is so virile his sex glands will go on functioning even after the rest of his body is dead."

The eighteenth-century duc de Richelieu, however, got there first. A precursor to the playboy, he was a distinguished figure in French history—diplomat, marshal of France, confidant to Louis XV, and the general behind important victories against the British, such as the brilliant capture of Minorca. He was also a "hero of the boudoir." "Profligate," adorable, and hypersexed, he lived so long and lustily, people thought he might be immortal. He sired a child in his eighties and died, still virile, at ninety-two.

He was no more handsome or clever than anyone else at the courts of Louis XIV and XV, but he had a sensual oomph, an "unbridled animal magnetism." With his sweetness, charm, and wolfish grin, he "could ruin a woman with a smile." Even as a boy at Versailles, his sexual precocity drew admirers, and at fifteen he was thrown into the Bastille for hiding in the Dauphine's bedroom. Afterward, women swarmed. He received ten to twelve love letters a day and made the rounds, romancing two princesses, tradeswomen, courtesans, and nearly every noblewoman in Paris. Women were "wild" for him.

So "wild" that Richelieu generated one of the most colorful scandals of the day. Two grandes dames who were competing for his favors decided to settle the matter with a predawn duel. On March 14, 1719, the contesse de Polignac and the marquise de Nesle arrived at the Bois de Boulogne "clothed as Amazons," leveled pistols at each other, and fired. As the marquise toppled to the ground drenched in blood, she cried that her lover "was well worth it." "Now," she shouted, "my love will make him wholly mine." She survived, but like his countless conquests, she was to be disappointed. This *vainqueur de dames* was too charismatic, too monumental a sexual force, to belong wholly to anyone.

Love of Women

Destructive, damnable, deceitful woman!
—THOMAS OTWAY, *The Orphan*

Ashton Kutcher is more than just another Hollywood hottie with a toned physique. Smart and multi-gifted, he has created and produced popular television shows (among them *Punk'd* and *Beauty and the Geek*), launched a most-visited Twitter site, and acted in over twenty movies. At the same time, he's— in fanzine-speak—"a honey-dripping chick magnet." Linked to many coveted women and once married to megastar Demi Moore, he has a unique brand of charisma: he "love[s] the company of women" as pals, equals, and lovers. Like many lady-killers, he has his mother and their close relationship to thank for it. She told him to "treat women right, to take care of them, to respect them."

Men who appreciate and enjoy women aren't that common. Boys are raised to boycott the girls' club and bond with each other. The "bromance" tradition is ancient and deep-dyed, a devotion to male friends that can be "wonderful, passing the love of women." In the extreme, it tips over into misogyny, as the "player" movement and movies like *Carnal Knowledge* and *Roger Dodger* attest. By contrast, ladies' men like women inside and out and seek their companionship.

Such gynephilia makes a man hum with charisma. Scientists track it to the mystery of connectivity. When someone empathizes and synchronizes with us, the effect is galvanic. Mirror neurons light up, explains MIT psychologist Alex Pentland, and our bodies kick off opiate-like endorphins. We endow rapport artists with "chemistry"—incandescent sexiness.

Mythology's premier ladies' man Dionysus was the one god who treasured women. Unlike the macho deities in the Greek pantheon, he grew up "surrounded by women"—flocks of foster mothers, mermaids, and sea goddesses. He was so fond of his mother, Semele, that he restored her to life and made her immortal. His traveling companions were throngs of female votaries.

Women-friendly seducers inevitably triumph in fiction. Anton Chekov's rake in "The Lady with the Dog" is gray and faded, but he enamors a spirited young married woman because he's a female aficionado; he's at ease and knows "what to say." Rowley Flint of Somerset Maugham's *Up at the Villa* is another unlikely ladykiller—ill-favored and slovenly—who profoundly "like[s] women" and lures a glamorous guest at a Florentine estate away from her rich, handsome fiancé. "Women are more important than baseball," says the hero of Jennifer Crusie's *Bet Me*, as he walks off with the pick of the town.

Casanova was never a man's man, although he excelled in daredevil masculine pursuits like spying and dueling. Coddled by his grandmother and other ministering angels as a boy, he was "madly in love with the eternal feminine," and preferred the society of women. Prince Grigory Potemkin was one of Russian history's most dashing figures—general, statesman, lover/advisor to Catherine the Great—and a sultan of seduction. Deluged by devotees all his life, "he loved women passionately" and was at home with them, having been pampered since infancy by his mother and six sisters.

Warren Beatty has the same pedigree. He was raised in a hothouse of strong, doting women—sister, aunt, and mother—

where he acquired a lifelong "sweetly endearing appreciation for females." "He's just wonderful to women," said Lana Wood, Natalie's' sister, "just wonderful. He genuinely likes them, *all* of them."

Jazz composer and orchestra leader Duke Ellington soared over the racial divide of his time, not only professionally but also romantically. An African American born in 1899 at the high tide of segregation and prejudice, he became a national celebrity, honored by the White House and the musical establishment. He became the ultimate "sweet man" in the process. Six foot one and deadly sexy, he enchanted women of all colors. "Spoiled rotten" by his mother and aunts, he "liked women as well as loved them," and drew them "like flies to sugar."

His love life was robust. Married once at eighteen and separated, he had three long-term mistresses over a lifetime: Mildred "Sweet Bebe" Dixon, a dancer at the Harlem Cotton Club; Beatrice "Evie" Ellis, a half-black, half-Spanish model; and white nightclub singer Fernandae Castro Monte, christened "The Countess." Then there were road ladies, colleagues, and squads of besotted fans, including two Chicago debutantes who got their hands on him. Women "absolutely adored him."

Throughout the high-volume sex, though, Ellington always revered and valued women. He regarded them "as flowers, each one lovely in her own way." Flirtatious and captivating, he would say to a secretary on the phone, "Is this the beautiful department?" or tell an actress, "Does your contract stipulate that you must be this pretty?" He played the piano for women; he pinioned them with his bedroom eyes. But perhaps the greatest part of his "charismatic presence" was something less usual: he truly appreciated and honored women and was "marvelous" with them.

Androgyny

The more feminine the man . . . the higher the
hit rate with the opposite sex.

—"The Evolution of Homosexuality," *The Economist*

In the swinging sixties, Essex Junction, Vermont, was the "in" place—a hippie enclave full of pony-tailed hunks and braless lovelies in search of sexual liberation. In that department, one man got all the action. Women trooped miles to his house in the woods for sleepovers—as did men. Clay's uncanny sexual magnetism was the talk of the communes. As frail and thin as the Little Match Girl, he had bad teeth, a Fu Manchu mustache, and a whispery alto voice. But he had a mantra: "Bi or Bye-Bye." In that hive of counterculture machismo, Clay cast one of the oldest sexual spells in the book: androgyny.

Counterintuitive as it seems, gender ambiguity is immensely seductive. In theory, the Darwinian he-man ought to get the valentines, but oddly enough, a man in touch with his inner femininity frequently has the romantic edge with women. As cultural critic Camille Paglia says, the androgynous person *"is* the charismatic personality." Why though? Why do gender-benders throw off such erotic magic and entice women as they do?

Scientists have located some clues. Researcher Meredith Chivers has found that women differ from men in their sexual tastes. When she attached female subjects to a photoplethysmograph while they watched erotic movies, she discovered that they shared a marked predilection for bisexuality. Other studies show women consistently preferring computerized images of feminized male faces and choosing more androgynous men in audio interviews.

This is not news to the psychiatric profession. Sigmund Freud and Carl Jung thought both genders posses an inner bisexuality in the repressed depths of the psyche. Later thinkers conjectured that we never lose an unconscious striving for a synthesis of male and female. This amalgam, writes religious scholar Mircea Eliade, represents ideal wholeness, the peak of "sensual perfection."

It's embedded in our cultural mythology. In many creation stories, the "great He-She" created life on earth, and the Hindu fertility god, Shiva, assumed both sexes to attain "divine sensual delight." Often shamans achieved their "mana" (air of sacred authority) by assuming a double-sexed persona. The "Man-Woman" Dionysus perfumed his curls and wore women's saffron robes tied with a flowery sash.

Erotic fantasies are replete with androgynes. Just when we expect a hulking warrior to carry off the heroine, we find the effeminate Paris abducting Helen in *The Iliad* and gentle Lanval of Marie de France's twelfth-century tale infatuating the queen of the fairies.

In a recent shift, romance idols have begun to blur gender. The "Woman Whisperer" Cash Hunter in Maureen Child's *Turn My World Upside Down* is a soul sister in the body of a linebacker. When his love interest suffers, he cradles her cheek, extracts her story, and bleeds for her: "Ah God. Empathy washed over him." Daniel of Anne Lamott's *Blue Shoe* not only behaves like a best girlfriend—baking, gardening, and church going—but he looks like one. He wears green silk shirts, sandals, and scented dreadlocks.

Whether subtle or pronounced, many great lovers have a distinct feminine streak. The Athenian *homme fatal* Alcibiades showcased his femininity, wearing his hair long and braiding it with flowers before battles. Casanova, too, had an overt distaff side—an aesthetic sensibility, a sentimentality, and a penchant for cross-dressing. Byron's androgyny was so apparent that the sultan Mahmud refused to believe he wasn't "a woman dressed in man's clothes." Emotional and epicene in dress and speech, Byron resembled a Renaissance blend of Greek god and goddess.

Ironically, the icon of tough, cool-guy masculinity, Gary Cooper, owed his fame as a ladies' man to his "ravishing androgyny." In more than a hundred movies over thirty-five years, he cemented the twentieth-century ideal of a "real man," the slow-talking honcho with quick fists and nerves of steel. But women saw a different side of him. Six foot three and "more beautiful than any woman except Garbo," he merged a feminine sweetness, tenderness, and artistic sensitivity with his masculine swank.

The hybrid proved knee-buckling. "Coop" was set upon by women the moment he arrived in Hollywood in 1925. Said director Stuart Heisler, they "fell over themselves to get him to take them to bed." And he complied. He slept with nearly every leading lady, from Carole Lombard to Grace Kelly and Ingrid Bergman, and moonstruck each of them. Helen Hayes said that if "Gary had crooked a finger I would have left Charlie and my child and the whole thing."

He was seriously loved. After their affair ended, twenties film star Clara Bow continued to come if he whistled, and actress Lupe Velez stabbed him with a kitchen knife when he tried to break up with her. He married socialite Veronica "Rocky" Balfe in 1933, who adored him so unconditionally that she endured his countless affairs, even a serious one with Patricia Neal. Attempting to explain his "hypnotic" effect on women, movie and TV personality Arlene Dahl referred to his "combination of unusual traits." The secret of that "combination," said actor-writer Simon Callow, was "the perfect balance between his masculine and feminine elements."

Creativity

Creative types have increased sex appeal.

—RUSTY ROCKETS, *Science a GoGo*

Adam Levy, a painter of dark, surreal canvases in the movie *Love & Sex*, looks like a date-challenged dork: he wears camp shirts over baggy cargo pants and has the face of an overfed hamster. But women engulf him, and he snaps up the smartest and prettiest of the pack. "That's why I started painting," he explains, "to get the girls in high school."

What is it about artists, those "unfit" creative guys who have all the luck with women? They may lack the right biomarkers—money, looks, and solidity—but they have sexual charisma to burn. As poet Rainer Rilke observed, art lies "incredibly close" to sex. Creativity is a knockout aphrodisiac, seductive at a gut level. Professional artists and poets, studies report, "have more sex appeal than other people and twice as many sexual partners."

Evolutionary psychologist Geoffrey Miller chalks it up to sexual selection. Art, he theorizes, originated as a courtship display. More than fitness and status, early womankind sought mental excellence, says Miller, creative intelligence in particular. The suitor who produced the best creations and delivered the greatest aesthetic pleasure won the prize females. Neuroscientist V. S. Ramachandran has located the center responsible for this artistic ability, the angular gyrus, and thinks prehistoric men may have wooed mates by advertising musical, poetic, and drawing talents as a "visible signature of a giant brain."

Primitive mythological and religious figures may factor in too. The shaman, "an archaic prototype of the artist," beamed with sexual charisma. It was his job to draw down the sex force of creation through magical song, drama, dance, and visual art. The cave paintings are thought to have been his handiwork, his inseminations "in the womb of the earth." The business of the sex gods was creation—new shapes and forms ad infinitum. Greek god Dionysus founded tragedy and comedy, choreographed dances, and composed "the songs of the night."

Artist-lovers seem always to have haunted the romantic imagination. Like the legendary Greek Orpheus, who charmed man, woman, and beast with his lyre, Chaucer's "Nicholas the Gallant" of "The Miller's Tale" seduces maidens by singing and playing his harp. Bob Hampton, the painter of *The Handyman*, barely has time to clean his brushes amid the pile-on of lust-crazed housewives. Creative heartthrobs fill movies, from *Titanic* sketch-artist Jack to the dishy novelist in *Purple Violets*, to Bleek the trombone-playing ladykiller of *Mo' Better Blues*.

A disproportionate number of ladykillers trade on the sexual charisma of creativity. History is chocked with poets, musicians, painters, dancers, actors, and "creatives" who prospered with women. A quick once-over reveals a list of banner names: Lord Byron, Alfred de Musset, Franz Liszt, Gustav Klimt, Frank Lloyd Wright, and Mikhail Baryshnikov. Casanova owed no small amount of his luster to his artistic achievements as a violinist, inventor, and author of poems, plays, and books.

Rock star "Mick the Magic Jagger" has made spectacular capital on this appeal. A throwback to the total theater of shamanistic rites, he admits that sex is at the center of his Rolling Stones' performances. He puts a sock in his crotch to simulate an erection, undulates like a "strip-tease[r]," and chants and rocks the audience to "mass orgasm."

He's an all-caps ladies' man, impossibly magnetic, lovable, and unleavable. Despite his nonstellar looks (the raddled features of a very old chimp), he has been bathed in adoration by a long line of superior women, including his wife, Bianca, Marianne Faithfull, Marsha Hunt, Carly Simon, Jerry Hall, Carla Bruni, and his current girlfriend of eight years, designer L'Wren Scott. He's neither mature, sober, nor faithful, and he would catch hell from a relationship counselor. But he has hundred-proof charisma on his side; as Marianne Faithfull put it, she felt as if she had "her very own Dionysus."

Artist Lucian Freud's draw, like Jagger's, was primeval. Poet Stephen Spender compared him to the "male opposite [of a] witch," and Freud himself equated his creativity with "phallic energy." Dubbed "the greatest living realist painter," by *New York Times* art critic John Russell, Freud did not paint canvases for calm contemplation. Warts-and-all portraits of nudes from odd angles, they are designed to "astonish, disturb, [and] seduce."

Seduction he knew. The British Freud, who died in 2011 at eighty-nine, had the career of a supernova lover. Married twice (once to siren Caroline Blackwood), he fathered at least nine children and was passionately involved with "umpteen" women. At seventy-nine, he shocked the nation by taking up with a waifish twenty-nine-year-old and later moving on to Alexandra Williams-Wynn, fifty years his junior. In a 2005 painting, *The Painter Surprised by a Naked Admirer*, she sits nude at his feet clutching his leg and caressing his thigh.

Every woman cited the same allure: his "intense sexual charisma." Being with him, said a lover, is like "being wired up to the national grid." Freud was an amorous master. He quoted poetry to his models, served champagne and delicacies between sittings, and gave "the best hugs." He was also an elegant figure,

with a fine, hawk-like profile, a cockade of gray hair, and a rakish scarf looped around his neck. But it was Freud the artist who
slayed women; it was his work, they said, that was the "potent
aphrodisiac." To sit for him, said a girlfriend, "felt like being
an apple in the Garden of Eden. When it was over, [she] felt as
if [she] had been cast out of paradise." This was the work of an
ur-artist, the sexual sorcerer with "the most primitive form of
charisma."

Quicksilver Man

Don't Fence Me In.

—COLE PORTER

Kurt is a thirtyish German photographer and downtown Casanova who looks like a dancer in an avant-garde ballet troupe.
He's a study in fluidity, with his loose jeans, ruffled dark bob,
and feline stride. Asked about the charisma for which he's
famous, he throws up his hands: "It's just part of you and you
radiate that in a certain way."

What he's radiating is the foxfire of free, unbound manhood.
Like many ladykillers, Kurt is a mover and quester, indifferent to
social constraints. At twenty-five, he gave up a banking career,
left home, built a photography career on pioneer techniques,
and now goes where the wind blows him. "I'm a boat-rocker,"
he laughs.

Charismatic men are laws unto themselves, renegade souls
who give the raspberry to the rule book. A zing of transgres-
sion defines charisma. People with that "irresistible magnetic
mana" flout authority and live on their own terms, unfettered in
mind and body. There's an intangible "apartness" about them.
Women, to official dismay, don't necessarily fall for providers

and staid nest-builders; they're often swept off their feet by free-souled nonconformists.

The charisma of these unbridled mavericks may not be accidental. Many psychologists contend that superior personhood demands psychic elbow room and a defiance of established norms. A woman in quest of alpha genes may do better with a restless rebel than a company yes-man.

Then again, archaic history plays in. Ancient deities like Shiva, Osiris, the Norse Freyr, and the Celtic Dagda defied conventions and traveled the earth dispensing fertility. The phallic Hermes was "God of the Roads." Perpetual wanderer Dionysus mocked institutions and social custom and "freed his worshippers from every law."

Free-range ladykillers have particular charms for women. "Libertines" hold out the seductive promise of escape from the traditional feminine fate of domestic stasis and conformity. The "eccentric" rover of Knut Hamsun's nineteenth-century *Mysteries* arrives among a group of restive women at just the right time. Over the course of the summer, he beguiles the entire female population of a Norwegian seaport with his mystic promise of freedom and revolt. Even the exemplar of feminine domesticity surrenders, crying, "You upset my equilibrium!"

One of the staples of popular romance is the solitary hero unburdened by sidekicks who disdains social dictates—roving renegades like Robert Kincaid of *The Bridges of Madison County*. In *The Ground beneath Her Feet*, Salman Rushdie takes the convention and transmutes it into great literature. "Bombay Casanova" Ormus Cama is a prismatic musical genius who renounces orthodox culture, slips the traces, and "step[s] off the map" into pure possibility.

Not every great lover bucks the establishment and goes his own way. But those who do exude an edgy excitement. Casanova was his "own master"—oblivious to regulations and in love with the open road—and no one could restrain pianist Franz Liszt, a vagabond spirit too overscale for civilized confinement. They're among a fleet of freewheeling originals: ladies' men such as Sir Walter Raleigh, Jack London, and H. G. Wells.

This footloose, anarchic spirit can be cerebral and work just as forcefully. Twentieth-century philosopher and *tombeur* Albert Camus was physically curtailed by tuberculosis, but inwardly was a dedicated maverick and roamer. Nonconformity and freedom were the watchwords of his "Absurdist" doctrine. "I rebel," he wrote, "therefore we exist."

Don Juan was one of his existential heroes, an enlightened lover who seduced women not to score but to spread amorous joy. "It's his way of giving and vivifying" before the axe falls. A romantic adventurer, Camus was as good as his word. Women found him drop-dead attractive—a French Humphrey Bogart—and he loved them "without bounds." The year before he died in a car crash, at forty-six, he was balancing three women in his life, plus a devoted wife. And he "managed to keep them all happy."

Had Camus known, he could have found his Don Juan across the channel: Denys Finch Hatton. Fabled lover, iconoclast, daredevil, and "eternal wanderer," Finch Hatton was immortalized as Isak Dinesen's überlover in *Out of Africa*. But Danish author Dinesen no more captured Finch Hatton in her idealized portrait than she did in real life. He eluded any attempt to pin him down. A born dissenter, he refused to be curbed by Edwardian social sanctions, raised Cain in school, and at age twenty-four fled to the wilds of East Africa for adventure and breathing room.

Women were mad for him. Six foot three and beautiful, he had enormous charisma, a valence that drew people to him "like a centripetal force." At one point "at least eight women were in love with him," and he chose fastidiously—strong, glamorous, bohemian individualists.

Dinesen, nom de plume of Karen Blixen, was his longest amour. They met in 1918 on her Kenyan coffee plantation, where she lived with her faithless husband, Bror, and entertained a revolving crew of tourists and big-game hunters. Their affair lasted until his death in a plane crash in 1931. She lived and breathed for his sporadic visits, catered to his whims, thought him a god, and hoped desperately to marry him.

But Finch Hatton "belonged to the wild nomadic world and he never intended to marry anyone." At the end, he paired up with the adventurous aviator Beryl Markham, who said, "As for charm, I suspect Denys invented it." The invention wasn't original; it was the "absolute magic" of the charismatic, unchained love god. He was "like a meteor," said a female friend. "He arrived only to go off again . . . he wanted the wild."

Flawed Manhood

The flaw that punctuates perfection
—HILLARY JOHNSON, *Los Angeles Times*

Every woman at the University of Virginia in the 1970s was a little bit (or a lot) in love with this professor. He had strut and movie-star looks—a trim red beard and safari outfits with biker boots and bush shirts. That day in class, he was talking about guilt in a Kafka story. "Say a policeman knocked on the door," he asked. "How many would think he'd come for you? Me? I'd know for sure."

He might have been right. Douglas Day was notorious: fast cars, exploits south of the border (in his own plane), and women everywhere. Married five times, he had window-rattling sex appeal, charisma that took your breath and heart away. More than his beauty and brilliance, it was his walk. He had a mysterious gimp leg, and when he limped down Cabell Hall, women dissolved.

Pop psychologists and coaches who tout ironclad confidence as the key to sexual charisma may need a reality check. A hairline crack in a man's aplomb, a hint of vulnerability—either physical or psychological—can turn a woman inside out. Joseph Roach traces this to the nature of charisma itself, the necessary flux of vulnerability and strength. To psychoanalyst Irvine Schiffer, minor defects, which he calls "straddling characteristics," create the highest sexual amperage; they encourage approachability and generate "instant glamour."

Women find a soupçon of fallibility in a man especially erotic. "The things I find most endearing" about lovers, says Erica Jong, "are their small imperfections." Perhaps maternal impulses are at work or an attempt to equalize the power imbalance between the sexes. Psychiatrist Michael Bader probes deeper; the female yen for injured manhood, he hypothesizes, stems from an impulse to neutralize fears of rejection and male violence. Author Hillary Johnson goes for the intimacy explanation. Scars and flaws, she writes, suggest "a way to get inside" masculine armor.

There's a mythic kicker too. Wounded men inherit some of the star shine of the earliest fertility gods. Adonis was gored in the groin by a wild boar, and like the maimed Osiris, Dionysus, and Freyr, he was healed and restored to life each spring. Just as shamans incur a "disease of God" during initiation to access the power source of creation, heroes acquire a permanent scar (similar to the tell-tale gash in Odysseus's thigh) in the archetypal male journey to maturity.

The trope lives on in hundreds of love stories, from the gouged Guigemar in Marie de France's story to the crippled and blinded Mr. Rochester in *Jane Eyre.* The emotionally or physically damaged man, says novelist Mary Jo Putney, is a hero of "incredible potency." Readers can find injured ladykillers for every taste on romance sites: a dyslexic duke, a Dominic with a deformed hip, and a psychologically impaired Lord Evelyn.

The sexiest man to enter a fictional bedroom is the one-armed biker Lefty, of Rebecca Silver's story "Fearful Symmetry." He caresses her nipples with the "delicate prongs" of his steel hook, then flings off his prosthesis, props himself on his stump, and flips her out of her senses on the futon. Women from one end of Texas to the other covet Hardy Cates, Lisa Kleypas's troubled "blue-eyed devil" who has been traumatized by a violent, alcoholic father in a seedy trailer park.

Great lovers with a "divine defect" are surprisingly numerous. Aldous Huxley and Potemkin were nearly blind, and Charlemagne, Talleyrand, and Gary Cooper limped. Lord Byron, with his club foot and bruised sensibilities, devastated women, just as Jack London's and Richard Burton's tortured souls played havoc with female hearts.

A grand prix identity that harbors a psychic wound can be an incendiary mix. "Great seducer" Jack Nicholson is a powerful presence with the strong ego of a talented actor and three-time Oscar winner. But what melts women is the fissure of hurt beneath the "King of Hollywood" persona, the insecurity intercut with confidence. Illegitimate, he was raised by a grandmother who masqueraded as his mother, and was so fat as a boy that he was excluded from sports and nicknamed "Chubs."

He's open about the scars and therapy, and his lovers are both protective and committed, with Anjelica Huston staying with him for seventeen years. Although he cheated openly on model-actress Cynthia Basinet, she explained why she couldn't leave him: "I saw such a wonderful vulnerable person . . . I vowed never to hurt him." It was, she said, part of "his spell," the "old Jack Magic."

The more extreme the flaws, the greater the need for compensatory attractions. Russian writer Ivan Turgenev may be one of the least heroic yet most lovable ladies' men of the nineteenth century. Author of such masterpieces as *Fathers and Sons* and *A Month in the Country*, he was plagued with neuroses, having been brutalized by a sadistic mother who faked death scenes to get her way. He was a weak-kneed, nervous "gentle giant," prone to hypochondria, hallucinations, and melancholy.

Nor did he strike a bold figure. Tall and stoop-shouldered, he had grayish eyes that gazed dreamily out of a "round, mild, handsome," somewhat feminine face. But he possessed surprising reserves of strength and an audacious, trailblazing genius. Ignoring his mother's curses, he expatriated, broke rank, and became a major "innovator" of Russian literature.

His weak/strong alloy, among other charms, made him a heart-stopper. Seduced by a chambermaid at age fifteen, Turgenev was avalanched by women, among them a Berlin mother of four, an aristocrat who called him her "Christ," and quintessentially, mezzo-soprano Pauline Viardot. She was besieged by suitors, but he scattered them all with his gifts and white-lightning compound of frailty and personal force. Viardot took him home to France, where she lived with him and her husband in a lifelong ménage à trois.

Despite the propaganda, bulletproof self-esteem and a perfect package aren't the ticket. It's an "enigmatic tang" of injury, a pinch of flaw in the confidence brew that fells women every time.

Charisma: Refining the Definition

Women can just *feel* a ladies' man on the premises. Suddenly the room is charged with ions and thrumming with sexual tension and promise. He doesn't need every charisma attribute: *joie de vivre*, intensity, creativity, titanic libido, tear-away originality, fondness for women, or manly self-esteem tinged with androgyny and fallibility. A great lover can throw sparks with just a few choice allures; they are that potent.

Erotic charisma, though, isn't easily coded and formulated. Mysteries remain. Why, for example, are men like Al Gore, Bill Gates, and comedian Robin Williams non-sizzlers when they fit the criteria? Why don't the standard recipes—big self-belief, expressivity, rapport, and communication skills—work? And what about the evolutionary psychologists' precepts, such as status, wealth, and stability?

The topic, as James M. Donovan highlights in the *Journal of Scientific Exploration*, is largely unexplored. Charisma, he writes, is "much more bizarre than commonly assumed," and bears little relation to any special personality type. Scholars agree: it's been relegated, they say, "to the back burner of research," and confusion reigns—even about the definition of the word. We can tease out traits, float theories, but we can't demystify that magic radiance—yet.

What we can say for sure, though, is that we know charisma when we see it, and are bespelled. When women encounter a magnetic man, they imbue him (similar to transference in psychotherapy) with their "forbidden impulses and secret wishes," investing him with what they crave and aren't getting. As such, the ladies' man is a valuable resource, a Rorschach of women's deepest, unmet desires.

Can men en masse acquire charisma, or is it an innate "gift" as the ancients believed? I ask Rick the fire captain, and he says he knows only one thing: you can't fake it. Biologist Amotz Zahavi and others have confirmed this in studies, and maintain that top lovers are authentic because women have always seen through false sexual advertisement.

"The feeling has to be real," Rick continues. And beyond that? Rick takes a sip of port, waits a beat, and sighs. "All I know is, life is good, I invent stuff, I travel. I never follow the crowd. And I *do* love women. Ever tell you about the time Vivien Leigh invited me up? She told me three times, 'If there were ever a real Rhett Butler, it would be you.'"

 Character:

THE GOODS

—

Character alone is worthy of the crown of love.
—ANDREAS CAPELLANUS, *The Art of Courtly Love*

His friends call him "The King"—the man who's invincible with women. When I meet Brian for lunch, I know what they mean when they say, "He could get the dogs off the meat truck." He greets me with a sunburst smile, looking more like a young Matthew Broderick at his First Communion than a twenty-six-year-old banker in a success suit and Hermès tie. But charisma, I soon learn, is only half of his allure. The rest comes down to character—qualities he has consciously cultivated.

"Oh sure," he begins, "there's the intrinsic stuff, loving women and *joie de vivre*. But I can shed some light on a few more things that work for me. I mean, you definitely have to be interesting."

In what way?

"Well," he quirks an eyebrow, "I'm incredibly active. I try to be all things at once. I read, keep up, I follow controversial topics—religion, politics, art. It's very important, too," he taps a sugar packet against the coffee cup for emphasis, "to deal socially with others, to have the ability to smile and charm. I like to keep in touch—all the lines open."

Open they are. Brian has "thirty or forty girlfriends" in his address book whom he contacts regularly, some for quick catchups at Starbucks, others for trysts throughout Europe. At the mention of the word *playboy*, though, he bridles. "Absolutely not! I count women among my closest friends. There are guys who are bad guys, but hey, I'm a good person. I don't mean any ill will. I try to be genuine and true to who I am."

His friends bear him out. Ladykiller that he is, Brian is a far cry from the stock lothario who lacks a mature identity or moral compass. Although base philanderers and scalp-hunters abound, real Casanovas are men of character who possess core traits that persist through time and cultures. Not that they are consistent or "right stuff" material; we have to expand the boundaries a bit. Instead, they are self-created originals with a unique mix of qualities designed to maximize life and love, and to fascinate.

Morality/Virtue

Good moral character is sexually attractive and romantically inspiring.

—GEOFFREY MILLER, *The Mating Mind*

Claude Adrien Helvétius was "the dread of husbands" in eighteenth-century France—the most desired, most sensual, and fickle of men. He was so handsome, with a cleft chin and ice-blue eyes, that Voltaire called him "Apollo." Every morning his valet brought his first bedmate, and every afternoon and evening he romanced the *ton* of Paris—the comtesse d'Autre, the duchesse de Chaulnes, among others—ending with the beautiful actress Mademoiselle Gaussin. Once when a rich suitor offered the actress six hundred livres for the night, she gestured toward Helvétius and said, "Look like this man, monsieur, and I will give you 1,200 livres."

Wealthy, witty, even a gifted dancer, he would seem to be a walking *ancient régime* cliché—a hard-boiled roué. Except he wasn't; he was also the soul of benevolence. No one, said contemporaries, "joined more delicacy to more kindness." When he met the right woman, he married, moved to the countryside, and devoted the rest of his life to good works. There he wrote *De l'esprit* (*On Mind*) and became one of the leading Enlightenment philosophers, advocating natural equality and the "greatest happiness for the greatest number."

Although some women *do* fancy wild and wicked reprobates (especially for flings), a bigger turn-on are men who scramble the good/bad categories and are nice with spice. Unalloyed virtue—or the appearance of it—has zero allure. Ladies' men stir it up. Morally mixed and inclined to bend rules, they are fundamentally decent and know the secret to the oldest conundrum: how to make goodness charming.

Virtue has long been entwined with romantic love. In the fourth-century BC, Plato defined eros as a love of goodness that led up a transcendental ladder to the spheres. Medieval amorists put moral excellence back into romance with courtly love, where it has remained in various degrees ever since. "Honesty [and] virtue" are "great enticers"; "No love without goodness": these rubrics still resonate today. Philosopher Robert Solomon believes ethical worth is a linchpin in love; partners must reflect and magnify our own virtues.

In studies, women seem to be of two minds about virtuous partners. On the one hand, say researchers, they want a nice guy, with "that old-fashioned quality: integrity"; on the other they want a fun, bold, bad boy. The problem is in the polarized choice, writes Edward Horgan in a Harvard University paper; after reviewing the literature, he concludes that women desire a combination of both—niceness commingled with deviltry, and served up seductively.

Seduction, in fact, may have been one of morality's earliest functions. Psychologist Geoffrey Miller speculates that prehistoric man deployed morality as a "sexual ornament," designed to intrigue and enchant women with the delights of fair play, generosity, decency, and concern for others. "You enjoy helping those who help you," writes psychologist Steven Pinker. "That's also why men and women fall in love." Particularly if the lover isn't too perfect.

The ancient love gods were the sexiest of all nice guys. A variegated species with their share of faults, they were glamorous deities who made virtue voluptuous. The volatile Dionysus was also kind and compassionate, and dispensed his benevolence through song, dance, and joyous celebration. Although a tricky customer, the phallic Hermes was the "giver of good things"—a luck-bringer, protector, and silver-tongued seducer. And the "too reckless" Cuchulain of Gaelic myth endeared Irish women young and old with his "pleasing" rectitude and "kindness" to everyone.

Female readers always rate Mr. Darcy of *Pride and Prejudice* as a romantic favorite because he is so deliciously decent. Fitzwilliam Darcy is both an odious snob and a man of honor who saves the Bennets from calamity and charms Elizabeth with his eloquent mea culpa: "You showed me," he says, "how insufficient were all my pretensions to please a woman worthy of being pleased."

Mass-market romances are supposed to be black-and-white morality fables, but the "nice" male protagonists in these novels are ethical crossbreeds. Harry, the straight-arrow accountant of *The Nerd Who Loved Me*, has an inner wild child. He's a covert Vegas buff who flirts with the Mob, beats a snoop to a pulp, and wins the heroine by advertising his good deeds through a series of seductive adventures.

Ladies' men are notorious admixtures. Casanova was not incapable of skullduggery; he exaggerated his exploits for profit and conned the wealthy dowager marquise d'Urfé out of a fortune by faking occult powers and staging a "rebirth" that entailed sex three times in a tub. But he brimmed "with kindness" and performed numerous charitable acts—a gallant visit to a dying inamorata and an impromptu gift of shoe buckles for a little girl.

Poet Alfred de Musset also misbehaved (as when he went on a brothel-bender in Venice while George Sand lay ill), yet he had a "sweetness of character that made him absolutely irresistible." So, too, Warren Beatty: at times a vain rascal and simultaneously, an "extraordinary, good person."

Rarely do you hear the terms *rock star* and *virtue* in the same breath. Unless, that is, you're talking about Sam Cooke. The rhythm-and-blues sensation of the 1950s and 60s who popularized such classics as "You Send Me" and "Wonderful World," Cooke doesn't look exemplary at first glance. He did jail time—brief stints for distributing a dirty book in high school and for "fornication and bastardy" in his twenties. He was stubborn, quick-tempered, conceited, and all hell with women. A "woman's man," he indulged in countless affairs, fathered four known illegitimate children, and was once discovered in bed with five women.

But the top note in his hybrid character was decency. Said friends, he conveyed "genuineness," generosity, and "instinctive kindness in every fiber of his being." Although a gospel singer in his early career and son of a Chicago Baptist preacher, he was not a by-the-Good-Book man; he lived by his own moral lights. Cooke seemed born for women. He had erotic crackle even as a teenager—energy, charm, vitality, and a way of talking to girls with "warmth, [and] kindness," as though each were the only person on the planet. Forthright and honest, he refused to game them, and so enamored Barbara Campbell, a neighbor four years his junior, that she had his daughter out of wedlock at eighteen and waited in the wings for him for seven years.

In the interim, Sam Cooke crossed over from gospel to mainstream rock and roll and became a celebrity with his sweet soaring voice. Women literally fainted when he sang, and stormed him backstage. He was "never crass, never vulgar" about it, but he capitalized on stardom: he fathered two more illegitimate children and married lounge singer Delores Mohawk. After that marriage ended, his high school sweetheart, Barbara Campbell, reappeared. They married and had two children, but he couldn't stay on the porch. Women mobbed him, mesmerized by his charisma and naughty/nice mélange.

Flawed, faithless, good-hearted, and an easy touch: he was each of these things—to his undoing. At thirty-five in December 1964, he hooked up with a party girl after a few too many martinis and took her to a cheap motel, where she changed her mind and bolted with his clothes and money. Enraged and dressed only in a jacket and shoes, he confronted the manager, Bertha Franklin, about the theft, and a scuffle ensued. In the process, Franklin pulled a gun on Cooke and killed him. As the bullet tore through him, he said with combined shock and disbelief, "Lady, you shot me." He died as he lived, "a real gentleman," who beneath the faults—anger, promiscuity, and more—was "a sweet, innocent young guy."

The ingénue of *Primrose*, an old musical, sings that her dream man "needn't be such a saint." Despite the imprecations of Platonists and love philosophers, women will never be persuaded to take perfect moral purity to their hearts. To be seductive, goodness needs sauce—joy, sweetness, and eloquence spiked with frailties. Better, though, to err on the side of the angels: kindness, Ovid reminded men, "will tame even the lions and tigers."

Courage

All true desire is dangerous
—ROBERT BLY, *Iron John*

The story is as old as time. The princess lies comatose in a haunted palace under an evil spell. Men perish in the attempt to rescue her, until one day two princes come along with their younger brother "Simpleton." At the palace they find a gray dwarf who tells them they must perform three impossible tasks to break the spell. As his two craven brothers fail and turn to stone, Simpleton boldly sets off into the forest. With the aid of the beasts he befriends, he collects a thousand pearls, dives to the bottom of the lake, finds the key to the princess's bedroom, and picks the "right" princess out of a choice of three. Simpleton isn't simple; he knows a cardinal ladykiller truth: only the good *and* brave deserve the fair.

Women, in a recent study, said they valued bravery even more than kindness in men. Moralists have long placed courage at the head of the virtues because without it none of the others would be possible. For centuries, valor and boldness of spirit have been seen as the latchkey to female affections. Ladies' men, however, do courage as unconventionally as everything else. They combine risk, perseverance, brains, starch, and inner mettle with decency and a distaste for gratuitous violence.

They need not be physically brave—broncobusters or smoke jumpers—but they have the right hearts and souls of steel.

They wouldn't, though, be great lovers without spine. Eros is dangerous terrain; intimacy is land-mined with threats. Women can be transported over the moon, but they can also be abandoned, engulfed, and driven mad by passion. Men, too, have special terrors of their own—performance anxieties and a witch's brew of other fears. In love, women want a man who's up to a challenge. As the Romans said, "Venus favors the bold," and god help the lover who recoils from the romantic fray and runs for cover.

Evolutionary psychologists argue that the female fondness for male mettle goes back to a physical need for provisions, protection, and status. Prehistoric women sought brave defenders to survive and prosper. Another explanation is more erotic: A woman may have been excited by exhibitions of courage in man-to-man combats because it thrilled her to think she was worth fighting for. Rather than a servile drudge, she became a prize for whom men risked their lives.

There may be a mythic tug on women too. Fertility gods were a staunch lot. The Sumerian "Fearless One," Dumuzi, descended to the horrors of the underworld and took the "ultimate adventure of the Lover," seducing the great love goddess Inanna. By nature unwarlike, Dionysus was intrepid in battle and routed the giants with his unholy uproar. He bravely came to Ariadne's rescue and stood his ground when King Pentheus imprisoned him. "How bold this bacchant is!" marveled the guards at his cool defiance of the king.

Women accord premier status to bold lovers in their fantasies. Romance novels teem with commandos, highland warriors, secret agents, and dukes who duel at ten paces, but their feats of derring-do are paired with psychological fortitude and moral sensitivity. Dr. Zhivago, a top romantic pick for women, is a portrait in courage—physical, psychological, and erotic. He braves the war zone, loves dangerously, and politically defies the Soviet state in the face of crushing odds.

Casanova, whatever his defects, strode out boldly. When the Inquisitorial police arrested him in Venice on trumped-up charges, he dressed in plumes and satin as if for a ball, then managed a daring escape from the impregnable Leads prison over a year later. He was equally valiant in his amours. At twenty, he fell hopelessly in love with a talented beauty of the wrong gender, the castrato singer Bellino. "He" had warded off every suitor, but Casanova persevered and discovered what he suspected: Bellino was a woman named Teresa equipped with a leather six-inch penis. He promptly declared himself, and asked her to marry him. "I am not afraid of misfortune," he explained to her; he counted courage and a sense of honor among his best qualities.

Though uniformly courageous, ladies' men range in degrees of physical and psychological valor. Fascinators, like air ace Denys Finch Hatton and bullfighter Juan Belmonte, fall on the action end of the spectrum. Belmonte, Hemingway's model for the matador-lover in *The Sun Also Rises*, was small, ugly, crippled, and tortured with fear, but he became a master in the bullring and in the bedroom. "The same energy that went into his conquering a bull also went into conquering a woman," said an unnamed famous actress, "and he was the greatest lover I ever had." More typical are ladykillers of moral fiber: Enlightenment intellectual Denis Diderot, who challenged the censors, and Albert Camus, whose credo was "courage" and whose underground Resistance work in World War II almost cost him his life.

Robert Louis Stevenson is the last person you might choose

for a courage hall of fame. But he's a prime candidate, in both word and deed, and a man beloved by women. Skeletal, eccentric, and sickly, he is remembered as the avuncular author of the classic novels *Treasure Island* and *Dr. Jekyll and Mr. Hyde*. But he was a paladin in full-tilt revolt against Victorian respectability, and a "fanatical lover of women." Despite poverty, "tatterdemalion" clothes, and a scarecrow appearance, he had enormous warmth, goodness, and charm, and bound "women to him with silken cords." He racked up scores of inamoratas: an Edinburgh belle; a "dark lady" named Claire; a noted European beauty; sundry mistresses and French *charmeuses*; and finally his wife, Fanny Osbourne.

In his courtship of Fanny, he displayed the high courage that marked everything he did. He was resolute against danger, whether scaling treacherous mountains or combating authority. "Keep your fears to yourself," he quipped, "but share your courage with others." He was not blind to the perils of passionate love. We are "unhorsed" by it, he wrote, cast into a hazardous zone which we explore like children "venturing together into a dark room." And Fanny was not the safest choice. Married with two children and ten years his senior, she suffered from depression and had to leave him mid-affair to settle accounts with her husband in America.

When he got her cable from California, he set sail, steerage class. By the time he reached her in San Francisco, he was penniless and ill, fluctuating between life and death. Fanny divorced her husband in 1880, and she and Stevenson married, after which he produced his best-loved works, *Kidnapped* among others. In deteriorating health, he remained an adventurer, ending up in Samoa, where he wrote, protested colonial injustices, and became revered by the Samoans. His friends envisioned him as "sly Hermes," the mythic seducer and spirit of fearlessness

who stole Apollo's cattle and Aphrodite's girdle. "Love," wrote
Stendhal, "is an exquisite flower, but it needs courage to pluck it
on the bank of a dreadful precipice."

Spiritual Cultivation

Eroticism is primarily a religious matter.
—GEORGES BATAILLE, *Eroticism: Death and Sensuality*

Peter K. wasn't the only Episcopal priest to run afoul that year.
It was 1974. A General Theological graduate with a Junior
League wife and small son, Peter was considered a catch for St.
M's—a small parish in a rural Virginia college town. He had
ideas and presence. Blond and lanky with an aquiline profile, he
loped down the aisle in his flowing chasuble and gold-brocaded
stole, drowning out the choir with his basso "Faith of Our
Fathers." He permitted children to take communion, chanted
the litany, and introduced a book club, soup kitchen, shut-in
outreach, and spiritual retreats to Mountain Lake.

The retreats were where it started: sobbed confessions on the
trail, a note squeezed into his hand in the prayer circle, and a
lay reader who burst into his room one night, nude beneath her
parka. He consoled too many. A vestryman's wife caught him
one afternoon on Bald Knob entwined with a parishioner on a
blanket, his clerical collar discarded on a boulder beside a bottle
of Mateus.

The man of God is one of the dark seducer's favorite guises.
A literary stereotype for hundreds of years (think of Chaucer's lecherous Friar) he's an all-too-real phenomenon in every
religion. The testimonials of women sucked in—and at times
abused—by a spiritual leader's aura could fill a dozen holy

books. The website "Boundary Violations without Borders" provides over a hundred links to such accounts.

Male spirituality is powerfully attractive to women, and many slick operators have turned it to sordid ends. Great lovers aren't among them. On the whole, they're nonexploitative, sincere, and untraditional in their beliefs. Kurt, a German Casanova and photographer I interviewed, is typical. Deeply pious, he espouses an eclectic Taoist-inspired faith that informs and augments his relationships. "I think you channel a force with a woman," he says. "Call it God—whatever you like. I don't go out to break hearts. I view this planet as a divine school."

The link between religion and desire is no accident. We ask passionate love to fulfill the same functions as belief: to plug the holes in our soul, sanctify and save us, defeat death, and raise us to seventh heaven. The loved one becomes our deity, our "will-to-meaning." From a sociobiological perspective, you might argue that spiritually grounded men make fitter mates. The Positive Psychology Center at the University of Pennsylvania lists the "Strength of Transcendence" as one of the six attributes of "character," and psychiatrists increasingly promote faith for healthy personhood.

Sex and the sacred also reach back to the dawn of humankind. Led by charismatic shamans, prehistoric peoples danced and drummed themselves into mystical raptures to merge with the vitalizing principle of the universe, divine sexual energy. Dionysian worship resembled a tent revival where celebrants sought redemption and transfiguration through ecstatic fusion with the phallic god. Psychologist Erich Neumann thinks these fertility rites have left a psychic imprint in the unconscious and influence our sexual proclivities today.

The love-religion meld is ensconced in modern culture. Religious rhetoric infuses the language of romance: ads, greeting cards, and popular songs assure us that we will be transported to "heaven's door" by angels we'll "worship and adore" forever. A troupe of Hollywood sex symbols portrayed cinematic holy men: Charlton Heston as Moses; Anthony Quinn as Mohammed; Cary Grant, John Travolta, and Warren Beatty as angels; and Brad Pitt as a Buddhist convert in *Seven Years in Tibet*.

Women's popular romances throng with men of the cloth. In the novella *God on a Harley*, the love hero is the Deity himself come to earth in jeans and a ponytail to spirit the heroine away on his motorcycle and redeem her. And they don't get more lovable than the handsome vicar Christy Morrell, of Patricia Gaffeny's *To Love and To Cherish*, with his humor, fierce doubts, and "edge of Woo." A "For the Love of God" romance website lists over forty clerical heartthrobs, not counting a six-book series about the "Rev. Feelgood," Nate Thicke.

Nineteenth-century pianist Franz Liszt enraptured women for many reasons, not least of which was his intense spirituality. As much inclined to religion as music, Liszt twice contemplated the priesthood, and at fifty, he took minor orders, donned a cassock, and wrote sacred music. His courtships centered on long conversations about God and eternity. To Countess Marie d'Agoult, who left her husband and children for him, he spoke only of the "destiny of mankind" and "promises of religion." Later, he captivated a Russian princess (who also abandoned her spouse for him) through spiritual communions in her crucifix-filled bedroom. She called him a "masterpiece of God."

The nineteenth-century John Humphrey Noyes is a less orthodox case. An "uncomely" loner from Vermont, Noyes saw the light one day at Yale Divinity School and envisioned a new religion—a perfected order of mankind. The Second Coming had already occurred, he preached, and ushered in a sinless, joyous age. To realize it, men had only to create a utopian society based on economic communism, righteous living, birth control, and free love.

The result was the Oneida Community in upstate New York, where men and women had sex with whomever they pleased and shared everything in common, creating their own schools, clothes, and cultural programs and supporting themselves with crafts. At its height Oneida contained over three hundred members and lasted thirty years, longer than any other utopian experiment in America.

During that time, Noyes was the group's supreme spiritual leader. He was "extraordinarily attractive to women," said his son, due to sexual "magnetism superadded to intense religious convictions." All the women were "eager to sleep with him," and he took hundreds of lovers.

The nature of his religious convictions may have enhanced Noyes's allure. God, Noyes professed, wanted women to be happy in bed. To that end, men were instructed to practice sexual pleasure as an art form, learning to court lovers with tenderness and gallantry and to withhold ejaculation so that women could have multiple orgasms.

Members had sexual freedom of choice so long as a woman held the power of refusal and neither indulged in the "claiming spirit." Noyes himself nearly fell into that snare. At one point he had a passionate affair with a resident, Mary Cragin, that developed into an "idolatrous attachment." "Anybody," he explained, who knew her "found her spirit exceedingly intoxicating—one that will make a man crazy." Providentially, she died in a shipwreck in the Hudson River, and he became an "exemplary lover" thereafter.

By his sixties, Noyes had sired at least nine of the fifty-eight children born in Oneida and was still active and virile. But there was dissension within and without. Fractious members lobbied for monogamy and free enterprise, and conservative clergymen in Syracuse banded against him. He fled to Canada, where he ended his days in the company of female loyalists, postulants to their prophet whose face "shone like an angel's."

Knowledge/Intelligence

The desire to know really is desire.
—CATHLEEN SCHINE, *Rameau's Niece*

Over vodkatinis in a Manhattan bar tonight, the city's "great Hungarian lover" is telling yet another woman, "When I make love to you, I will go very slow and you will have multiple orgasms." What more could a lady want? For a grand passion, she might want something else he provides: brains. As one of his lovers tells me, "You know what his real secret is: he's very smart. Smart is sexy." Laszlo speaks five languages, and if you find him on his favorite bench beside the boathouse in Central Park, he'll be deep into Lacan, Maimonides, or Primo Levi. Intellect even enhances his promised assignations: *Tristan and Isolde* on the Bose and pillow talk about Modigliani. "The ecstasy," says this recent conquest, "is unbearable."

You don't see the 1960s bumper stickers and tee shirts anymore that say, "Intelligence is the Ultimate Aphrodisiac." Now it's more about chiseled abs, bespoke shirts, tactics, and two-comma incomes. But the brain is the biggest sex organ, and a woman's second (maybe first) most loved part of the male anatomy. Studies show women favor intelligence over beauty or wealth, even for one-night stands.

The fourth-century sex manual *Kāma Sūtra* alerts men that without knowledge nothing is possible, and assigns an ambitious curriculum for a lover: fourteen sciences, seven religious traditions, the Vedas, and six other tomes. To be loved by a woman, say each of the great amorists, one must acquire "distinction of mind." It's easy to see the parallels, writes philosopher Martha Nussbaum, "between sexual desire and the desire for wisdom."

Yes, but. Anyone who has slept through Econ 101 or dated a leaden Proust scholar knows that super-smart doesn't always mean super-sexy. Women-charmers understand how to make intelligence seductive; they sparkle with mental energy, surprise, amuse, instruct, up the drama, and surf the whole realm of knowledge—high-, middle-, and lowbrow. And they really can look like Woody Allen on a bad day.

Evolutionary psychologists have several explanations for the sex appeal of male IQ. Ultra-Darwinists believe ancestral women valued intelligence in men because it predicted economic and social success. Geoffrey Miller puts a sexier spin on this. Bigger brains evolved the same way penises did, he theorizes; they "reached inside women's pleasure system." Men with the most cerebral bells and whistles gave women a better time and edged out the dim bruisers.

None of the mythological love gods was slow-witted. Ganesha, the Hindu Lord of Letters and Learning, acquired his elephant's head because he so enthralled the goddess Pavarti that her husband, Shiva, had to decapitate and deform him. Dionysus brought civilization to the world in his wanderings, and Hermes the Seducer was the "Clever One" and culture hero. The Irish folk hero and sex god Cuchulain was a scholar of Druid lore with gifts of "understanding and calculation."

Recently intellectuals haven't fared well in mainstream fiction. They're portrayed as sex-driven, debauched scoundrels whose trips to the library are euphemisms for trysts with young lovelies. Scholar-satyrs who exploit the erotic hit of knowledge doubtless exist, but women prefer to see them otherwise in their fantasy literature. Intellectuals proliferate, and professors are one of the eight archetypes of romance novels.

When they appear, as in Nora Roberts's *Vision in White*, they are sober good guys, like Carter whose mojo with the heroine, Mac, is his mind. "He made her think," she muses, "the man was charming." In Norman Rush's *Mortals*, two pedants in Botswana duel with their learning to gain the affections of the heroine. Ray, her husband, realizes what women want: not "buns or dick size," but "intellect," and he wins her back with his brains.

A number of unlikely ladies' men used their heads to enchant women. The diminutive eighteenth-century philosopher Voltaire—a polymath of immense range—kept the tall, brilliant beauty Émilie du Châtelet interested for thirteen years. He challenged her to scientific competitions, staged plays and poetry readings, debated politics, and traded repartee with her over four-hour dinners.

And then there's mathematician Bertrand Russell. Gaunt and small, with a "Mad Hatter's" features, bad breath, and a high, fluty voice, he disheveled women, accumulating four wives and many lovers. (One was my great aunt Barry Fox, who collared him in New York and gave him "several enjoyable evenings.") In just one night's fireside chat, he pitched bird of paradise Ottoline Morrell into a grand amour. "In spite of myself," she wrote, "I was carried away, but fate sometimes throws a ball of fire into one's life."

Aldous Huxley's fabulous love life has to have been a case of mind over matter. Nicknamed the "Ogre" as a child, he was over six foot four with coke-bottle glasses and an enormous head atop a spindly frame. Yet women adored him. Of the distinguished Huxleys, Aldous, said his brother Julian, was the "one genius in the family." The scope of his mind and achievements was astounding; he wrote well-known novels like *Point Counterpoint*, *Brave New World*, and *Island*, as well as poetry, short stories, travel books, screenplays, and twenty-three volumes of essays on subjects from science and politics to parapsychology. His *Doors of Perception* about his experiments with LSD made him the father of the hippie movement.

When he arrived at Oxford nearly blind from an incurable eye infection and smarter than anyone, "he made a tremendous impression," especially on his female peers. Highly sexed, unpuritanical, and fond of women, he was much sought after. One infatuated young playwright remembered how he "threw open a whole world" to her—French poetry and the arts—and how much she wanted to kiss him. His choices were gifted, unconventional women such as violinist Jelly d'Arányi and artist Dora Carrington. With Carrington, he spent nights on the roof talking about books and ideas and singing ragtime tunes.

In 1919, he married Maria Nye, a cultivated Belgian beauty who devoted herself to his welfare and consented to the most unusual of open unions. Without a touch of rancor, she abetted his extramarital affairs, selecting lovers, arranging rendezvous, and sending books the morning afterward with appropriate risqué French inscriptions. He enjoyed sex and women, she reasoned, and needed escapades as a relief from his mental exertions.

Included among his lovers were a Romanian princess, the political activist and writer Nancy Cunard, and one of Maria's bisexual friends, Mary Hutchinson, who lived with them in a ménage à trois for almost a decade. Several had marital designs, but Aldous and Maria had a close—albeit unique—relationship that lasted thirty-five years. At her death Maria handpicked her successor, a violinist and psychoanalyst twenty years Huxley's

junior who gave up music and dedicated herself to him, nonex-
clusivity and all.

Pictures of Huxley cannot account for the spell he cast on the
female sex. He looked, Virginia Woolf observed, like a "gigantic
grasshopper." But five minutes in his company and the necro-
mancy of his learning put stars in women's eyes. Said one: when
he talked "he was ribald and cynical and brilliant." As his son's
marriage was breaking up, he told him his secret: "Intelligence,"
he wrote, "endows love with effectiveness."

Social IQ

Loving well requires a full social intelligence.

—DANIEL GOLEMAN, *Social Intelligence*

Social circles are full of men who talk shop, blow their own
horns, and tune out women. Real-estate mogul Mort Zuckerman
isn't one of them. He's attentive, plugged in, and "one of the
best dinner-party companions," says Barbara Walters, she has
"ever known." He navigates social waters like a sonar-guided
submarine, from beach barbecues, business deals, and high-level
politics, to black-tie penthouse parties.

None of this is lost on his romantic life. He's a swami with
women and has dated such A-listers as Betty Rollin, Nora
Ephron, Diane von Furstenberg, and Marisa Berenson. He's
"fun to be around" and mind-reads the feminine heart. Gloria
Steinem said he wrapped her in an emotional "sheepskin jacket"
when she was at a low ebb. Former girlfriend Arianna Huffington cited his "gift of intimacy" and compared him to the god
Hermes, "the master of love magic" who is also socially "wise"
and knows how to "deal with strangers."

In seduction there are two ways to be smart: IQ and EQ.

Cognitive brilliance, the light-and-laser show of learning, has potent charms, but so does emotional intelligence. Only recently recognized by academic researchers, social dexterity is now regarded as a crucial life skill, increasingly correlated with success in love and work. What it boils down to is savoir faire: a radar for other people's feelings, mastery of synchrony, and the practical skill to get the answer yes. Social IQ may or may not make the course of love run smoother, as some advocates claim, but it can release the floodgates. Ladies' men are master hands.

Science writer Daniel Goleman says they have to be: the rational brain alone can't manage romance, which is a subcortical activity and requires the complex coordination of three different brain systems. A great lover needs his social wits about him. None of which is new, Goleman admits; it's just being ratified by social neuroscience.

Two millennia ago, Ovid provided a crash course in social competence for lovers-in-training, prescribing courtesy, tact, and intuition. Every amorous guide since then advises men to shine up people skills. Geoffrey Miller thinks we owe civilized behavior today to women's preference throughout history for interpersonal finesse—empathy, rapport, and good manners—over brute physical prowess.

Arch-seducers, though, practice an elite form of erotic intelligence. Whether through talent or practice, they have an "eighth sense" (as they say of Warren Beatty) with women. These experts possess an almost paranormal sense of a woman's hidden desires and the optimal way to handle the moment. Sexologist Havelock Ellis referred to this as a "fine divination," and philosopher Ortega y Gasset, as "*tacto*," an intuitive grasp of another's psyche and needs.

Sex gods had that magic touch. The Sumerian deity Dumuzi intuits the source of love goddess's Inanna's anger, and senses how to placate her and bring her around. He promises her heart's desire: equality, no women's work, and a husband who will be a father and mother to her. Dionysus soothes the jilted Ariadne with divine delicacy, approaching gently, praising her to the stars, and promising fidelity: "I am here for you a lover," he says, "faithful."

Like Dionysus, romantic heroes lavish heroines with their social gifts. Empathy, attunement, the apt gesture: even the most callous rakes supply them in women's love stories. Explaining why she's hooked on a certain guy, the heroine of a popular romance says, "I think he's just really, really, *really* good with people. Empathetic." Czech lothario Tomas of Milan Kundera's *The Unbearable Lightness of Being* has an extra gene for social aptitude, with a knack for "emotional telepathy."

Although social savvy, say psychologists, has fallen out of fashion, women-charmers are adroit practitioners. David Niven was a virtuoso. His bonhomie, warmth, and wizardry with people opened all the doors—and bedroom doors—in Hollywood. Inconstant as he was, women excused his defections in exchange for his tuned-in "concern and affection" and interpersonal brilliance.

Sometimes social prowess in love can migrate into politics. The synergy of the two was Sir Walter Raleigh's fortune and downfall. An obscure soldier without rank or connections, Raleigh arrived at court in 1581 with only his "caressing manners" and uncanny ability to wrap people around his finger. As soon as he finagled an audience with Queen Elizabeth, he became her darling. He gave her a taste of the "bumptiousness" she craved, mixed with wit, passion, drama, and shrewd praise. For twelve years he advanced from post to post until the queen discovered his secret marriage with one of her maids of honor, Bess Throckmorton, and imprisoned him in the Tower.

Prince Clemens von Metternich, the nineteenth-century "Knight of Europe," allied love and diplomacy with greater success. Handsome, elegant, and a social maestro, Metternich was one of the most stellar statesmen of his age. As Austrian minister, he brokered the 1815 Congress of Vienna, which redrew the map of Europe after Napoleon's defeat, and steered the Austro-Hungarian Empire for the next thirty years. Through his dexterity in managing intricate negotiations, he extracted compromises, maintained a balance of power, and created the European Alliance that prefigured NATO.

He was no less smooth with the ladies. Raised by his sophisticated mother on the finer points of politesse—adaptability, social telepathy, rapport, and grace—he was an "Adonis of the Drawing Room," with a high-bridged nose, sensuous mouth, and slate-blue eyes beneath crescent eyebrows. When he left home, his mother said presciently, "He is pleasing to women . . . He will make his way."

While still at university, he was spotted by one of the most beautiful women of France, taken to her home, thrust into an armchair, ravished, and swept into a three-year affair. As he moved up the diplomatic ladder, he "made every woman fall in love with him," even his wife, an heiress whom he had wed in a marriage of convenience. And he loved them in return, often two or three simultaneously. He said he "cared for all in a different way and for different reasons."

His mistresses were many—titled, married, and select. There was the wife of a Russian general who appeared like a "beautiful naked angel" on his doorstep in Dresden; Napoleon's sister, whose bracelet of hair he never took off; and two duchesses, one of whom cost him Bavaria when he overslept with her during the Congress of Vienna. Altogether, Metternich had nine major amours, including two more wives after his first one died. His last was a spitfire Hungarian and aristocrat thirty-two years his junior who bore four of his children. At seventy-five, widowed and in exile in England, he was visited by all his surviving lovers, including a seventy-six-year-old ex-mistress still in love with him.

Metternich was "extremely handsome" right into old age, when his face was sunken and seamed and his hair, shock white. But what made him such an unsurpassed "*homme à femmes*" was his exquisitely tuned social antennae and arts of ingratiation. It made him, too, a dominant figure in European government up until 1848. "Politics and love," he believed, "went hand in hand."

Pleasure

Pleasure considered as an art is still
waiting for its physiologists.
—HONORÉ DE BALZAC, *The Physiology of Marriage*

The cast of male characters in Woody Allen's *Vicky Cristina Barcelona* comes straight from a Social Darwinian lineup. They're good physical specimens, rich, stable, respected, devoted, and free with goodies: yachts, maids, and mansions with tennis courts. But they leave the two heroines cold. Instead, the women fall for a stranger who makes them an offer one night they can't refuse. A sultry Spanish painter approaches them at dinner and says, "I would like to invite you both to spend the weekend. We'll eat, we'll drink wine, we'll make love. The city is romantic, the night is warm, why not?" A *maître de plaisir*, Juan Antonio leads them down the pleasure path that weekend and thereafter, serving up gourmet delights of mind and body: art, travel, cuisine, poetry, music, beauty, frolic, and passionate sex. In the process, the "right choice" men fall by the wayside—revealed in all their robotic drabness and undesirability.

You might ask, What's pleasure got to do with it? To evolutionary diehards, not much, except as an adaptive by-product, candles on the mating cake, or "spandrels," as biologists call them. Women want men, they contend, for weightier reasons. Desire, however, has an inconvenient way of ignoring reason; falling in love, writes psychiatrist Michael Liebowitz, is "having your pleasure center go bonkers." "Love is pleasure," as the ballad proclaims. And ladies' men are deluxe pleasure-providers, adept in the whole repertoire of enjoyment.

Although we're awash in entertainment options, men who deliver full delight in love are relatively rare. The default position in the animal kingdom, notes Geoffrey Miller, is apathy; the select few favored by "hot choosers" in prehistory were men talented in the arts of pleasing, from the sweets of the sense to the charms of the mind. Women may have inherited an internal pleasure-meter and pick men who move the needle.

A second theory keys off from Freud's pleasure principle, the idea that the unconscious contains drives for gratification that must be repressed in the interests of civilization. According to a school of neo-Freudians, this repression is both excessive and toxic. What's wanted—craved deep in our ganglia—are men who will shed restraints and restore sensuosity, satisfaction, and primal joy.

Sex gods like Dionysus, "the delight of mortals," were pleasure freedom-fighters. They released "everything that had been locked up," and drenched the earth in delectables: wine, dance, joy, and satisfactions of soul and body. "Pleasure" was "the image of the divine state" in ancient Shiva worship.

Are women more susceptible to these blandishments?

Maybe, if scientists are right. As sex researcher Marta Meana observes, female erotic fantasies focus on getting pleasure. Perhaps this stems from the extra vigilance and life tensions women bring to the bedroom, or a heightened sensuous receptivity. Their hearing, vision, smell, and tactile senses are sharper than men's, and they furnish their imaginative sex scenes with a sensorium of props: votive candles, silk sheets, mood music.

The mantra of romance heroes is "relax, gorge your senses, let me show you a good time." Josie of Eloisa James's *Pleasure for Pleasure* is deflowered by the "adorably beautiful" Earl de Mayne on a sofa in a moonlit cottage amid a scented rose garden.

Mary Gordon's novel *Spending* speaks to every woman's starvation for joy and relief from strain and overwork. Monica Szabo, a middle-aged painter, meets a fantasy muse, a wealthy commodities broker who offers to give her what she needs: R & R (dance, gourmet dinners, perfumed baths), sexual solace, and trips to see art galleries and bask in the Old Masters. Pleasure-soaked, she produces her great work.

Men's love manuals have always emphasized the arts of the delight. The *Kāma Sūtra* devotes volumes to the minutiae of intoxicating a lover through hedonistic allures, from a sumptuously fitted-out "chamber of love" with soft cushions and games, to festive evenings of song, music, and flower battles. Ovid was less specific; just "endeavor to please," he exhorted. The mindset is what counts, wrote Balzac in the nineteenth century; a man must interest himself in the "science of pleasure" to prevail with women.

Casanova, a thinking woman's voluptuary, studied the subject at length and concluded that "pleasure, pleasure, pleasure" was man's highest calling—if and only if it were treated intelligently. There must be a spiritual component, he wrote, combined with connoisseurship and variety. His three happy months with Henriette were carefully calibrated: scholarly studies, sex, rest, and different diversions and operas each day.

During the nine-to-five work crackdown of the 1950s, romancer Porfirio Rubirosa asked a subversive question: "What's wrong with pleasure?" It doesn't take a PhD in psychology to guess the consequences. Standing "head and shoulders above the international pleasure pack," "Rubi" was gallant, sophisticated, and a genius of enjoyment. He knew how to keep delight fresh and soul-satisfying, and tailor it to each woman.

He wooed Doris Duke, his third wife, with a pleasure tour designed specifically to her tastes. He took this cosseted, libidinous heiress (daughter of tobacco mogul "Buck" Duke) to louche Left Bank hangouts and anything-goes Antibes, where he treated her to "the most magnificent penis" she had ever seen.

After their divorce, he conquered Zsa Zsa Gabor through a different tack. For the stressed-out movie star, he delivered sabbaticals of Hungarian food, getaway weekends, and uninhibited all-night revels where Rubi drummed with the band and led musicians home for ham-and-egg feasts. "We were like two children," recalled Gabor, "pleasure seeking, hedonistic." "I am, and always will be," he said, "a man of pleasure."

It's no feat for a king to have mistresses; ambitious beauties will hurl themselves at any crowned head. But to have them love you is another thing. Charles II of England adored women, and they repaid him in kind. Called the "Merry Monarch," he came to the throne in 1660 after Oliver Cromwell's harsh nine-year puritanical rule, and reintroduced the pleasure principle. Fun returned from exile. And the king led the way, "charm[ing] all who came near him" with his affability, ease of manner, and talent for enjoyment. He turned the palace into a garden of delights—sports, dances, comedies, exotic birds, verdant parks, and the arts and sciences—and populated it with Eves. He had nine mistresses, at least, whom he treated to this fare, and none was indifferent to Charles. His French *maîtresse en titre* Louise de Keroualle thought him "the love of her life"; comic actress Nell Gwynne sincerely loved him; and his often-betrayed wife, Catherine of Braganza, worshipped the ground he walked on.

Despite the rampant hedonism and sexual license of modern life, pleasure may be on the decline. Studies show that Americans tend to defer fun and enjoyment; we work longer hours and work at play and relationships. Which isn't how eros operates. As Johnny Depp's character in the movie *Don Juan DeMarco* explains, "I give women pleasure if they desire. It is of course the greatest pleasure they will ever experience."

Self-Realization

I am large, I contain multitudes.

—WALT WHITMAN, "Song of Myself"

Don Juan of Steven Millhauser's story "An Adventure of Don Juan" is the seducer at the top of his form and so jaded by success that he decides to visit an unprepossessing English squire for a change of scene. Once at the estate of the round-faced Augustus Hood, he sets his sights on his wife, Mary, and sister-in-law Georgiana; they're both easy prey, he muses, he's "never wrong about such matters."

But he has underestimated his host. Hood, despite his schoolboy looks, is a dynamo, a "man of many projects" who has turned Swan Park into a highbrow Disneyland. When not in his library or workroom, he gives guided tours of his simulated Elysium and hosts erudite dinner-table debates. Don Juan begins to feel progressively off his game. With his seductions stalled, he takes matters in hand one night and winds his way through Hood's labyrinthine mansion (an image of its owner), to Georgiana's boudoir. He opens the door and sees that he's been outmatched by a greater seducer: Hood is in bed nude with his siter-in-law.

Complete, multifaceted personhood is the peak of character development—and seductive allure. Philosopher Jean-Paul Sartre thought this was the all-access pass in amour. "The lover," he wrote, "must seduce the beloved" by besieging her with "his plenitude of absolute being" and intriguing her with his "infinity of depth." Which is a tall order. Full self-development takes drive, courage, and a robust ego. Not every ladies' man is up to the task, but most are strong-selved, replete personalities. Actualized individuals, note psychologists, report "richer, more satisfying love experiences," which may be related to the fact that they're desired more. We love souls that are "overfull," that evoke "wholeness."

A rich-natured ladies' man compels women—regardless of his rank, income, or looks. When women in surveys express a preference for "achievers," they seldom mention tangible assets; they cite intelligence, energy, ambition, and all-round excellence. They seek, as psychiatrist Ethel Person explains, an "authentically powerful" selfhood. Supermodel Carla Bruni said former French president Nicolas Sarkozy conquered her through the force of his prolific personality. "He has five or six brains," she told an interviewer, "which are remarkably well irrigated."

Sexual selection and ancient myth favored high evolvers. Ancestral women, surmises Geoffrey Miller, were less impressed with material resources than cerebral ones, preferring polysided, potentiated men over one-dimensional swells. And fertility gods were individuated on a heroic scale. Khonsu, the ancient Egyptian love deity, fertilized the cosmic egg and commanded health, architecture, time measurement, hunting, travel, and wisdom. As for the thousand-named Shiva, he contained the entire cosmos, and Dionysus was the lord of "diversity" and "inexpressible depth."

Storied ladykillers often display manifold characters. Odysseus is a *kalokagathos*, "complete man"; Cuchulain, a many-gifted wonder; and the knight Lanval, of Marie de France's medieval *Lais*, such a model of total manhood that both Guinevere and the queen of the fairies proposition him. The duc de Nemours of Madame de La Fayette's seventeenth-century *Princesse de Clèves* is unsurpassably self-actualized. A court paragon—multi-accomplished, integrated, and zealous—he enamors the married princess, with tumultuous results.

Heroines still fall hard for these full-selved heroes. Grace, a poor girl in the Alice Munro story "Passion," is happily engaged to the wealthy, "sterling" Maury until she meets his complex "deep unfathomable" brother and flees with him into the night. The polymathic doctor Davis Morel has the same effect on the wife of CIA agent Ray Finch in Norman Rush's *Mortals*. Abundant male personas pervade women's fantasy fiction, from the mega-versatile Christian Grey of *Fifty Shades of Grey* to history professor Lincoln Blaise in *The Cinderella Deal*. "There were so many layers to Linc," moons the heroine as she realizes he's the one.

Although ladies' men can be loved without this amplitude of being, a number have large, geodesic identities. The sixteenth-century Florentine Filippo Strozzi was a politician and banker, then papal diplomat, and finally, leader of the 1537 rebellion against the Medici stronghold in Rome. Known as the "siren," he also wrote love sonnets, designed a pleasure palace, and sang "The Passion" at a professional level each Holy Week. After his romance with Camilla Pisana ended, the renowned beauty mourned him until she died.

Carl Jung, psychiatrist and popularizer of such concepts as archetype and the collective unconscious, thought good relationships depended on self-development and a complexity of mind "comparable to a gem with many facets as opposed to the simple cube." He should know. A man of phenomenal appeal to women, he explored the depths of the psyche, wrote about it (with illustrations), and studied Eastern and Western philosophy, alchemy, sociology, astrology, literature, and the arts well into old age.

Had Jung searched, he would have found an alter ego in America. Benjamin Franklin was another champion self-actualizer who wore so many hats he has become a national legend and inspiration to millions. One of those hats—recently dusted off by scholars—is that of ladies' man. He's an illustration, par excellence, of the sex appeal of an optimized, multi-faceted personality. A successful newspaper printer, civic leader, and author, he retired from business at forty-two to devote himself to his studies. He experimented with electricity; invented a stove, bifocals, and the lightning rod (the list goes on); and launched a political and diplomatic career that lasted forty years. Vibrant and brilliant, he "continually reinvented himself."

But a ladies' man—with his bald pate, spectacles, and paunch? Yet Franklin was lusty and charming and "surrounded himself with adoring women." As a young man in Boston and England, he did his share of wenching and fathered an illegitimate son, William, whom his wife Deborah agreed to raise. During their forty-four years of marriage, they spent only eighteen together. The rest of the time, whether in America or England, he entertained young women like Catherine Ray and Polly Stevenson with his élan and conversation, and perhaps slept with Polly's mother in London for fifteen years.

At seventy and widowed, Franklin was still attractive to

women. When he arrived in Paris in 1776 to secure support for the new nation, he created an amorous furor. Women wore cameos with his likeness, fêted him nightly, and stopped him on the street to have their necks kissed. It's your "gaiety" and "gallantry," said one admirer, that "cause all the women to love you." Improbably enough, he became the center of a sex scandal that almost cost him his job. The lady in question was no ingénue but a sparky *salonnière* of sixty-one.

Minette Helvétius, widow of the acclaimed philosopher, held court in a home on the Bois de Boulogne that attracted the intellectual and political elect of the day. Serious discussions took place in an atmosphere of relaxed festivity where Franklin played his harmonica, composed drinking songs, and debated atheism. After seven weeks, he was so in love that he told friends he intended to "capture her and keep her with him for life." She refused his marriage proposals, but they remained lovers, exchanging notes, visiting regularly, and kissing in public.

The affair grew shocking. Abigail Adams met Helvétius and was horrified; she was a "very bad" hussy, pawing Franklin in public and "showing more than her foot" on the sofa. Future president John Adams was as "disgusted" as his wife and stormed back to America, where he tried (unsuccessfully) to ruin Franklin politically.

Like all national icons, Franklin was cleaned up for posterity and mythologized as an asexual folk hero and statesman. But Franklin was more: he was a darling of women and a total man whose myriad interests, talents, and charms worked both to build a nation and to captivate female hearts.

Character in a New Key

Character is power.

In none of the standard character instruction is there a word on how to be lovable and sexually fascinating. (Franklin kept his charm secrets under tight wraps, concealed beneath a Poor Richard facade.) But the ladykillers' qualities deserve equal time. Great lovers are undeniably shot through with flaws— infidelity, vanity, intemperance, irresponsibility, and more. Their personalities, though, are custom-crafted to gain and sustain female desire. It's just a question of a perspective shift and a broader definition of character.

Casanova, ever ahead of the curve, was an ardent advocate of cultivating desirability. His "character," he asserts in his memoirs, was the product of his own efforts "to make himself loved by [women]"—and was nothing to be ashamed of. He freely admits his shortcomings, then spends the next twelve volumes documenting the qualities he acquired to be adored: intelligence, bravery, "honorable" behavior, spirituality (he always "worship[ed] God"), hedonistic artistry, social wizardry, and optimal selfhood. With his acute insight into women's "fears, hopes, and desires," he ingratiated himself with every class, from servant girls to Catherine the Great, who became "sweet and affable" in his presence and granted him four interviews.

"If you want her to love you," Ovid advised, "be a loveable man." That, insists Brian the banker, can be learned. He has groomed his personality to the height of charm through deliberate self-cultivation. "And it wasn't because I was a knight or anything like that," he says. "It was just fun." Renaissance man and social maven that he is, he admits he doesn't have it all. He's not as bold as he would like to be or as spiritual or as advanced in the arts of pleasure. But, he adds, "the quiver doesn't have to be fully stocked. If you have eight out of ten characteristics, you're already about seven steps ahead." He cuts me a sly smile: "It's a wide open field."

Lassoing Love

You must not imagine it is such a simple matter to catch
that noble animal, a lover.

—SOCRATES

As a rule, a ladies' man can't just radiate charisma and character and expect women to flock. Only half of erotic conquest is who you are; the other half is what you *do*. "The man," decrees Havelock Ellis, "must necessarily take the initiative." In Part Two, we'll watch the great seducers in action, practicing a lovecraft that doesn't come from how-to or gamer playbooks. They handle passion as an art, "a creation of the human imagination," and draw on principles from a long, sophisticated erotic tradition.

First, there's the "catch"—landing the loved one. Inspiring desire entails more than checklist skills: pat lines, the right look and approach. Passionate love is a "violence of the soul," hyperbole, and theater. Amorous artists supply that excitement and snag women with a nuanced array of erotic lures: sensuous charms, grand overtures, praise, intimacy, and the strongest spell of all, conversation.

Conversation is the endless turn-on. The real test in love is the ability to retain passion. Left to its own devices, desire devolves through familiarity and habit into *blah* togetherness. Master lovers don't let that happen. They keep the sparks flying and maintain the ecstasy, using techniques of an uncommon, creative variety. After deconstructing the process, we'll place the ladykiller in the here and now. Does he have a future? Can this be taught, and does anyone care? We'll canvas critics, talk to some twenty-first-century Casanovas, and "hot choosers," and ask if French philosopher Jean Baudrillard is right: "Seduction is destiny."

PART TWO

The Seducer's Way

CHAPTER 3

Lassoing Love:
THE SENSES

—

Love is the poetry of the senses.
—HONORÉ DE BALZAC, *The Physiology of Marriage*

In desire the senses claim us first. A touch, a scent, a gaze, a hoarse vibrato can make our hearts do handsprings. Later, cerebral charms take over and summon the serious passions. Luke, a Baltimore computer jock referred to me by four ex-girlfriends, is a master of both mental and physical spells, but he leads with sensuous appeals—and in a unique, often counterintuitive, fashion.

His looks aren't in his favor. A thirty-one-year-old British transplant, Luke is a too tall six foot seven, with chipmunk cheeks, a receding hairline, and rectangular geek glasses. Yet he's an erotic mage with a flair for the pleasures of the flesh. His appearance is soon beside the point, or rather it is the point. "When I first meet someone for coffee," he explains, "I arrive a little scruffed up in my biker shorts so they see me at my worst; then everything else is *kaboom*—a bonus."

His bonuses are good. On a second date, he turns up in a

Savile Row jacket and jeans and delivers what he calls "the big throwdown," a sensual blitz. Rather than a routine restaurant dinner, he mounts road trips—say, to the Maryland shore for boiled crabs eaten under a tent.

Later, he takes dates to his place, the unlikeliest of seduction lairs. Luke's home is a fixer-upper in a derelict Baltimore neighborhood that he stripped to the studs and emptied of everything except a yoga mat, a file cabinet, and color swatches on the mantel. "It's a fantastic lure, believe it or not," he says. "I ask their opinion and ideas, and after that it's . . ."

At this point, his dates get lucky. Sincerely fond of women—their minds and bodies—Luke is a passionate, generous, and dextrous lover. His motto is "Make sure she has double before you have a single," and he makes a production of it: foreplay in the bathtub, laughter, "touching every part of a woman," and handholding before and after. At almost any time of day or night, there's a car at Luke's curb with yet another woman bearing armloads of "food parcels" and hoping to find him alone. "They're intelligent women," he concludes, "and the best part is seeing their smiling faces as they drive away waving."

Luke would be the last person to claim, like some scientific materialists, that love can be reduced to "the physical part"—a neurochemical perfect storm. "You have to have some depth," he cautions, "or that bubble bursts very quickly." The big guns of seduction are 90 percent psychological. Nevertheless, physical allures are powerful enticers, particularly for women, whose senses are generally more attuned and acute than men's.

Ladies' men are artists at this. Like Luke, they avoid standard-issue male ploys and add imagination, originality, and style to their sensual seductions. They may not be as radical as Luke with their lovecraft, but they can alchemize sensory charms into transcendent desire, an out-of-body rapture.

Appearance

Appearances belong to seduction.

—JEAN BAUDRILLARD, *Seduction*

He's a feast for female eyes. Although slight by Darwinian standards and without a "manly" jawline, movie superstar Johnny Depp is the idol of women. They voted him the best-looking man in America in 2010 and the celebrity they would most like to sleep with the year before. Twice selected as *People* magazine's "Sexiest Man Alive," he doesn't come packaged as usual—in tees and board shorts with beefcake bulges.

Instead, Depp ornaments himself for maximum erotic impact. Playing to the nostalgia for male plumage, he embellishes his body with tattoos and invents traffic-stopping ensembles: fedoras, blue glasses, bracelets, rings, and layered shirts festooned with beads, chains, and scarves. Raves a fan, "I luve [*sic*] the way he dresses." His own stylist, he designs the looks in his movies, such as the bespangled pirate Jack Sparrow in his flowing sashes, rakish tricorne, and bucket boots. His outfits, say critics, are "mysterious—always—and magical." One costar, Missi Pyle, said that at the first sight of him on set, "a party [went] off inside" of her; and another, Leelee Sobieski, said, "He really *is* as sexy as he's cracked up to be."

The Body Beautiful

He was a brown eyed handsome man.

—CHUCK BERRY

Ladies' men don't have to be pretty; some are eyesores, like the "disproportioned" one-eyed Russian general Potemkin or the unsightly Jean-Paul Sartre. Beauty, though, factors in. Contrary to myth, women may be just as turned on by visual stimuli as men. Their vision is keener than men's, and their eyes and cervixes dilate when they see an attractive man. Hooked up to a lie detector, they pick the best-looking guys regardless of other factors.

Handsome has curb appeal: average height, pleasing proportions (a waist-to-shoulder ratio of .60), and symmetrical features in which the right and left sides match. A hero, instructs a Harlequin book editor, should be "incredibly good looking," with a sleek build and impressive "thunderstick." As Nancy Friday discovered, "Women do look," covertly fly-watching and sizing up faces and physiques.

Fashion and Grooming

The greatest provocations of lust are from our apparel.
—ROBERT BURTON, *The Anatomy of Melancholy*

Clothes, however, can remake the man. Psychologists have long argued that you can transform a toad into a prince with a simple makeover. If you take a non-looker, groom and clothe him in pinstripes and a Rolex, most female subjects will choose him over a male model in a fast-food uniform. This suggests that nothing does it for women like dark, staid success suits, which signal solidity, power, and status.

But it isn't necessarily so. The repressed male peacock has a perverse way of erupting into the gray-flannel status quo and staking its ancient claim on the female libido. Ladies' men are fashion plates; they glam up to steam the sexual imagination. Aware of women's more astute sense of smell and scent's erotic importance to them (ranked number one in choosing a mate), ladykillers pay attention to fragrance. And they dress for sensuosity and show.

Masculine embellishment is too entrenched in human history to be easily suppressed. Our Stone Age ancestors, anthropologists tell us, "were adorned rather than clothed." One 25,000 BC alpha man was found in a robe garnished with almost three thousand beads, a fox-tooth-encrusted cap, and twenty-five ivory bracelets. Sumerian kings bedizened themselves for sex. At fertility festivals, they arrived in tufted sheepskin skirts and perfumed headdresses studded with jewels. In most cultures throughout time, "men ornament themselves more than women" to attract mates.

The first deities of sexuality were resplendent male specimens. The Indian Shiva wore a tiger-skin loincloth, a braided conical coiffeur, and a snake looped around his blue-tinted neck. In godlike fashion, each adornment stood for one of his cosmic attributes. Dionysus also adopted symbolic dress, adding another aspect of eros—sexual ambiguity. Swathed in phallic totems, he flaunted feminine dresses and capes and styled his long hair like a woman's.

Fantasy ladies' men dress to kill. Before Odysseus courts Princess Nausicaa and later, his wife, the goddess Athena whisks him off to the wardrobe room. She bathes him with aromatic oils, clothes him in shapely tunics, and coifs his hair so that his curls tumble to his shoulders "like a hyacinth in bloom." Emma Bovary may never have gone astray if she hadn't seen Rodolphe from her window caparisoned in a green velvet coat and yellow gloves. When woman-slayer Bobby Tom Denton enters the scene in the romance novel *Heaven, Texas*, he's turned out to a fare-thee-well: showered, shaved, and poured into butt-hugging jeans, a silk shirt, and purple cowboy boots.

Great lovers hone and work their fashion sense. Casanova,

an amateur costume designer, turned heads wherever he went. Decked in suits of taffeta and lace-trimmed velvet and scented with "secret perfumes which controlled love," he wore gold watches, medallions, and rings on every finger.

Regency romancer Lord Byron was as much a poet of attire as of verse who carefully crafted his ensembles for evocative effects and multiple messages. His auburn curls in artful disarray, he garbed himself in white pantaloons (instead of black breeches) and embroidered shirts garnished with chains and "swashbuckling accessories." He exuded sartorial sex: a mysterious foreignness, combined with mixed gender-and-class signals. Women wilted over the ambiguous "wild originality" of his look.

Military men have a long tradition of self-adornment, which many ladies' men parlayed into seduction, from the feathered and pearl-encrusted Sir Walter Raleigh to the theatrically kitted-out Gabriele D'Annunzio in the First World War. One of the great commanders of the ancient world, Julius Caesar, was both a flagrant dandy and a celebrated ladykiller.

A plain-featured man with a comb-over and too full face, Caesar compensated with a wardrobe of standout glamour and singularity. Rather than the customary short-sleeved senator's tunic, he swanned around in a long frock, belted loosely at the waist, with fringed sleeves that reached his wrists. He was oiled, scented, and fastidiously close shaven—even down to his nethers. Everything about him advertised exceptionality and erotic mystique, including a tang of androgyny.

Men aped his look, and women orbited around him. His love affairs were prolific and notorious, and usually with smart, aristocratic married women. During the Gallic Wars, soldiers sang of him as they marched: "Romans, lock your wives away!" Liaisons continued throughout his three marriages and culminated in his most famous one with Cleopatra.

During her four years with him (three in Rome), the Egyptian queen exercised a strong influence on Caesar, which perhaps extended to her talent for costume drama. While she was his mistress, he made his fateful entrance at the Lupercalia fertility festival. He appeared like Cleopatra in one of her operatic goddess moments, accoutered in a golden wreath, the purple robes of a conquering general, and the high red boots of Italy's legendary kings through whom he traced his descent from Venus. His rivals saw the threat of despotism in this regalia and murdered him the same year, in 44 BC.

Male appearance may have entered a new epoch. More and more men "rock cool threads," indulging in cosmetic surgery, fragrance, and guyliner, and following the lead of metrosexuals like soccer star David Beckham with his sarongs and pink toenails. *New York Times* clothing maven Bill Cunningham speculates that we may see a "return of the peacock" in the future, men who become "the sex and fashion objects of women."

Setting

Location, location, location
—REAL ESTATE SLOGAN

Weeks before her wedding to a prominent lawyer, Allie Nelson, the heroine of Nicholas Sparks' *Notebook*, sees a photograph of an old boyfriend's house in the paper and can't help herself. She drives off to the North Carolina boondocks, where the power of place overcomes her. The low-country landscape brings back a "flood of memories," and once she steps on Noah's front porch, the setting works its magic and delivers her back to his arms. He serves her seasoned crabs in his cozy kitchen, and takes her the next day to a secret lagoon, where they're drenched by a thunderstorm. They dry off before a fire and resist until they can resist no longer. She unbuttons his shirt and it's all over, her marriage to the lawyer and her respectable life in Raleigh.

Ladies' men are poets of what Roland Barthes calls "amorous space." They shun clichés—romantic suites with rose-petal turndowns—and go for impact, a sensual skylift. "Passion," writes critic Jeff Turrentine, "is catalyzed by the erotic pull of place," such venues as a curio-filled "office" atop London with a bed concealed in the wall, or an abandoned bench in a garden maze, or an "otherworldly" castle of high-tech surprises. Passionate love sweeps us out of the mundane into a magical, exalted elsewhere, and location—artfully arranged—can help spirit us there.

Both genders are erotically susceptible to space, but women are especially sensitive to location. Biologist Richard Dawkins attributes this to a "domestic bliss" strategy in which our female ancestors sought secure nests and solid resources from mates. Women, though, may have been somewhat pickier. Geoffrey Miller thinks they also looked for beauty, prompting men to adorn the premises, "be they caves, huts, or palaces." The embellishment of place in seduction is called "priming," and it can be eerily effective. Psychiatrist Cynthia Watson tells of a patient who followed an unattractive man back to his apartment, where the elegant "highly charged environment" made her see him anew; by the end of the evening, she was smitten.

The erotic diablerie of setting may also well from the collective unconscious. We may retain memories of space as sacred and yearn for the time when cave-chapels served as shrines suffused with erotic images and the *mysterium tremendum* of divine lust. In 4000 BC Sumer, the king and priestess performed their ritual copulation in the holy of holies of the ziggurat, and the acolytes of Dionysus coupled each year in a secret sanctum, the "Bull House." The mythological Adonis and Psyche wed in an alpine love temple filled with rare treasures and conceived with the "cunning of a god."

Since tales were told, women have been transported by aphrodisiacal milieus. In *Paradise Lost*, Eve beds Adam in a "blissful bow'r" walled around with fragrant roses, jasmine, and irises. And Emma Bovary yields to Leon in a voluptuous hotel room softly lit "for the intimacies of passion." Romance heroines have amorous sensors for settings and take in details like estate appraisers. When Ann Verlaine first sees Christy Morrell's bedroom in Patricia Gaffney's *To Love and To Cherish*, she catalogues the layout—the handsome fittings, flock wallpaper, and crochet-draped tester bed—and wonders, "Why was it, again, that she wasn't marrying him?"

Gabriele D'Annunzio was a "born interior decorator" who mined poetry, myth, and drama for his settings and believed "love was nothing without the scenery." When asked why he never went to "their place," he replied, "[And] sacrifice my privileged position of sorcerer, surrounded by my philters and incantations?"

His apartments were calculated to intoxicate and levitate the senses. Tuberoses scented the rooms, shades muted the light, and the décor was late Djinn Palace: velvet cushions, arcane bibelots, and a red-brocaded boudoir furnished with silk kimonos and a wrought-iron bedstead. Later he dialed up the drama to elicit an "excitation transfer," the erotic frisson of fear. At Lake Garda he built a villa designed to unnerve the boldest lady friends: warrens of claustral parlors, pillows stuffed with lovers' hair, lugubrious war souvenirs, and a "Leper's Room" lit by an oil lamp.

D'Annunzio utilized another potent scenic spell: nature. Dancer Isadora Duncan recalled a rendezvous with him in the forest that—perhaps evoking Dionysian rites in the wild—lifted her spirit "from this earth to the divine region." D. H. Lawrence, no stranger to sexual myth, has Lady Chatterley experience her erotic awakening with Milord in the woods where everything is "alive and still."

One of America's most noted architects and ladykillers put this erotic charge of nature to spectacular amorous ends. A short elfin man with neither looks nor wealth, Frank Lloyd Wright married three times and had numerous affairs. Women found him irresistibly magnetic, and none, writes his biographer, "ever wanted to let him go."

Although gallant and charming, his chief attraction was his revolutionary-design genius. Deliberately invoking the numinous aspect of setting, he brought the natural world within. In his pioneering structures he opened a room to the outside so that it resembled a "woodland chapel."

His female clients who saw these "artful, enchanted" places were entranced—and often with the creator himself. Mamah Cheney, a cultured Chicagoan, went further and abandoned her children and husband, running off with Wright (then married with six children) to Europe. They returned a year later, and he built a sanctuary for Cheney on two hundred acres of Wisconsin wilderness called Taliesin, named after the Welsh bard and fertility god.

When a crazed servant burned Taliesin to the ground three years later, killing Cheney, her two children, and four workers, women flocked to console Wright. Miriam Noel, a glamorous aesthete with a monocle, led the pack. Finding Wright "unpre-possessing" at first, she changed her mind after she saw one of his houses—"as lovely as a miniature Palace of Baghdad." They married, and for seven years thereafter she alternately "kissed his feet" and tore his eyes out in jealous rages until they divorced in 1928. Wright then married a third time, a young Russian who consecrated herself to the "master" and his architectural vision for the rest of his long life.

Setting isn't everything; a real romance, as the song goes, doesn't need a designer "hideaway" or "blue lagoon." Some ladykillers such as Jimi Hendrix, Warren Beatty, and Picasso operated out of distinctly unsavory settings in their early years. Picasso's Bateau Lavoir studio in Paris was a squalid, cold-water dump littered with garbage and half-squeezed paint tubes. A true ladies' man upstages any stage set—regardless of the trappings.

Nevertheless, as anthropologists say, "space speaks." And when it functions erotically, it doesn't need to follow formu-las—deluxe spreads with expensive toys or couples' retreats with beachfront villas and travertine soaking tubs. Instead, set-tings that seduce are the work of artists of ambiance—charmed sanctums designed to ravish women and raise the roof.

Music

A sweet voice and music are powerful enticers.
—ROBERT BURTON, *The Anatomy of Melancholy*

In the late 1950s a Massachusetts resort town had the envied rep-utation as a safe haven for teenagers; they sailed, danced to soci-ety bandleader Lester Lanin, and had good clean fun. Mothers used to say—justifiably—there was no sex at The Point. That is, until Bordy appeared. A Harvard freshman and poor relation of an old family, he had been given a fisherman's shack on a cousin's private beach for the summer. He arrived on a Vespa dressed in sandals and jeans, with bed hair, a baby face, and most lethally, a guitar on his back.

Suddenly there were beach parties, with Bordy playing licks on his Gibson and leading the group in "Bye Bye Love" in his cashmere baritone. Nice girls clustered around and began to behave not so nicely with him behind the dunes. The yacht club lost its luster. The place to be was Bordy's shack, listening to his walking bass versions of "Crawlin' King Snake," and "doing it" for the first time. He didn't make it through Labor Day. A jealous Miss Porter's senior made trouble, and Bordy was sent packing to the Cape to continue his sing-along seductions elsewhere.

Music assaults the mind and torches the libido like nothing else. It's "the most ecstatic of the arts" and inseparable from love and sex. Although a ladies' man can manage without music, he's passing up a prime aphrodisiac. Women have a keener, more refined sense of hearing—a subtler ear for higher tones and auditory nuances—and have been serenaded into bed since the dawn of culture. In studies they rank men sexier after listening to rock anthems. Music *is* "the food of love"—an entrée laced with deep elixirs.

The fourth-century author of the Indian *Kāma Sūtra* was insistent on the subject. "It's a matter of experience," he preached, "that music reaches the center of female sexuality." For that reason, men must prepare themselves accordingly—learn to sing, play string and percussion instruments, and master the "science of sounds." One medieval caliph was so alarmed by the female weakness for music that he tried to ban it from the land: it loosened "self-control," incited lust, and led to "unacceptable practices."

Why music churns up such an erotic tumult is still uncertain. A melody or cadenza, for instance, can "rattle" us "to the core," "raise gooseflesh," and render us "almost defenseless." One explanation is music's ability to express the inexpressible emotional life; another is its whole-brain engagement and precision punch to the limbic nodes where we experience sex and cocaine highs.

Darwin proposed an evolutionary answer; music, he conjectured, originated to charm the opposite sex. Male rutting calls pervade the animal kingdom: whales sing to females miles away, frogs croak, cats caterwaul, crickets whirr, and fruit flies vibrate their wings like scrapers in a jug band. Very likely, Pleistocene men followed the same courtship strategy, staging drum, whistle, and clapstick jamborees to seduce women.

Music's erotic force may also derive from the sacred. At the earliest rites, worshippers channeled cosmic sexual energy through concerts of bone flutes, rattles, tom-toms, and bull roarers. If we're all alloys of our ancestral past, we may still hear subliminal echoes of the sex gods' pipes and drums—Krishna's flute that seduced nine hundred thousand cowgirls or Dionysus's haunting aulos and tambourines. Orpheus, an avatar of Dionysus, charmed stones, beasts, and the beautiful Eurydice through the strains of his lyre.

The sorcery persists. Salman Rushdie's Orpheus, Ormus Cama in *The Ground Beneath Her Feet*, maddens women and makes sidewalks sway with his music. An opera's "diabolic" force drives the librettist of Doris Lessing's *Love, Again* into a passion for two men, one half her age. And the "Kreutzer Sonata" of Tolstoy's novella so enraptures a wife when she plays it with her violin teacher that her husband kills her in a jealous rage.

Music can be just as ecstatic in a mellower mode; a slow, steady womb-beat rhythm is intensely seductive. The fairy-tale

Beast soothes Beauty with soft airs over dinner, and Nicholas woos the rich miller's wife in *The Canterbury Tales* by playing a dulcet "Angelus" on his harp. Tea Cake's largo blues piano lulls Janie into his arms in *Their Eyes Were Watching God*. However they do it—whether through easy-listening music or tempestuous pulse-racers—ladykillers bewitch women through their ears; one romance novel even comes with a CD by the "hero."

Lovers have always been wise to the effect of music on women. During the reign of courtly love and throughout the Renaissance, a man was expected to be musically proficient to earn a woman's regard. Men who can play anything—the violin like Casanova or the saxophone like Bill Clinton—hold a strong charm card. When Warren Beatty was a bit actor with acne, he won Hollywood beauty Joan Collins by improvising at a baby grand during a party.

Franz Liszt was one of the great musical seducers, a pianist and composer who touched off a "Lisztmania" throughout nineteenth-century Europe. At his concerts, this bravura showman performed with such soul-sizzling passion that women went wild. "Trembling like poor little larks," they stalked him, fought over his discarded orange rinds, tucked his cigar butts in their cleavages, and swamped him with love letters. Too kind-hearted to decline, he took droves of lovers, two of whom left their husbands for him and forgave his many transgressions. In old age, women were still "perfectly crazy over him," twice threatening him with loaded pistols to regain his favors.

His closest twentieth-century counterpart was conductor Leopold Stokowski. Tall, blond, and as handsome as a central-casting Viking, "Stoki" combined titanic musical gifts with torrid sex appeal. His prospects were not promising when he first appeared in New York City in 1905 as a poor organist at St. Bartholomew's Church with just four years' training at the Royal College of Music in London. He had only three assets: tremendous talent; a dramatic, virtuoso delivery; and a flair for women.

Within a year, he had conquered the famous concert pianist Olga Samaroff, who married him and gave up her career to foster his. He went on to become conductor of the Cincinnati Symphony Orchestra and the Philadelphia Orchestra—as well as a high-profile ladies' man. His caprices were so numerous that the Curtis Institute of Music (where he taught part-time) was called the "Coitus Institute." Eventually his wife left him. By then, he was the toast of the music world, a celebrity known for his iconoclastic innovations such as freehand conducting and fortissimo finales, which were compared to "twenty-two minute orgasms."

His love life matched his music. At forty-four he dropped a nineteen-year-old debutante to enter into an open marriage with maverick aviator and spiritualist Evangeline Johnson, heiress of the Johnson & Johnson fortune. Convinced that Stoki required affairs to fuel his music, she looked the other way for eleven years. Then came the screen siren Greta Garbo, who saw Stokowski conduct and was electrified. Their much-publicized romance was too much even for Evangeline, and she divorced him in 1937. His third marriage to Gloria Vanderbilt lasted seventeen years, after which he retired to England in the company of two handmaidens from the "Coitus Institute." He continued, "glamorous to the end," enamoring women and making spectacular music until he died at ninety-five.

There are other ways to make spectacular music. The male voice in song can be as seductive as an orchestra in full Wagnerian flight. The root meaning of *enchant, incantare,* is to bewitch through singing. In ancient Rome a young patrician heard a suitor sing to her and decompensated: "I am undone," she cried to her sister. "Oh how sweetly he sings! I die for his sake." Maggie Tulliver of George Eliot's *Mill on the Floss* is overtaken by the "inexorable power" of a gallant's "fine bass voice," and never recovers.

Frank Sinatra, a songmeister and seducer of the first order, should have been a Darwinian discard. Skinny and jug-eared with a "dese-dose" accent and Hoboken address, Sinatra began his career with a string of failed employment attempts and an empty wallet. But as soon as he stood up and sang in those early dives, "broads swarmed over him." He "wasn't the best singer in the world," but he had "dick in [his] voice,"—a lush, intimate lyricism—and used the microphone "like a girl waiting to be kissed."

Women were insane for him. They snatched his handkerchiefs, begged barbers for his hair clippings, bared their bras for autographs, and threw themselves in front of his car. Although a difficult man by any gauge—subject to temper tantrums, mood swings, and capricious no-shows—he was a love pasha. To seduce a woman, he would tilt back in a chair, hot-eye her, and sing, "I've Got a Crush on You." Lauren Bacall, Sophia Loren, and Marlene Dietrich adored him. His second of four wives, Ava Gardner, hyperventilated: "Oh god, it was magic. And god almighty things did happen."

Smart lovers envelop girlfriends and wives in a sonic bath of sensual melody and song. "Sing," Ovid exhorted, "if you have any voice." As the sign in a St. Thomas music store says, "No matter how ugly you are, if you play the guitar, you'll have a way with women." "Love," wrote Elizabethan amorist Robert Burton, "teacheth music."

Kinetic Voodoo: Body Language and Dance

You got to let your body talk.

—DADDY DJ

Psychologist and ladies' man Jack Harris doesn't simply walk into a room; he glides. He settles on the sofa, pulls a leg under him, stretches an arm over the back cushion, and pins you with his eyes. Reminiscing about his romantic life, he begins, "It sort of exploded in my thirties, and I'll tell you what it was: dancing." It happened, he says, by accident. During a teaching stint in San Antonio he wandered into a bar and discovered Tejano, a South Texas couples' dance that involves complex spins and fancy footwork. One of his students offered to teach him. "It was amazing," he recalls, "when you dance it's like turning on a light. If you're a good dancer—and I *am* a good dancer—women want to dance with you, and the attraction ensues from that."

Body Language

Bodily movements may appeal to the eye quite
as much as bodily proportions.

—THEODOOR HENDRIK VAN DE VELDE, *Ideal Marriage*

Ladies' men are kinesthetic shamans, masters of body movement and (usually) dance. "Besides spoken language," proclaims the *Kāma Sūtra*, "there is also a language of parts of the body." Gifted lovers are fluent in this idiom. As well they should be: women have an enhanced ability to decipher gesture, posture, and facial expressions, and psychologists estimate that 50 to 90 percent of our communication, especially in romantic relationships, is nonverbal. Ovid understated when he told trainees, "You can say a lot with gesture and eye."

Our faces do most of the talking. In the first three or four seconds of meeting a man, a woman will subject him to a face scan, spending 75 percent of the time on his mouth and eyes. Within five minutes she will have sized him up. And it's curtains if he gives her a frozen poker face. Women like features that are plastic, expressive, and vibrant.

Eyes are heavy artillery, "the purest form of seduction." Ancient cultures such as classical Greece thought they possessed occult powers and could infect the unwary with an airborne "*bacillus eroticus*." Kama, the Hindu god of love, directed his gaze at victims and they swooned with desire, while Dionysus radiated the light of Aphrodite from his eyes.

Some men just know how to look at a woman. They create a "lustline"—they gaze a fraction longer and tight focus as if she's the only person in sight. Love giants like Aly Khan, actor Richard Burton, and reggae singer Bill Marley were renowned for their "eye sex." Lord Byron's trademark was his infamous "underlook"—his upper lids lowered at a woman as though he were in the throes of sexual excitement. Women, significantly, rank men's eyes as their favorite feature.

At the same time, women watch men's mouths with "close attention." If a man is interested, his lips will part slightly, redden, and engorge. Nineteenth-century female fans loved poet Alfred de Musset's full "vermillion lips," and modern romance readers demand descriptions of a hero's mouth. Dallas Beaudine's looks like it belongs "on a two-hundred-dollar whore" in *Fancy Pants*, and the heroine can "barely breathe" when he smiles.

A smile is a female sweet spot. The genuine "Duchenne" kind, where cheeks lift, teeth flash, and eyes crinkle, is a "powerful courtship cue." Brian, the New York banker, says he is a compulsive smiler; instinctively, he insists, it sets up an attraction and a smile-back reflex. Warren Beatty, like so many darlings of women, gives "the best smile in the whole world." Herbert Beerbohm Tree owed much of his romantic (and professional) success to his mastery of facial expression. Founder of the Royal Academy of Dramatic Art and His Majesty's Theater, he was a luminary in Edwardian England, both as a manager and character actor and as a world-class Casanova. In his youth, he pored over Darwin's *Expressions of the Emotions*, and soon became fabled in the theater for his protean impersonations. Seducers were Tree's specialty.

Off stage, he practiced what he played. He had a preternatural ability to fascinate and draw women. Although he was nothing to look at—a tall, rawboned man with red hair and sand-colored skin—his eyes were extraordinarily "expressive and alert," and were said to have "transfixed" his wife, actress Helen Maud Holt, into marrying him.

He used them to the same erotic effect on mistresses, including leading ladies and a secret second wife who bore six of his ten children. One inamorata said he seduced her at a spa simply by gazing at her like a "true artist"—with "deep admiration." At close quarters even great actors can't fake this; involuntary micro-expressions give us away. Tree genuinely loved women.

In seduction, the entire body gets in on the act. Gestures have to work in sync and send the same message. Every courtship move—open palms, subtle shrugs, posture mirroring, taut carriage—has to match the love language of the face. And to enrapture, it should be done with grace and feeling. Tree finessed this art as well, captivating women through his eloquent hands, "cat-footed" stride, and regal carriage.

The male animal in motion has a primal hold on the female

libido, harking back to the remote past when men strutted on sexual parade grounds to procure women. In studies, women show distinct preferences in men's gait; they favor a long, light step, swaying torso, and assertive arm swing. Rhett Butler rivets Scarlet with his "lithe, Indian-like" walk, and the young officer of *A Hero of Our Time* has a "careless, lazy" stroll that captivates belles at a Caucasus resort. Writer Katherine Mansfield recalled being spellbound by a stranger's walk: "I watched the complete rhythmic movement, the absolute self-confidence, the beauty of his body, and [felt] that excitement which is everlasting."

Zsa Zsa Gabor claimed that Porfirio Rubirosa snagged her just by the "primitive" way he sauntered across the Persian Room at the Plaza Hotel with an "intriguing spring" in his step. It was no accident. Rubi cultivated the art of movement. From adolescence, he studied every sport—boxing, fencing, swimming, and horsemanship—and kept limber with yoga.

Dance

And then he danced . . .
—LORD BYRON, *Don Juan*

Dance, however, was Rubi's real ace. Asked for his secret with women, he replied, "I take them dancing a lot." An expert dancer, he mastered the merengue, the twist, and everything in between, and romanced all his lovers on the dance floor. As study after study has shown, "Men with the best dance moves have the most sex appeal." Researchers Cindy Meston and David Buss found that women will often have sex with a man just because he dances well. In one survey of five hundred women ages twenty-five to sixty, they ranked dancing above financial success or sexual prowess as the most desirable trait in a man.

Dancing is intrinsic to mating. Animal life is a continual

The great Casanova

The great Hindu sex deity, Shiva, dancing the Dance of the Cosmos

The penultimate sex god Dionysus seducing Ariadne

"Second Dionysus," Alcibiades, ca. 450–404 BCE

"Hero of the boudoir," Louis François Armand, duc de Richelieu

"The most remarkable lover of his time," Gabriele D'Annunzio

*The "mad, bad, dangerous to know" romantic poet
and ladykiller, Lord Byron*

"Sweet man" Duke Ellington pursued by women

"Fanatical lover of women," Robert Louis Stevenson

Irresistible Rubi, (Porfirio Rubirosa), the "last playboy"

Crooner and "woman's man" Sam Cooke

Former President Bill Clinton turning on the charm

round of rollicking courtship dances. Male grebes enact "water ballets," and certain species like fallow deer and sage grouses gather in groups called "leks" and leap, stamp, and do-si-do to attract females.

Havelock Ellis speculated that primeval men cavorted in a similar vein, vying in vigor and grace to obtain the best women. Evolutionary psychologists ascribe this to a fitness contest. Men whose feet smoke, they claim, prevail because they demonstrate greater symmetry, health, strength, coordination, speed, and— if they vary their steps and style—higher levels of testosterone. They also exhibit playfulness and artistic creativity.

But there's more than evolutionary logic to women's lust for a dancemeister. While dance arose for multiple purposes, a key function was aphrodisiacal; prehistoric peoples danced at fertility rites to draw down divine sexual energy. By miming intercourse, they channeled cosmic eros and worked themselves into a copulatory lather.

In myth, the sex gods enter dancing. Vishnu, the Indian Adonis, greeted postulants with a crotch-swiveling Tandava, and Shiva, lord of eros, danced with his penis in his hand and enacted nine routines—the basis of classical Hindu dance. Dionysus, "the leader of the choral dance," jetéd throughout the countryside followed by a corps of nymphs and bacchantes. He so intoxicated Ariadne with his gyrations that she "could scarce sit still," and flew into his embrace.

Traditional cultures contain a full repertoire of erotic dances, from the Chilean *cueca* to the Hungarian *friss*, a "violent couple dance." Men of the Wodaabe tribe in Niger stage all-day dances to compete for brides. Adorned in black-and-white face paint and dressed in tight sarongs, white beads, and ostrich feathers, they undulate for hours until three women pronounce the winners and give them the choice of mates.

Fictional ladykillers waltz divinely and dance women into love with them. Olga in Alexander Pushkin's *Eugene Onegin* loses her heart to her fiancé's best friend during a mazurka, and Anna Karenina falls for Vronsky over a quadrille. When Hardy Cates gathers Liberty Jones into his arms for a two-step at a country fair in Lisa Kleypas's *Sugar Daddy*, Liberty is flooded by "uncontrollable" desire and follows him off the floor to a back lot. The most cherished chick flicks feature "honeys who can swing," such as the snaky-hipped Patrick Swayze in *Dirty Dancing*.

Casanova took this primordial turn-on seriously. He hired ballet master Marcel to teach him the minuet, and acquitted himself like a professional, executing a *furlana* in 6/8 time. Similarly, French eighteenth-century duc de Richelieu was "one of the best dancers" at court, and a generation later, philosopher and heartthrob Claude Helvétius performed with the Parisian ballet.

Mikhail (Misha) Baryshnikov was the "Russian superstar Casanova," both a dance wonder and an *homme fatal*. An unlikely premier danseur, he was too small, stocky, and gamin by ballet standards. But when he made one of his gravity-defying, shoot-the-moon leaps, he brought down the house—and women. Ballerina Gelsey Kirkland thought him a poor piece of work—an "adolescent"—until he soared onto the floor. After that, she pronounced him "the greatest male dancer on earth" and "fell in love with him then and there."

Theirs was just one of his many affairs. Among his romantic partners were Isabella Rossellini, prima donna Natalya Makarova, Liza Minnelli, and Jessica Lange, who lived with him for six years and had their daughter Shura. (He now has three children with his longtime companion Lisa Rinehart.) The women he didn't take to bed dreamed of it. "Baryshnikov leaps higher than your heart," raved a poet in *The New Yorker*. "You swoon back in red plush," she wrote, until you feel "as wild as nineteenth-century hopeless love."

Through no fault of their own, many men are kinesthetically challenged. It's understandable. Men are socialized to mask emotions, hang tough, and shun "sissy" pursuits like dancing. Pop man-guides perpetuate the problem, peddling expressionless, cool body language, and "seductive" war moves. "Dancing with a woman," they instruct, is "not the ultimate goal"; "the dance floor is not the natural habitat of the alpha male."

If "alpha" means king of the hill in the boys' game, they're right. But enswooning women is an adult art, designed for animated, poetic body-speakers and princes of the ballroom. As the French put it, "Love teaches even asses to dance."

Sexpertise

Banging, nailing, and screwing isn't sex; it's carpentry.
— The Secret Laughter of Women

Wynn is the last person you'd pick on Match.com for a lust-soaked rout. He's on the wrong side of sixty, with a staid address and a job as an antique dealer. But women swear by him. He meets me at a fashionable uptown bar; he's a little stout, wears a tweed hacking jacket, and has his gray hair slicked back European style. "Listen," he says over a martini, "I don't have money, power, or youth anymore, but I think I know what women want. And," he slants me a glance over his half glasses, "I'm very good at that."

He runs through the usual reasons—good conversation, TLC, love of women—before he gets to sex. Then he grows expansive. "Typically," he begins, "I ask the woman. 'Tell me what you want.'" He is serious and puts his heart into it. "I do bond during sexuality; love is when you have a partner for whom nothing is too much trouble."

For months, he courted a West Coast academic by email and didn't mince words. At one point he wrote, "How do you accomplish your orgasms?" She flew to New York soon after, and he seems to have listened. "It's not the gun," he explains, "it's the man behind it. It's what you can do. I mean, I've got a long tongue with an eggbeater on the end of it!" Not surprisingly, the professor relocated to New York and moved in.

She knew a good thing when she found it. Increasing numbers of women don't have the sex life of their dreams. Despite a "go-girl" culture of sexual license, graphic guides, therapeutic aids, and bedside toys, a significant number of women experience sexual problems. In a landmark 1999 study, 43 percent reported difficulties such as lack of desire or inability to achieve orgasm. A more recent five-year survey of a thousand women found that 50 percent "have trouble getting aroused," and when they do have sex, it's often for such uninspired reasons as stealing a friend's mate (53 percent) or keeping the peace (84 percent). According to several 2010 polls, only 65 percent of women said they had had an orgasm in their most recent encounter, and two-thirds of wives would rather do anything than make love.

To be sure, women and sexuality is fraught territory. The female body *seems* a setup for hyperpleasure: the clitoris has eight thousand nerve fibers (twice that of the penis), and orgasms are stronger and last longer than a man's, and can be multiple. But a woman's sexual response is capricious and delicate. It's a "whole-brain operation" that depends on a perfect mesh of the rational neocortex and passional hypothalamus. Then there are psychic killjoys like stress, fear, fatigue, self-image, and cultural bogies. To complicate matters further, women need to be warmed up first—sometimes for up to a half hour—and the clitoral hot button is in the wrong place, about an inch from the vaginal strike zone.

Under these tricky circumstances, what's a man to do? Classic male guides stress technique: tongue-manship, Frisbee grips, python positions, and delay tactics. Therapists add intimacy and communication and emphasize deference to individual proclivities. "Ecstasy" researchers raise the bar higher: for a woman's optimal pleasure, men must also show "gender empathy" and prime the narcissistic female libido with passionate praise. Ladykillers cover all these bases and more: skill (customized to specific tastes), emotional engagement, generosity, adulatory ardor, and quality climaxes.

If great lovers didn't exist, they would have been imagined. As studies have revealed, plenty of women care about good sex. Surprisingly, they're often the ones you see at the checkout counter with a romance novel, the best-selling and steamiest book genre. At the center of these stories is explicit sex and ladykillers who wax sentimental, ring all the right chimes, and grant heaven-scaling orgasms. Jack Travis in Lisa Kleypas's *Smooth Talking Stranger* tells the heroine after an aria of sweet nothings, I want to "have sex with you until you scream and cry and see God." He's as good as his word.

In ancient history, sex of this caliber was the measure of a man, physically and spiritually. Dumuzi, the Sumerian fertility god of the third millennium BC, copulated with the goddess Inanna in a sacred wedding ceremony that culminated in a mystical union with the Almighty. The epiphany depended on Inanna's pleasure. "Murmuring words of love," Dumuzi "tongue-plays" Inanna fifty times, strokes her thighs and loins "with his fair hands," caresses her tenderly, and "plows [her] holy vulva" until she comes and cries, "He is the one my womb loves best."

These early civilizations assumed that sex could not scale such heights without cultivation. Archeologist Timothy Taylor estimates that by 5000 BC, coitus had become a spiritual discipline, and classicist Paul Friedrich describes at length the advanced love arts of ancient Greece. The *Kāma Sūtra* devotes hundreds of pages to the study of ecstatic sexuality. To pass muster and attain "beatitude of being," a man must know how to set the mood and "relax the girl," as well as conduct elaborate foreplay and handle sixty-four coital positions. If he does not succeed, "if he is scorned by women in the art of love," he is a "dead man."

Casanova's bedmates, by his account, had no complaints. Enlightened for his day, he believed sex was meaningless without intellectual rapport and a woman's satisfaction. He demanded "complete harmony of mind and the senses" and received "three-fourths" of his enjoyment from his partner's pleasure. In an age of perfunctory in-and-out, he discovered the clitoris-climax link (just published in a 1710 English sex manual) and once provided a lover with double-digit orgasms in one night.

Physical virtuosity, though, was only part of his *in excelsis* lovemaking. Before he slept with Henriette, an accomplished French adventuress, he laid the psychological groundwork. He told her he had never "felt such an urgency" or love for a woman, supplied voluptuous preliminaries, and treated her to a night of quasi-religious rapture. He conducted their love affair and others "like a work of art outside space and time."

Peak sex for a woman takes time. Love, as Ovid taught, is "never a thing to be hurried." Ladies' men subscribe to the slow-sex movement; they take the longest route home. Rick, the retired fire captain, savors his lovers for prolonged pleasure. "It's the touching," he says, "that's the best part. I go slow and sort of feather-stroke with my fingertips—places you wouldn't expect, like the back of the knee or small of the back."

Rick is onto something. Women have more sensitive skin than men and place touch at the forefront of their sexual fantasies. They're also better served by light, silky caresses and a gradual circuit from the least to the most stimulating erogenous zones. Skin is the largest organ of the body—the "most urgent of the senses"—and so sexually responsive that a hot hand can set a woman on fire. A hero's ankle play with his little finger takes the heroine to the brink in Jennifer Crusie's *Tell Me Lies*. "She'd definitely come if he put his hands on her," she muses. "Anywhere."

A kiss is turbocharged touch, and women prize "good kisser[s]." It's the quintessence of sensuality and demands more skill than neophytes imagine. There's the matter of timing, synchrony, and mastery of an infinite range of "mouth music" from the degree of pressure and tempo to tongue play. And the media usually gets it wrong. Instead of rabid tonsil-hockey, women are most roused by soft, wispy moth-kisses. The grand amorist Gabriele D'Annunzio was a proverbial kisser. A Michelangelo of oral pleasure, he fondled eyelids with his tongue and planted "stinging kisses" on necks and genitals throughout his long "intoxicating nights."

For the main act, andante has the edge. Since women take longer to climax than men (fifteen minutes on average versus two and a half minutes), carnal artists pace themselves accordingly and delay their orgasms. The 1950s lover Porfirio Rubirosa was supposed to have been a "Tarzan of the Boudoir" because of his jumbo package, but performance may have been his true claim to fame. Like Aly Khan who studied imsak (the ancient

art of semen retention) and who "could control himself indefi-
nitely," Rubi guaranteed his partner's gratification and often
lasted hours at a time.

John Gray claims in *Mars and Venus in the Bedroom* that
"a woman can be just as fulfilled without having an orgasm."
Maybe. But she'll be missing something: the convulsive pel-
vic contractions and the flood of chemicals—prolactin and
oxytocin—that saturate every pore with euphoria, warmth, and
satiation. With the right man she can be turned inside out and
flung to numinous heights. "This was all she ever needed to
know about god," exclaims the wife in a short story by Udana
Power after an orgasmathon with her husband.

Few ladies' men have given more thought to transcendent
sex than Jack Nicholson. An early strikeout, with PE (premature ejaculations) and predatory-male syndrome, Nicholson
went through years of Reichian psychotherapy, a treatment
based on removing emotional armor and releasing "orgone"—
primordial sexual/cosmic energy. He confronted his demons,
shed defenses, and embraced a new model of freed-up, holistic
lovemaking.

"Most sex is about nonfeeling," he observes, but "you can
feel the difference when you make love and there's love there,
and . . . there's not." Attuned to women's psyches and idiosyn-
crasies, he deftly massages them into the mood. A British actress
recalled her fear and self-consciousness, and how he "carried
[her] up to his bedroom," where he was "very gentle, very loving, very romantic."

During sex, said another, he was "indefatigable," but also
"close" and "very oomp!" soliciting verbal feedback throughout. He wants to make women insanely happy: "He satisfied me
like no man before," gushed one, "he was only concerned with
my pleasure"; he's a "perfect practitioner of love; God put [him]

on this planet to love women." And Nicholson puts God into the act. Girlfriends claim he often became "spiritual and talked about the sanctity of what was happening." "I felt in my heart every time," he once confessed. "I was in the sublime sexual embrace." Men aren't born with a good-sex gene that tells them how to pull this off. Training and inclination are necessary. But not even a workshop with a tantric master under the direction of Dr. Ruth can turn out a supernatural lover. To hit the high notes in bed, a man has to be "all in"—body, soul, and sensual intuition. And it helps if you adore each other. As the *Kāma Sūtra* admits, no instruction or advice "will be needed by those who are properly in love."

Gifts and Wallets

Gifts persuade even the gods.

—EURIPIDES, *Medea*

Beacon Hill was baffled for years afterward. The Cobb boy (of the old Boston family) had been nothing if not magnanimous, commissioning a portrait of his fiancée Ann, a Smith scholarship student from god-knows-where. This was 1932, and the artist, the cook's nephew, needed work. Angus was an Irish émigré with a nervous laugh, a blond cowlick, and a wrestler's body that seemed in perpetual motion. The sittings took place in the Cobb vaulted library, and whenever the husband-to-be dropped by, he noticed odd things: a pair of spectacles painted with a winking eye, a soap sculpture satyr, dandelion chains around Ann's neck, and once, an envelope in her hand.

Before the portrait was finished, the wedding was off. Ann had boarded the train to Mexico with the penniless Angus, leaving the handsome heir and his millions behind. The next day, the maid found a letter in the library under the settee: a sketch of Ann as Venus on the half shell, with a fan of caricatured faces in her hand (some of them Cobbs), and a dolphin at her feet that spouted, "I love you, Ann."

According to a recent poll, most women would have stayed with Cobb & Co; two-thirds of the female respondents said they were "very" or "extremely" willing to marry for money. In another 2009 survey, 50 percent of women reported they would marry an ugly man if he were rich. Pragmatically speaking, the impulse makes sense. Even in a postfeminist world, the spoils aren't evenly divided. Women still make eighty cents to a man's dollar and pick up a disproportionate amount of housework and childcare. There's also the practical voice of Stone Age grandmothers: tribal chiefs provide social power, deluxe extras, and freedom from want, care, and predators.

But desire isn't reasonable. Although mating has been a commercial transaction for centuries, with women as objects of exchange, money and sexual love are unnatural bedfellows. The economic motive, psychiatrists explain, is the antithesis of eros, passion displaced into "non-human" rationality and calculation. That's why Freud said, "Wealth brings so little happiness"; it's not an archaic, erotic wish. As Robert Louis Stevenson remarked, "Falling in love is the one illogical adventure." Romantic passion, writes psychologist Rollo May, is a transrational "exhilaration" that money can't buy.

At the same time, gifts—whether bought or homemade—have their charms. They're embedded in the feminine ideology of love. Women put stock in presents; they take them to heart and regard them more intimately than men. A gift signals a man's interest and, later in a relationship, his commitment. Receiving love tokens from men has been practiced since antiquity, and is so widespread (found in 79 percent of societies) that it may be indispensible in courtship. "The path to a lasting intimate relationship," claims sociologist Helmuth Berking, "is lined with presents." Evolutionary psychologists interpret this ritual as a sex-resource exchange. Men barter for brides by proffering financial protection and superior resources. Just as female scorpion flies pick mates by the size of their nuptial gifts, women choose men on the basis of largesse. Generosity pays. According to Amotz Zahavi's "handicap principle," the man who shows how much he can afford to squander has the courtship advantage. As philosopher Julia Kristeva points out, profligacy is the seducer's calling card; "he spends extravagantly."

Romantic gift giving, however, isn't a clear-cut transaction. Presents, noted Ovid, are "quite an art." They're hard to get right, easy to botch, and spring-loaded with signifiers. A man's gifts give him away—who he is and who he thinks *she* is. Implicit in trinkets, too, is a delicate power dynamic of creditor and debtor. Gracie Snow of *Heaven, Texas* ditches her wealthy beau when she discovers he's ruined their erotic parity by secretly paying her boutique bills.

Practicality is also a no-no in presents; hold the smoke alarms and robo-cleaners. Gifts must fulfill their primal, first function, when they were objects of magic and enchantment in the past. "At its finest, the true gift is transcendent," wrote author Stuart Jacobson, it "lights up the other person." And to really shoot the works, it's an object of beauty as well. In essence, says one scholar, a gift is an "emanation of Eros." And like eros, an ideal gift carries a kick—a *ta-dah!* of theater that proclaims pleasure, passion, novelty, creativity, male effort, and extravagance.

Mythic givers were lords of magnificence. Phallic deities embodied the spendthrift extravagance of nature, "the tumultuous surge to spill forth" and gave like gods. Dionysus, the "giver of riches," conferred bounty on the earth each spring and pulled out the celestial stops when he courted Ariadne. He anointed her queen of the skies and placed her crown among the stars as a constellation. Odysseus bestowed a ravishing wedding present on Penelope—an exquisite, hand-hewn bed that concealed a mystery known only to them.

Courtly love in the Middle Ages encoded gift giving into romance. The lady had to be propitiated with bibelots, bouquets, and poems to her taste, and the transaction, kept secret. Claudius in John Updike's "Hamlet" novel deploys this convention with a twist. Surreptitiously, he sends the queen an emblem of their blind, savage (and suppressed) passion: a falcon with "lethal talons" and "sewn-shut eyes." She capitulates. No romance hero comes courting empty-handed. Cal Morrisey of Jennifer Crusie's *Bet Me* divines the heroine's pet fancy—bunny slippers with French heels—and delivers them with fanfare, in private.

Master lovers have a genius for presents. Julius Caesar gave Cleopatra a gold statue of herself, which he placed in the Temple of Venus, raising her to the ranks of the gods. Casanova, who spent money on women like a drunken sailor, regarded gifts as an art form. He presented one lover with a spaniel, another with an ode, and another with a made-to-measure dress of the "best Valenciennes lace."

White game-hunter Denys Finch Hatton brought Isak Dinesen a trove of treasures each time he landed on her African farm: cheetah pelts, marabou feathers, snakeskins, records, books, and a rare Abyssinian gold ring so soft that it could be molded to the finger. The "absolutely irresistible" nineteenth-century poet Alfred de Musset produced customized poems. After he read George Sand's novel *Indiana*, de Musset sent her verses that made romantic history. He pictures her "in her attic, smoking a cigarette," while her secretary "still drunk from yesterday / is cleaning out his ear / in the most meticulous way." Within days they were a couple.

Riches raise the stakes; "wealth creates obligations"—for more enthralling effects to be pulled out of gift boxes. Women didn't fall in love with Aly Khan because of his fortune, but because of the spells he spun with it. Instead of minks and diamonds, he gave women two a.m. boat rides and all-expense-paid trips to parts unknown, leaving the city and reality behind. "It was like a flight aboard a magic carpet," a mistress effused, "a woman's gyroscope went out of whack."

Fiat titan Gianni Agnelli was cut from the same iridescent cloth. Unlike run-of-the-mill moguls, Agnelli was less interested in business and profit than in creating transcendence—of the amorous kind. Women were crazy about him (both Jackie Kennedy and Pamela Harriman wanted to marry him), and "there was no one he couldn't seduce." He furnished total theater that took women away from "mere existence" into "a world of pure pyrotechnics"—picnics on his black racing yacht and cocktails on a sun-drenched roof, his *tappeto volante* (flying carpet), overlooking Turin.

The Edible Gift

The loves of most people are but the results of good dinners.
—Sébastien-Roch Nicolas de Chamfort

George Duroy, the ladies' man-on-the-make of Guy de Maupassant's *Bel-Ami*, nabs his first society lady at a post dinner party in the private room of a restaurant. Sensual dishes follow one after another—oysters like "dainty little ears," trout "as pink-fleshed as a young girl"—and Duroy turns the talk to love and sex as he homes in on the rich matron, Madame de Marelle. She hands him the bill, and by the time they are in the cab he has her in a deep clinch and at his bidding.

Food for sex—almost no courtship gift can rival its libidinal appeal. "After a perfect meal," says German scholar Dr. Balzi, we are most "susceptible to the ecstasy of love." Taste is the multisensory sense that incorporates vision, scent, hearing, and touch and is hyperresponsive to social and psychological cues. (The wrong word can wreck an *homard flambé*.) Although men have the same number of tongue receptors, women are finer tasters. They distinguish flavors better and are more sensitive to strong doses of sugar, salt, and spices. They also long to be romanced over meals. Eating is intrinsically sexual. The language of desire is steeped in food metaphors (melons, nuts, buns, and jellyrolls), and aphrodisiacal food lore has thrived for eons.

Wining and dining women also goes back to our primate past: courtship feeding. Just as animal species entice females with tasty morsels, proto-humans, according to social anthropologists, wooed prospective mates with shares of the kill. Fertility gods did erotic business the same way. Dionysus gave honey (his invention) and the "gift of wine" to his female votaries, and Dumuzi plied Inanna with "rich cream" and produce from his garden. In rural Peru, a suitor typically brought his sweetheart panniers loaded with food and "amber chichi," a sweet national drink.

Love stories are storehouses of gastronomic seductions. Drouet captures Sister Carrie of Theodore Dreiser's novel with a mushroom and steak dinner, and Robert beguiles Edna Pontellier in Kate Chopin's *Awakening* over a shared roast chicken on an excursion to Grand Isle. Steve, the motorcycle stud of *Wilde Thing*, dispatches the heroine by finger-spooning a caramel Frappuccino into her mouth. "Definitely rich, creamy, and seductive," she sighs. "I think I just discovered a new aphrodisiac."

Casanova was a gourmet who relished "highly seasoned dishes"—gamey meats and overripe cheeses. But for amorous repasts, he catered to the more refined feminine tastes and laid in delicacies such as smoked tongue, oysters, Cyprus wine, bread, fresh fruit, and ice cream. He was also a master of culinary theater. To seduce the burgomaster of Cologne's wife, Casanova staged a Lucullan banquet, designed to whet the palate and the imagination. He set the table for twenty-four with damask linen covered with vermeil and porcelain, and served a three-star menu from truffle ragout to a dessert buffet "representing portraits of the sovereigns of Europe." The next day she promised to be his.

Casanova's romantic dinners downplayed drunken excess. Aware that alcohol lowers inhibitions but impairs performance, he drank sparingly. Warren Beatty, with an alcoholic for a father and a sexual reputation to preserve, "was never inclined to drink." Even a gourmand like Prince Grigory Potemkin didn't overdo it. His fabulous fêtes of champagne and "exquisite and rare dishes" were dramatic preludes for the "lover's hour" afterward.

When a ladykiller also cooks, it's culinary courtship on high flame. A man can tailor the cuisine and ambiance and trade on the ur-appeal of the male hunter-provider. Dirk, a twenty-six-year-old law student I met recently, tells me that his walk-up apartment is a sorcerer's kitchen. "I adore cooking," he says over coffee at Starbucks. He's a wiry John Cusack look-alike, with blue eyes that flare as he warms to the topic. "I'm a great cook! I mean, this Valentine's I'm going to surprise my girlfriend with an amazing chicken tagine my mother taught me. Along with . . . hey! I was a drama major."

Dirk is surfing a trend. Television chefs are the new sex gods, and movies like *No Reservations* feature fetching young men in white aprons who can rock a stove and a woman's heart with the flip of a spatula. Food researchers point to a growing breed of male "gastrosexuals" who "pursue cooking as a way to attract women." Writer Isabel Allende argues that for women few things are "more erotic than culinary skill" in a man.

THAT SAID, WOULDN'T a woman rather have a kitchen staff, compliments of a rich provider, than a guy with a frying pan? After all, a magnate can afford serious pleasures of the senses: designer wardrobes, opulent sets, concert tickets, haute dinners, exclusive dance clubs, and expensive spas and therapy, if required. Then there's the added charm of security in a harsh, uncertain world. Money, says book and magazine editor Hilary Black, "symbolizes so much for so many people."

But money doesn't always fill the symbolic bill. In Pedro Almodóvar's movie *Broken Embraces*, Penelope Cruz's character, a poor secretary, succumbs to a sugar daddy for safety, status, and the good life. The luxury rush, however, wears off quickly as the "hedonic treadmill," the tendency for material upgrades to wane over time, takes hold. Her mogul lover proves dull, cruel, and physically revolting. At the price of her life, she escapes with a filmmaker, an artist and dramatist of the world of the senses.

Romantic passion, by definition, is a heist to a higher state of being. The senses are potent and can vault us there. But they can be damped by false creeds and consumerist promises, and the corrosive effects of habit, satiety, and overload. Ladies' men exploit the full force of sensual lures, adjust them to women, and soup them up with ancient spells that work on the deepest recesses of the human psyche. They seduce us out of our skins, and catapult us to another world.

CHAPTER 4

Lassoing Love:
THE MIND

—

Love looks not with the eyes but with the mind.
—WILLIAM SHAKESPEARE, *A Midsummer Night's Dream*

A Casanova can go far with sensory artistry, but to cinch the lasso, cerebral skills are key. Vance, a gourmet-store owner and ladykiller who earlier credited his charisma to "just passion," agrees to expand further on his appeal to women. This time we meet at a local coffee bar, and as before, he seems more vestryman than ladies' man, with his Leslie Howard features and oxford button-down. "You've got to feel it," he begins, sipping an espresso ristretto. "It really stems from within."

Which does not mean he neglects sensual allures. Recalling his heyday in the sixties and seventies, he tells me he put a premium on seductions of the senses. He danced "very, very well," dressed in fringed shirts and opera capes, flew dates to Jamaica for dinner, produced *aha!* gifts, and always made women's sexual pleasure his priority. "Only the clothes have changed," he laughs.

But he attributes something less tangible to his numerous "catches." "I don't shilly-shally," he says. "I wear my heart on my sleeve." By way of illustration, he recounts a story that sounds like a Hollywood set piece. At an art gallery, he chatted with a Norwegian model, forgot her name, then ran down six flights of stairs to meet her as she walked off the elevator. Taking her hand, he said, "Tell me who you are. I've *got* to be with you!" She followed him, and they were a couple for two years.

Vance adores women and wants to make them feel fabulous. But flattery, he points out, has to be done with a difference; "you have to take the edge off." When he first met the love of his life (and partner until her recent death) at a Nassau party, he opened with, "Anyone tell you you have a Darwin's tubercle? That little quirk on the tip of your ear? It's pretty rare—legacy from the raunchy apes." What grabbed her, though, and made her leave her husband was Vance's flair for intimacy. He's a connector, emotionally plugged in. "We struck a mutual chord," he explains. "We were woven together. An artist could not have created a bonding like ours." How does he do it? "I'm interested in what makes people tick. Forging ties. That's how I run my store and my love life."

In a post-romantic age of sex friends, practical partnerships, and polyamorism, Vance may sound as outdated as his fringed disco shirts. Who needs to expend all this mental effort—hot pursuits, compliments, and intimacy—to get a woman? You don't have to for casual or practical purposes, but igniting passionate desire requires cognitive craft. The mind is the body's most erogenous zone. Romantic love is a psychological takeover, which cannot, as philosopher Irving Singer observes, "be fully explained in terms of sight or touch or any other sense."

Women may be particularly susceptible to mind spells. Meredith Chivers, a leading figure in female sexual research, notes that women are more aroused by mental stimuli than men. In desire, their brains are busier, sussing out streams of cultural, social, situational, and emotional data. The conscious part of the female mind that inhibits action and appraises feelings (the anterior cingulated cortex and insular cortex) is larger, and the amygdala in the unconscious subcortex "remembers" amorous events in detail, as opposed to men, who pick up only the gist. From a woman's perspective, the heroine of the film *Juliet of the Spirits* has a point: "The powers of seduction," she says, "are all inside."

Certain cerebral charms are especially lethal to the female libido. They transcend time, trends, and culture and target women's deepest desires. Ladies' men, even when it's unfashionable, have been roping women this way forever. Unlike amateurs, though, they don't practice these "throws"—passionate approaches, praise, and connection—by the book. They enlist imagination, drama, ardor, novelty, originality, brains, and a sixth-sense sensitivity about what each woman wants.

The Royal Rush

Who loves, raves.

—LORD BYRON, *Childe Harold's Pilgrimage*

Sebastian D. knows a thing or two about love and seduction. He has written novels and made movies on the subject, and at age forty, he has the reputation of one of the "really exceptional ladies' men" of today. At the moment, he's busy promoting his new indie film, but he accepts a lunch date to chat about Casanovas, himself in particular. True, he *is* stunning—a fine-boned British version of Javier Bardem in a Brioni suit and vintage swing coat. But he exudes something else: a sexy, nervy energy. "I'm not sure what it is," he says in a cut-glass Cambridge accent. "I mean, I'm fascinated by women constantly, and if you want to get that girl, of course, there are tactics . . ."

The more he talks, though, the more "tactics" recede. Instead, he riffs on Freud and "fascination," and reminisces about girlfriends past and present. By dessert, his main strategy is out of the bag: a full-on frontal assault when he "fancies" someone. For instance, he once met a Persian woman at an LA nightclub, and at the end of the evening, turned to her and whispered in Farsi, "*Esh-ghe-mani*"—You touch my soul. They were together for almost a year. "The important thing," he writes later, "is that it's sincerely expressed. We Casanovas fear the wrath of Eros should we misuse that word for cynical, seductive means." He told the woman, with whom he now has a daughter, on their first date, "I want us to be lovers; I want to make you sigh like no man has made you sigh before."

What woman is going to buy this? More than you might expect. Although women prize their right to the sexual initiative and accept erotic "cool" as the new normal, most secretly like a man who floors it. Romantic love, by nature, is a "furious passion," and women want to be furiously desired and pursued. High-mettled lovers who throw caution to the wind impress them more than they like to admit. My own father won my mother with a proposal on day one: "My hat's in the ring," he announced.

Scientists speculate that women's sex drive may need displays of avid desire for peak efficiency. It takes a greater jolt to "switch on a woman's libido," writes University of Nevada psychologist Marta Meana. "Being desired is very arousing to women." Over half of female fantasies reveal a wish to be sexually irresistible and, in some cases, "ravished." What a woman craves, explains Meredith Chivers, is a passion so intense that it shatters constraints, fires desire, and allows her to be "all in the midbrain." An ardent advance is also a "woman's moment of power," giving her the high ground of erotic choice.

For millennia men have been hectored to haul out. "Let the man be first to make the approach and entreaty," Ovid enjoined. "Ask her outright!" The Hindu author of the *Kāma Sūtra* directed suitors to take command and confess endless devotion. In the Middle Ages, courtly lovers were expected to storm "the door of love's palace." Robert Louis Stevenson, a ladies' man himself, berated "anaemic and tailorish" men who dithered in desire; a man should be so overcome by passion that he runs out "with open arms" and declares himself. People feel only aversion, wrote psychologist Henry Finck, for lovers who hang fire and are "neither hot nor cold."

Women may be intrinsically repelled by tepid Romeos. According to cultural psychologist Matt Ridley and others, males are the seducers in 99 percent of animal species and are genetically programmed to take the initiative: "Women may flirt, but men pounce." Anthropologist Helen Fisher traces this to deep history when a man had to go the distance to persuade a woman he was worth the investment. Evolutionary psychologists see the male courtship offensive as a commitment ploy; persistence and passion telegraphed a "faithful nester" to our female forebears. Whatever the motive, argues neuropsychiatrist Louann Brizendine, the fervent male suitor isn't an outmoded stereotype; it's built into the "brain architecture of love."

Myth also mandates the male initiative. In Greek mythology, Dionysus swoops down on Ariadne and says without preliminary, "I am here for you, a lover. You shall be mine." And when Freyr, the Norse fertility god, sees his future wife, Gerd, from Odin's window on the world he is "consumed with desire." He gives his servant his all-powerful magic sword and sends him to

LASSOING LOVE: THE MIND   *139*

plead his case. After she agrees to marry him in nine days, he agonizes: "One night is long. Two nights are longer. How can I bear three?"

Lancelot, an anglicized version of the Celtic phallic god, was an even more headlong lover. When Meleagant abducts his liege lady Guinevere to the land of no return, Lancelot embarks on a rescue mission. "For pity's sake, Sir, calm down," Gawain beseeches, but Lancelot rides his horse to death, crosses the sword bridge, fights bloody duels, and rips the bars off Guinevere's bedroom, cutting his finger to the bone. After he returns her to Camelot, he's so distraught by her loss to the king that he wanders, demented and destitute, through the land for two years.

The Prince Charmings prefigure almost every romantic lead to come. Count Vronsky chases Anna Karenina to St. Petersburg amid passionate avowals, and Valmont of *Dangerous Liaisons* is "violent, unbridled," and determined in his conquest of Madame de Tourvel. "I shall on no condition be your friend," he tells her. "I shall love you." And this fortress of feminine virtue caves in the end, as women have for eternity, to men who give them the royal rush and won't relent.

When women write about ladies' men, they invest them with go-getter ardor. The duc de Nemours of Madame de La Fayette's *Princesses de Clèves* glimpses the princess at a ball and is dumbstruck. His love is earth-shaking, and he tells her so in a four-page paean. In Mary Wesley's 1987 novel *Not That Sort of Girl*, an impoverished tutor, Mylo, proposes to Rose the moment he discovers her in the library at a house party. "Let's get some tea," he says. "I have so much to tell you. I feel faint with love." Material obstacles impede them, but they conduct a covert affair for over three decades before finally marrying in the end.

Popular romance heroes are walking billboards of the impetuous, perfervid lover. In the first chapter of Maureen Child's *Turn My World Upside Down*, Cash informs the heroine, "Ignoring me won't make me go away." "The man," she realizes, "is determined to seduce her." When Reggie Davenport of *The Rake* realizes he loves Lady Alys, he swings into action, untying her braids and moving in for a caress. She crumbles: "The desire in his eyes was a potent aphrodisiac, releasing the hidden part of her nature." Seduction, in this genre, is always "intense and aggressive, with the woman the treasure rather than the treasure hunter."

Ladies' men have their faults, but being lukewarm isn't one of them. The twelfth-century troubadour Peire Vidal, in a tale that sounds apocryphal, toured southern France singing the praises of a chatelaine named Loba ("Wolf") and dressed in wolf skins in her honor. It almost cost him his life. A hunting party of dogs and shepherds mistook him for their quarry and left him for dead on the roadside. Providentially, the lady Loba passed by in time and conveyed him to her castle, where she nursed him lovingly back to health.

Italian Renaissance cavaliers wooed courtesan queens just as vehemently. They carved lovers' names on poplar groves, composed reams of verse, and became their personal paladins. The Florentine banker and statesman Filippo Strozzi romanced the great Tullia d'Aragona so feverishly he made a "public fool" of himself. He churned out love sonnets, challenged rivals to duels, and leaked state secrets to her, blowing his cover as a secret agent and jeopardizing his life.

Casanova was equally passionate. When he saw the Duke of Matalona's mistress at the theater, he seized the moment. After a volley of aperçus about love, he found that Leonilda lived sexlessly with the duke. "That is nonsense, for you are a woman to inspire desire," he exclaimed. "I have made my declaration." He asked her to marry him, and all was set except for the approval of her mother. But the interview went badly. The mother took one look at Casanova and fainted; she was his old mistress and Leonilda, his daughter.

Benjamin Constant, French nineteenth-century romancer, political philosopher, and author of the novel *Adolphe*, seemed congenitally unsuited to erotic conquest. By temperament he was a timid, melancholy soul, beset with "doubts, qualms, [and] scruples." But when it came to seduction, he was a samurai. Sexually precocious, he began his siege on female hearts as an adolescent, firing off florid declarations and once, in extremis, swallowing an overdose of opium to win over a lover.

By his late twenties, Constant was a veteran ladykiller, with a wife and a mistress, and a dangerous reputation, despite his looks. He was scrawny and bow-legged with a red ponytail, green glasses, and a face stippled with acne. It was then that he met Germaine de Staël, a famed *salonnière*, seductress, and intellectual, and found his fate. He wasted no time, literally galloping after her in hot pursuit, stopping the carriage, and proclaiming his intentions. "My whole life is in your hands," he might have said, like his fictional seducer Adolphe. "I cannot live without you." Their affair lasted twelve tumultuous years, during which they produced a child, Albertine, in 1797, and some of their best work. As they drifted apart, Constant took several mistresses, two of whom never recovered from his full-bore amours.

At first, a romantic putsch often proceeds without words. This was Jackson Pollock's preferred mode. The abstract painter fastened on Ruth Kligman, his last mistress, at the Cedar Bar and stared at her with "such intensity" and "such hunger" that she felt impaled. At her apartment afterward, she remembered, he cinched the deal by sobbing, "I want you," "I need you," "I've been looking for someone [like you] my entire life."

Seduction prophets like Mystery and his henchmen would jeer at Pollock. To nail "targets," real men feign "lack of interest," and let women chase *them*. A woman "will do almost anything for your approval," promise pickup gurus, if you're "cool" and keep her guessing. According to *Maxim* magazine, the "three treacherous syllables" are "I love you." Only clueless losers race up to prospects and bare their souls.

If so, some losers are getting lucky; hell-bent, do-or-die lovers still captivate many women, both in reality and fantasy. Warren Beatty put his cards on the table from the start with Annette Bening, revealing his interest at the upshot and telling her later after a wrap party that he wanted her to have his child and marry him. She conceived that night.

In the 2010 movie *How Do You Know*, George wrests the heroine, Lisa, away from her baseball pitcher beau with a no-holds-barred courtship. He gate-crashes a party for Lisa at the pitcher's penthouse, pours his heart out, and tells her he'll wait for her at the bus stop for as long as it takes. Journalist Tom Terell read a stack of romance novels for a *Salon* story and decided men needed a course correction. To enamor women they must "move in without invitation," and "express the depth of [their] passion" "right out of the chute."

Women, declares Stanford University anthropologist Carl Bergstrom, "*do* appreciate men who court energetically." Charleen, a character in the documentary film *Sherman's March*, tries to clue in her friend, Ross McElwee, on how to get women: "I don't care, Ross!" she tells him. "Passion is the only thing that matters! You must say to her, 'You are the only woman to me. I live for you. I breathe for you, I would die for you. Please for God's sake be with me!'"

The Wine of Praise

O flatter me, for love delights in praises.

—WILLIAM SHAKESPEARE, *Two Gentlemen of Verona*

When his wife, Lisa, dies in the film *The Other Man*, Peter (Liam Neeson) discovers a dark secret: she had a lover for years. He then embarks on an obsessive pursuit of the mysterious Rolf. What Peter finds, though, isn't what he expected. Rolf, played by a winsome Antonio Banderas, is a mere janitor who pretends to be a polo-playing aristocrat. During a series of chess games between the two, in which Rolf takes Peter's "queen," the truth unfolds. Lisa knew Rolf's scam from the start, supported him, and loved him anyway. Her reason? Rolf possesses a unique talent: he "makes women pretty . . . prettier than they would be otherwise." "I was made for the ladies," Rolf tells the bewildered Peter, "and the ladies for me."

Women are fools for flattery. As clichéd and passé as it seems, praise is a royal road to the female libido. In love we all seek an inflated image of ourselves, a perfected Me. The man who makes a woman feel like that ideal, photoshopped self can write his ticket. Yet flattery is a complex art that demands subtlety, imagination, discrimination, wit, and infrared vision into a woman's personality.

According to erotic theorists, ego enhancement is inherent in romance; with loved ones we seek priority and a grander identity. Love, by definition, writes philosopher Robert Solomon, "maximizes self-esteem." Some extremists, like psychiatrist Theodor Reik, believe that the central drive of passion is vanity, the "dream of a nobler self." Sex may be the first violins of amour, but the ego is the concert master. Love means knowing you're somebody special.

For women this lure carries particular weight. They accord higher importance to romantic compliments than men do and are more erotically stoked by ego boosts. Female sexuality, say current researchers, may be flattery-operated. A woman's seat of desire, asserts Professor Meana, is narcissistic rather than relational; she wishes to be "the object of erotic admiration." Philosopher Simone de Beauvoir made the same point in "The Narcissist" and expanded it, arguing that women seek self-exaltation in love due to impoverished personhood.

Centuries of culturally imposed inferiority have contributed to the female yen for praise. Although women are no longer the "devil's gateway" or male chattel, the legacy of the "lesser sex" lingers on. Many women can still use a shot of confidence. Fifty-five to eighty percent of women are unhappy with the way they look, and across the board they report low self-esteem. Then, too, notions of masculine superiority continue in Western culture. Women often need a prestige hike just to even the erotic match.

Neurochemistry also factors into the feminine relish for flattery. Women are biologically primed to base self-esteem on intimate relations with others and have a built-in "negativity receptor." Their mental worry station, the anterior cingulate cortex, is larger and more active than men's and craves validation. As Chaucer's Wife of Bath says, "A man can win us best with flattery."

Kudos does wonders for the brain's esteem center. In what's called the "applause response," we get a reward rush from compliments that simulates a drug high, bathing the brain in amphetamine-like chemicals and heightening our sense of self. We feel exhilarated, "more attractive," confident, and competent.

The classic love guides counseled men to applaud women. "Flattery works on the mind as the waves on the bank of a river," wrote Ovid. "Praise her," right down to her "fingers and toes." In the medieval *Art of Courtly Love*, adulation of the beloved was canonical. No man could expect a woman to smile on him unless he hymned her to the skies, and with skill. A middle-class lady might be swayed by tributes to her beauty, but a noblewoman required more rarefied homage. Lord Chesterfield in the eighteenth century cast aside all these distinctions; a man should flatter women "as much as possible," he told his son, "whenever possible in any way possible."

More recently, amorous thinkers have reassessed and finetuned the role of praise in love. Psychoanalyst Adam Phillips speculates that ego inflation may be crucial for passion. "What if our strongest wish" in desire, he asks, "is to be praised?" He's seconded by many theorists who contend that idealization is indispensable in relationships.

The craft of praise itself has received new scrutiny. Complimenting well, say investigators, is an astute business. A man has to be alert—cultivate creativity, humor, and sincerity; add a dash of bitter to the sweet; and suit the praise to the person. The worst gaffe is half-hearted flattery; one study found that most people, in an "above-average effect," will believe superlatives about themselves. Fulsome plays best in love.

Fertility gods knew how to pour it on; they enthroned and glorified women. The Indian Shiva, Sumerian Dumuzi, and Egyptian Osiris lauded their queens and placed them on high altars. Dionysus rescued his mother from the bottom of the sea and crowned her (and Ariadne) with immortality. At the rites of these sex deities, women served as high priestesses, avatars of the goddess, with a direct line to the divine.

Seducers of fable and fiction historically buff up women for less honorable ends. Such is female inferiority throughout history that a woman can be a pushover for praise. The arch-flatterer Odysseus deftly exploits the female longing for status under Greek patriarchy. When shipwrecked on the island of Scheria, he endears himself to Princess Nausicaa (and gains an entrée to the court) by "mistaking" her for an exalted being. Rather than the subjugated nonentity she is, Odysseus calls her a goddess who alone has the power to save him: "I marvel at you," he cries, "pity me."

The serpent in *Paradise Lost* plies a similar form of ego massage. Again, he goes for the status jugular. The Eve that Milton portrays is a member of the seventeenth-century underclass— "weak," disenfranchised, and subject to male authority. The wily Satan manipulates her like a cosmetic shill. She will be an "Empress" (as she deserves), and "more than equal" to Adam if she'll bite the apple.

In Edith Wharton's socially stratified world of *Summer*, the déclassé heroine is just as easy pickings as Eve. The cosmopolitan architect Lucius Harney visits a rural backwater for the summer, finds a raw, insecure mountain girl, Charity, and courts her with a social promotion. He admires her "difference," he says, and suggests she's one of the elect as he leads her off to an abandoned cabin. "He was praising her," she exults as he kisses her knuckles, "and praising her because she came from the mountain."

Daryl Van Horne uses a twentieth-century version of this strategy to seduce the housewives of John Updike's *Witches of Eastwick*. Amid the domestic gulag of 1950s America, this Satan dangles the apple of distinction to three stifled "witches."

They're "onto" him but are so starved for professional recognition that they succumb to his puffery. He touts Alexandra's female figurines as museum-quality art and convinces Jane the cellist of her superior talents. Sukie the town reporter, he harangues, should quit hackwork; she's an intellectual who can "think" and comprehend his abstruse chemical experiments.

The post-feminist Kate Alexander of Gael Greene's *Blue Skies, No Candy* lacks all these bygone insecurities; she's a successful screenwriter, with money, looks, and class, and handpicks devoted lovers who praise her properly. They assure her she's perfection (plus a "spectacular good fuck") and she soars. She's "Remarkable," she crows, "Wonderful [and] lovable."

Romance novels probe deeper into fantasy territory. Here women want what psychiatrists claim lies at the core of the unconscious—to be a man's deity, the only woman in the cosmos. The "good," authentic heroes in these stories are staggered by the heroine; she is the "most magnificent female" in creation, a goddess who obliterates other women. Rick Chandler of *The Playboy* has done the rounds, but as soon as he views the leading lady, he has a religious conversion: "Rick had been exposed to many females in his lifetime and none had ever shaken him this badly." He tells her so without cease, itemizing her merits in grandiloquent detail.

The only thing better are two heroes who do this. In *The Sweetest Thing*, an Olympic-medal sailor and NASCAR star vie for the love of the peerless Tara Daniels. To Logan, the race car driver, Tara is his one-and-only and idol, and he won't leave town until she accepts him. The sailor, meanwhile, is even more full-throated: no other woman has ever attained such heights of female perfection, and he says he'll be her "sex slave" if she'll have him.

Real ladies' men are brilliant praisers who make much of

women. Like Casanova, they're creative and code-read the female heart. As a young apprentice priest, Casanova romanced an advocate's wife in a public carriage during a trip to Rome. He first said in the presence of her husband that she had destroyed his wish to be a monk, then addressed her alone. Excusing his ardor, he pronounced her an "angel," the "one Lucrezia" in "all Italy." In a stroke, he vaulted her from the anonymous property of a dull lawyer to a celestial heroine in a cosmic love drama. By the time the carriage rolled into Rome, she was his mistress.

Certain lovers are prodigies of praise. Sir Walter Raleigh became the "Darling of the English Cleopatra," Queen Elizabeth, through an ingenious flattery offensive. Instead of the rote compliments of court toadies, he appealed to Elizabeth's brains and brio. He etched a clever couplet to her with a diamond on the latticed window of the palace, extolled her in witty badinage, and wrote love poems filled with word games and intellectual conceits.

Gabriele D'Annunzio was a flamboyant flatterer. With him, each lover received a new semi-divine identity and name, and an entry into a select society. The lady was "alone of all the world," the noblest hearted, most radiant of beings. Vouched dance diva Isadora Duncan, "To hear oneself praised with that magic peculiar to D'Annunzio was something like the experience of Eve when she heard the voice of the serpent in Paradise."

Twentieth-century British statesman Duff Cooper was a testament to the power of praise over every physical and practical consideration. Not only was he plump and saucer-faced with an oversized head; he lacked the evolutionists' sine qua nons of sex appeal, wealth and rank. Yet as a lowly London civil servant, he achieved the romantic coup of the decade. Lady Diana Manners was the celebrity beauty of her age, an aristocrat of slender means with a taste for "the things money could buy" and a coterie of rich, titled suitors. But she could not withstand Cooper's worshipful courtship, his barrage of letters that called her the "the brightest color, the sweetest warmth, and the one dazzling light of [his life]."

Their marriage turned out to be more of an "arrangement" than his letters presaged. With Diana's tacit consent, Duff acquired a stable of mistresses during their thirty-five years together. He never saw an attractive woman he didn't want to ego-fan into an affair. Actress Catherine Nesbitt, another great beauty, was classic. Cooper dexterously enumerated her best performances, pronounced his passion for her, and begged to kiss her feet, which he had seen nude on the stage. She rolled down her stockings and obliged.

When he campaigned for the princesse de Broglie, he focused on her hands. He kissed them as they drove around in her Hispano Suiza, and followed up with a poem: "Two lily hands are all my desire / They hold my hope, my pleasure / My despair." She relieved his despair, providing a love nest for them in London and taking him on holiday flings to her villa on the French Riviera.

Cooper's most notorious affair, though, was with France's "empress of seduction," Louise de Vilmorin, a poet, novelist, and siren who had discarded three husbands and just returned to Paris. At first glance, she saw little of interest in the new English ambassador. However, after a night of his expert blandishments at dinner, she followed him to the door and "returned [his] kisses."

"You are a treasure," he wrote the next day. "I want to be the miser." She complied, and moved to the embassy, where she lived with the Coopers for three years in a scandalous ménage à trois. He idolatrized her: he admired her poems, bravoed her guitar recitals, and translated her famous novella, *Madame de.*

Then, nearly sixty, he seduced the twenty-nine-year-old Susan Mary Patten, a diplomat's wife who later married journalist and John F. Kennedy's friend, Joseph Alsop. With his usual panache, Cooper deluged her with droll, hyperbolic fan mail until she confessed that she loved him so much it made her "ill."

Author Evelyn Waugh called Duff "Cad" Cooper. But women—even his indulgent wife—never thought him a cad. He ministered too expertly to the feminine (and universal) longing for applause, distinction, and an enlarged, glorified self-image.

In a climate of romantic skepticism, pragmatic pair-bonds, and transient love, the art of praise has petered out. Hip dating instructors promote anti-flattery, "negs" that cut women down to size with zingers like "Your ex-boyfriend must have really hated that about you," or "Is that your real hair?" And the greeting-card industry has devolved into generic schmaltz or sarcastic digs.

All of which leaves the game and the girls to ladies' men. One I talked to recently—an MIT business school student—credits his romantic popularity to targeted praise: "Flattery will get you everywhere," he remarked, "but it has to be smart and selective." And sincere: a secure woman always knows the difference. As philosopher William Gass concludes, ultimately "love is a form of flattery."

Soul Meld / Intimacy

They other self, / thy wish exactly to thy heart's desire.
—JOHN MILTON, *Paradise Lost*

The lady is a lost cause. Addicted to laudanum, prone to hysteria, panic attacks, claustrophobia, and fainting fits, Mrs. Carleton of Gilded Age New York has been written off as hopeless by ten doctors. That is until Dr. Victor Seth, a charismatic neurologist, takes over. As soon as Lucy Carleton encounters his penetrating gaze in Megan Chance's novel *An Inconvenient Wife*, the "cure" begins. Dr. Seth has a unique talent—the seducer's almost clairvoyant gift of intimacy. (He also has a way with a newfangled vibrating wand, but that's another story.) When Lucy arrives for her first appointment, he sits beside her as if they "were lovers embarking on an intimate conversation," and hypnotizes her in order to sound her depths.

Over the course of her treatment, he discovers the "wellspring of [her] inner life," prompting her to strike off her genteel shackles, defy her despotic husband, and fall hopelessly in love with Seth. "I understand you, Lucy," he says during the ensuing affair. "Look at me. You know it's true. I know what you want." Which triggers the novel's violent dénouement. Desperate to be with the man who understood her "as no one had," she shoots and kills her husband, escapes punishment, and runs off to Europe with "Victor the magician."

There's no end to what a woman will do for male intimacy. As shopworn a canard as it is, women do want men who plumb their innermost selves and connect with them emotionally. They plead for more closeness with partners: openness, empathy, soul-to-soul rapport, and the promise of deep togetherness. Practical seducers answer their prayers.

Love is constructed to make us yearn for this. We seek, say erotic philosophers, "total union with a loved one," psychic transparency, and the loss of "I" into a transcendent "We." Plato provided the master myth of the idea in *The Symposium*. In his fable, a race of double-sexed creatures once inhabited the earth and grew so powerful that Zeus divided them, dooming mankind to an eternal quest for wholeness and his other half.

While both sexes crave ego fusion in love, women seem to

covet it more. In surveys they chronically complain of inadequate intimacy with men, and say a frequent motive for sex is the hope of an "emotional connection." Researcher Lisa Diamond believes the drive to bond is one of the four cues of female desire, and so forceful a woman will reroute her affections. Women are setups for intimacy. Even in the womb, their brains are hard-wired for emotional contact, and in adolescence, an estrogen surge promotes a powerful impulse to empathize and affiliate. A man who acknowledges that need, who engages and has the "gift of intimacy," wrote a 1901 *Cosmopolitan* columnist, can secure women with "links of steel."

Storytellers have long chronicled the erotic pull of intimacy. In the ancient Egyptian myth, Isis is as attached to Osiris as a "brother," and when he's torn to shreds by his enemy, she mends him and draws "his essence into her body." Kali, the Hindu energy of the universe, likewise, enters Shiva's inner being and "melts into his heart." Becoming "one" with his female votaries was the goal of Dionysus's mystic rites.

Perhaps uncoincidentally, women of fairy tales and myth mix the philters which bind lovers into a "complete and united" whole. Iseult's mother blends the potion her daughter accidentally consumes with Tristan (instead of her intended, King Mark), thus igniting their fatal romantic union. In a twelfth-century Italian legend, three good witches of Benevento create an intimacy brew. They concoct a liqueur of seventy herbs (bottled and sold today as "Strega"), which they give to Princess Bianca Lancia, who promptly soul-bonds with the "red, bald, and short-sighted" Frederick II, and lives with him until she dies.

The German author Goethe thought science was behind this urge to merge. Eduard of his 1809 novel, *Elective Affinities*, invites his wife's niece for a visit to his castle, and chemistry seizes control. Impelled by the same force that draws physical particles together, the young Ottilie develops a spiritual affinity for Eduard that soon subsumes them both. Ottilie's thoughts and handwriting match his; her headaches on the left side mirror his on the right; and their improvised musical concerts echo the harmony of the spheres: "They were one person, one in unreflecting perfect well-being." Drunk on a more gothically inspired potion, Cathy Linton of Emily Brontë's *Wuthering Heights* tells the narrator, "Nelly, I am Heathcliffe!" He is "my own being."

Modern heartthrobs of fiction are well versed in this drug. Ludovic Seeley, the foxy charmer of Claire Messud's *Emperor's Children*, has an infallible maneuver with women—intimacy, "or the impression of it." He leans in, speaks in a confiding whisper, regards each with an unbroken gaze, and causes erotic mayhem. Another seducer, Jonathan Speedwell, in James Collins's *Beginners' Greek*, makes out like a bandit in love because he gets "into the heads of women." "The human heart, baby!" he tells a married beauty before bedding her on the country club lawn. "That's what I'm all about."

Romance heroes take women further into the primordial, mythic domain of erotic twinship and oceanic oneness. These dream men insist on shared selfhood and have telepathic insight into the heroine's psyche. Juliet of Christie Ridgway's *Unravel Me* marvels: her lover "can read her mind!" Critic Amber Botts argues that he *is* her; the romantic male lead is actually a projection of the heroine's shadow self, her disguised double.

"You're not really a bloke are you?" Libby asks her boyfriend in Jane Green's *Mr. Maybe*. "You're a girl." Nick is intimacy personified, a mind-melder who breaks barriers, exchanges confidences, shares secret wishes, and makes her feel so comfortable that she joins him in the tub the first night. He's a broke, disheveled writer-wannabee, but Libby jilts her wealthy fiancé for Nick. Nothing matters, she says, until "you've got your other half."

The leading men of daytime television (and its successor, chick flicks) are fanatical bonders as well. They interlock with heroines, intuit emotions like psi (parapsychological) detectives, and murmur, "I would do anything to spare you heartache." "The desire for intimacy," writes Professor Martha Nochimson, "propels the storyline of soap operas." Amorous guides throughout recorded time have put intimacy at the top of a man's skillset. The *Kāma Sūtra* schooled students in how to interpret female feelings, and regarded transcendent unity as the aim of love; couples' lives should be joined "like two wheels of a chariot." Ovid was an ardent advocate of up-close seduction. Get intimate fast, he told suitors, gauge and mirror her moods, endear yourself as a friend, and shower her with "attentive devotion." Stendhal adjured men, in a chapter on "Concerning Intimacy" in *Love*, to cultivate naturalness and transparency for erotic accord.

More, however, may be necessary. Recent critiques of intimacy caution that a total soul graft may not be ideal. The concept of spiritual union is extremely seductive, promising an end to existential loneliness and the fulfillment of infantile fantasies of fusion. But unrelieved togetherness can also depress sexual desire and breed demons: codependency, suffocation, and boredom. Francesca and Paolo's punishment in Dante's hell is to be permanently soldered together and condemned to circumnavigate the same claustrophobic round for eternity.

Vibrant, sexy intimacy, instead, maintains the tension between attachment and separation, togetherness and privacy, and preserves self-differentiation. This is a nuanced operation, not designed for erotic triflers. It calls for resolve, tact, and sensitive emotional antennae.

Casanova, long vilified as an emotionally avoidant rake, was one of the subtlest and most masterful engineers of intimacy. He strove to fathom women's psyches and sought "the kiss that unites two souls in bed." With the castrato Bellino, he alone pierced "his" facade, revealed the true Teresa beneath, and launched an ecstatic affair with his "double." Yet Casanova always sustained a here-there interplay in his intimacies. He liked games of disguise with Teresa, faked then confessed his true wealth, and advanced and retreated from the altar.

The Reverend C. L. Franklin isn't a household name in the annals of seduction. But he was an Afro-Baptist sensation in the 1950s, a preacher and woman slayer whose specialty was empathic, heartfelt connection. A gospel pioneer with his sung sermons (he's the father of Aretha Franklin), and a civil rights leader, he was also a consummate ladies' man. As Mary Wilson, an original member of the Supremes, said, women "absolutely loved him" and dozens cycled through his life, including two wives and R & B celebrity Ruth Brown. Asked why, the answer was always "his uncanny ability to address the deepest recesses of another's soul"—while retaining an "inner wall of privacy."

In the beginning, Monica Lewinsky was underwhelmed by President Bill Clinton; he was an "old guy" with a "big red nose." That was before the 1995 rope-line incident when he lasered her with his "look," and she fell like a shot bird. For all his squalid delinquencies and sexcapades, Clinton is beloved by women—insanely so. As Gail Sheehy observes, he knows how to make them "purr." His secret: heat-seeking intimacy. Says an old girlfriend, "he makes you feel like you were the only one on this earth." He dollies in and seems to "crawl into your soul."

Many inamoratas have stayed close to Clinton, and his wife, say intimates, remains "besotted" with him. At the same time, he has a cagey, inaccessible side that only ramps the I-we dynamic.

Psychiatrist Carl Jung was an intimacy virtuoso of a different caliber. He, too, had a fix on women's interior life and a genius for connection. But he made the exploration of "inner space" the focal point of his career, becoming a founding father of analytical psychology. A lifelong student of romantic love, Jung resurrected Plato's trope of the search for a twin soul and gave it a depth-psychology spin. Each of us, he theorized, possessed an image of our other self in the unconscious—an anima for men and an animus for women—which explained why certain people entrance us.

Jung, "a great lover" by his own admission, was often entranced. Although he attracted his share of women in his youth, he encountered his first anima at twenty-one: a fifteen-year-old girl in braids whom he saw on a staircase and married six years later. He and Emma Rauschenbach had five children, but as his psychiatric practice grew, so did his female admirers and extramarital interests. It was, he realized (before the censure of doctor-patient involvement), the nature of the job. In therapy, patients projected onto him aspects of formative figures in their past, a process called "transference" that can create "unreal intimacy" and erotic yearnings. The yearnings must have come easily. Jung's manner invited intimacy, and he was strikingly handsome—a six-foot-one "bull of a man" with piercing eyes and rugged features.

His first mistress, Sabina Spielrein, had been diagnosed as a hysteric and sloughed off on Jung as an incurable case. Through a revolutionary regimen, he released her buried repressions and in the process discovered their "deep spiritual affinity." Their affair lasted two years, and contrary to modern taboos against analyst-analysand liaisons, she recovered fully and became a noted psychiatrist. Later in Zurich, he attracted a seraglio of society women—known as the "Jungfrauen." They packed his lectures and scheduled sessions with him in their homes, which often included sex.

In 1910 another patient, Toni Wolff, crossed his threshold, and the thirty-five-year-old Jung was struck again; here was his complementary cerebral half. "What would you expect from me?" he shrugged. "The anima bit me in the forehead and would not let go." The ménage à trois lasted forty years. He brought her home to live with Emma and their five children, and spent part of his day and some nights with Toni, part with his wife, and the rest with women famished for comprehension and contact. None seems to have been injured by these unorthodox unions.

Despite Jung's interest in self-completion through sexual love, however, he resisted unalloyed two-in-oneship. Emotional interdependence, he thought, was death to identity and romance. The libido, he said, was "like the two poles of a battery"—a continual oscillation of opposites. A complicated man, he encouraged confidences with his warmth and openness, yet he habitually retreated into long, ruminative silences. Jung wrote that the "story of [his] life" was that of his "inner experience." But it was also a story of seduction on a grand scale via a sophisticated aphrodisiac—concentrated intimacy, cut with differentiation, and the dream, however briefly, of one flesh/ one spirit.

The word *intimacy* makes many men head for the hills. It has become a pop sanctity and couples' therapy billy club. It evokes the rap of the relationship police at the door, a strip search of the soul, and life without parole in a hot box of overshared emotions. As a result, nervous seduction coaches caution men to maintain "good mental armor," to "back off and go bland" for success with women. But real success—gaining a woman's entire, lifelong passion—requires engagement, perceiving her unspoken self, inviting alignment, and mixing it up with a vital flux of selfhood and symbiosis.

Even the best-cast psychological "throws," however, can miss the mark. A man can charge in, applaud a woman until he's blue in the face, and offer an astral union of souls. But it won't work without words—the right ones. If he can't talk, if he bores or runs a line of BS, he'll never lasso the lady, regardless of sensual or cerebral charms. Conversation is the slipknot in seduction, the first move to master—and the most neglected—for landing and locking in love.

CHAPTER 5

Locking in Love

—

Conversation

——

Love consists almost always in conversation.

—HONORÉ DE BALZAC, *The Physiology of Marriage*

"Believe me," one of New York's top hostesses tells me, "every woman I know would kill for this man. Talk to him, you'll see." When I first meet George Reese at her home for a pre-dinner drink, I emphatically *don't* see. He looks like a Southern sheriff in a Sunday suit: a thick-set build, bushy salt-and-pepper eyebrows, and a suggestion of a jowl above his Windsor collar.

Then we sit down in the den, and he shoots me a larky, high-beam look: "Love your barbed-wire bracelet," he says in a basso Georgia drawl. "I'm safe, right? Now tell me, how did you wind up in New York?" As I ramble on, he *uh-huhs* and chuckles along. "But you!" I catch myself, "I hear you're pretty popular with the women in town."

"Suzanne [our contact] is a peach and all that," he answers, sipping his Manhattan. "But I'd give myself a seventy on a scale of a hundred." "Well," he finally admits, "I *have* always enjoyed the ladies. Back in Shiloh High when I ran for president, I had a female support group—they called 'em 'Reese's Pieces.'"

"Why the appeal?" I ask. He pauses and says, "Let's see: I suppose in my case it's conversation. I mean, I wasn't a football type the girls chased after. But talking was always easy. And I do think it's an advantage with women." He angles forward and splays his hand for emphasis. "Still, it's got to be spontaneous. I have a lot of interests, and I try to figure out what a gal wants to talk about. And a little drama, too, goes a long way, don't you think?"

At dinner, he's not the headliner I expected. Only after the soup course does he emerge from a genomics debate with his female dinner partner, a blonde surgeon, and address the table. He mentions weddings, and stories start to ricochet: the nude groom in a top hat, a ring bearer who swallowed the ring, the poodle "bridesmaid," and the accident in the aisle.

Reese's contribution isn't remarkable. He tells about the time he waltzed with a gay usher at his son's high-society wedding. But he "throws the gift," as they say down South. Reese sets the big-tent scene with wry details, mimics the in-laws' whispered invectives, and builds up to the moment when the priest cut in and escorted him off the floor. The women at the table are riveted. The surgeon beside him slips him her card, and he leaves with a just-divorced Swedish journalist.

A seductive conversationalist does more than verbally connect; he conjures enchantment—of a prepotent kind. A man of winged words and colloquial gifts, no matter how ill-favored, can gobsmack a woman. "Give me ten minutes," bragged Voltaire, "to talk away my ugly face and I will bed the Queen of France." And keep her bedded, if he wishes. Conversation is a long-acting charm that fires and feeds female desire and potentiates with time. "Women," wrote Victorian novelist Wilkie Collins, "can resist a man's love, a man's fame, a man's personal appearance, and a man's money, but they cannot resist a man's tongue, when he knows how to talk to them."

Perhaps for good reason. Not only is a woman more verbal and communicative than a man, but she's also erotically "lit" by conversation. The XX-chromosome brain is built to savor speech. Women have a larger communication center than men, possess faster verbal circuits, and process language more emotionally. The emotional-linguistic parts of their brain are extensively meshed and hypersensitive to social nuances. When women connect via talk, explains Louann Brizendine, they get a huge dopamine and oxytocin rush, the biggest neurological reward outside of an orgasm or a heroin hit.

All too often, male conversation isn't providing these rushes. In poll after poll, women complain about men's inability to give good dialogue—to listen, engage, and interest them. Silence is the number-one gripe. Studies suggest that the fallout may be serious, accounting for a high percentage of fights, divorces, and women's affairs. Sociolinguists attribute the problem to an innate gender gap in speech styles, and say "cross-cultural communication" can't be helped. But that's cold comfort to many women who yearn, as *New York Times* columnist Maureen Dowd writes, "to be in a relationship with a guy they can seriously talk to."

The female fantasy world is full of such men. In Madame D'Aulnoy's seventeenth-century fairy tale "The Blue Bird," the King Prince transforms himself into a blue bird who visits his truelove's prison cell each night for seven years and talks to her for hours. In more contemporary tales, heroines leave perfectly good lovers the moment they encounter talented talkers. Irina McGovern of Lionel Shriver's *Post-Birthday World* discards her loyal partner of nine years for conversational sorcerer, snooker star Ramsey Acton. In and out of bed, he bespells her with his

"soft, thick" down-market accent, his intuitive ear, funny stories, and off-color gabfests where he extemporizes with her until
dawn, gesticulating with his fine, thin fingers. In Elin Hilderbrand's *Summer Affair*, a Nantucket artist and mother two-times
her "nothing-to say" cute husband with an overweight, bald-
ing retiree who'll discuss "her work," culture, and "important
ideas" with her.

Mass-market romance heroes answer women's wildest
dreams: they're talkative girlfriends embodied in 210 pounds of
Mr. America muscle mass. Lisa Kleypas's four Travis brothers
in her Texas trilogy are ripped hunks, but they talk up a storm—
about dreams, ambitions, psychic wounds, love, and the heroine's endless attractions. The chiseled six-foot-six Mat Jorick
of Susan Elizabeth Phillips's *First Lady* is a conversationalist
from female heaven. Smart, empathic, and gregarious, he love-
swoons a hitchhiker (a president's widow in disguise) on a trek
in his RV through his sparkling, in-touch dialogue.

Mythic love gods, predictably, possessed the celestial gift of
gab. The Irish Ogma was "honey-tongued," and Hermes, "the
god of eloquence," wore a gold chain dangling from his lips and
deciphered the hidden meanings in language. Dionysus not only
founded dramatic dialogue in comedy and tragedy, he drew the
wrath of King Pentheus with his "clever speech" and "slippery
words." And Paris seduced Helen of Troy by such "sweet and
persuasive" speech that it affected her like "witchcraft" or the
"the power of drugs."

Gifted conversationalists may also have been the erotic king-
pins of evolutionary history. According to many theorists (Darwin included), men who were good talking partners had the
romantic edge over the grunters and club-wielders and monop-
olized the prime women. "Verbal courtship," states Geoffrey
Miller, "is the heart of human sexual selection." Language itself

is "made out of love" since speech may have evolved as a mating call or from the shamans' spell-magic at fertility rites. Conversational fluency in general is a mark of "mating intelligence" and a male plumage display. Great communicators fantail empathy, humor, brains, psychological health, and social aptitude, and suborn women away from the mute studs.

For centuries amorists have implored men to get their colloquial skills up to speed. "Women are conquered by eloquent words," proclaimed Ovid in ancient Rome. The European, Arabic, and Indian love literature was equally emphatic: a man must be "good at the art of conversation" and render a woman "rampant" with honeyed rhetoric. He is "no man," said Shakespeare, "if with his tongue he cannot win women." From Balzac to the present, the advice has persisted. "Speech is the true realm of eroticism," writes Professor Shoshana Felman. "To seduce is to produce language that enjoys," that "takes pleasure."

By conversation these writers didn't mean solo flights of glittering oratory. Although a command of words, subjects, and narrative drama is part of conversational charm, the rest is interactive, a dialogue that resembles a complex, erotic *pas de deux*. Ladies' men are master choreographers. They both shine alone and coordinate conversation for two—talk that soothes, amuses, entertains and informs, and poetically enchants. And not all of talk is spoken; much depends on how a man moves, uses his voice, and listens. A great seducer provides verbal and nonverbal eloquence, shows a woman to her best advantage, and creates an improvisational "zone of magic" that's charged with drama and sexual sorcery.

Unspoken Eloquence:
Gesture, Voice, Listening

There was speech in their dumbness,
language in their very gesture.

—WILLIAM SHAKESPEARE, *A Winter's Tale*

You can miss his SoHo shop if you aren't looking for the small plaque, "Bryce Green, Couturier," on a black nondescript door. But you can't miss his edgy, neo-fifties' designs in fashion circles, or the man himself. He's tall, rail thin, with a mane of sandy hair, and on the day of my first visit, he's dressed in black jeans, a fitted checked shirt, pink socks, and matador shoes. In his world, heterosexuals are rare—rarer still are beloved ladies' men like Bryce.

"Ladies man!" Bryce protests when we sit down in his studio. "That has a rather negative ring; I prefer a man who loves ladies." His voice is soft, plumy, and dusted with his native Scottish burr. He cants forward, drapes his long arms over his knees, and says, "I was a late-bloomer—married twice—and now here I am with a string of lady friends. Must be a dearth of decent men," he laughs.

"There's more," I coax.

"Oh, absolutely," he spreads his arms. "I make a woman feel appreciated. Like most good lovers, I expect?" Then I'm off on Casanova—his gifts, veneration of women, and adventures—while Bryce beams and listens: "Right!" "Right!" "Yes." "Exactly!" The phone trills, a client is here, and he shows me to the door, with a light hand on my shoulder: "Let's talk again. Fascinating." Back on Broome Street, I'm suddenly struck by what Bryce *didn't* say, the spell of his voice, supple gestures, and avid listening.

Gesture

Conversationally, we speak volumes without words. At least 60 percent of conversation content is "silent." Women read this nonverbal subtext better than men, and attend closely to men's paralanguage, especially in romantic exchanges. In a Harvard University study, 87 percent of women versus 42 percent of men correctly interpreted the content of a couple's conversation when the sound was turned off. A woman is on high alert for unsaid messages—wise to nuances of body movement.

Unlike ordinary men, great lovers are pros at wordless communication. T. C. Boyle depicts an adept in his novel about Alfred Kinsey, *The Inner Circle.* "Sexual Olympian" Corcoran seduces the narrator's fiancée, Iris, with a polished nonverbal "rush," sidling over and mimicking her smile for smile, move for move. Most men, say body-language students Barbara and Allan Pease, display few facial expressions (only a third of women's) in conversation, and use mutual eye contact just 31 percent of the time. But Corcoran gazes fixedly at Iris, his mobile features alight with animation. Before long, she's packing her bags for a liaison.

Gabriele D'Annunzio was celebrated for his "speechless" eloquence. Although handicapped by a homely face and squat build, he bewitched women with his amorous gestures. In a photograph of him talking to his Russian mistress, he stands tilted toward her, head inclined, arm extended, and one foot pointed forward. As kinesics experts explain, this was a fine-tuned erotic move. An inclined, asymmetric posture communicates immediacy and engagement; a head nod, rapport; a swerved foot, inclusiveness; and an open arm sweep, attraction. Expressive hands—a female favorite—were a D'Annunzian specialty as well. Actress Madame Simone found the poet's looks repellent, but she conceded that he spellbound her as soon as he spoke, "waving his beautiful white hands in the air."

It takes an agile romancer, too, to manage personal space successfully. He needs radar for mood and timing and a working knowledge of female "proxemics." During intimate talks, a woman tends to stand closer and may become more generous with her favors if a man touches her lightly. Conversational doyen Bill Clinton excels in this lexicon. When he speaks to women (and men), he's "almost carnal," squeezing their hands and wrapping his arm around their shoulders as he locks eyes with them.

Voice

Along with his way with words, Casanova had another conversational gift that made him irresistible to women: his sonorous voice with its "seductive inflections." As the *Kāma Sūtra* recognized, a woman "can be hypnotized by a man's voice." The female weakness for vocal seduction has been featured in folktales since ancient Egypt, where the vulva was called "the ear between the legs." Women hear better than men and listen with their libidos. Even as babies, girls are better at detecting tones of voice, and they remain good at it, sizing up potential mates by the sound of their speech. Vocally expressive themselves, women favor inflected male voices that are deep, low, and musical, which may be related to the fact that a "singsongy, lilted voice" correlates with stronger empathic abilities.

Skilled seducers spoon up rich, creamy baritones. An actor once enrapt a female audience by mellifluously reciting the names of vegetables in French. "A voice," writes author Alice Ferney in *La conversation amoureuse*, "can enter deeper inside you than a man's sex"; "[it] can inhabit you, lodge in the pit of your stomach," and whip up desire as "the wind whips up the sea."

For the fullest seductive effect, soft is the charm. Hermes, the Greek god of seduction, was "the whisperer"; in primitive magic, love spells had to be crooned *sotto voce* to work. Vronsky accosts Anna Karenina (with fatal results) in a "soft, gentle, calm voice," and the ladykiller Lorcan of Marian Keyes's *Last Chance Saloon* ensorcels women by talking to them in his "soft-spoken" melodious brogue. Popular romance heroes, like Rick Chandler of *The Playboy*, may make content-free conversation, but their "bedroom voices" drip "charisma."

A great lover can voodoo women with his voice. Lady Blessington visited Lord Byron in Italy and enthused that "his voice and accent are particularly clear and harmonious, not a word is lost." One clue to Aldous Huxley's success with women (despite his beanpole appearance) might have been his famous voice. It was "an instrument of music," said violinist Yehudi Menuhin, "beautifully articulated, modulated, [and] silvery." Duke Ellington too spoke, recalled bandmates, as if he were singing, with "an extraordinary range of pitches, inflections and rhythmical patterns." Mika Brzezinski, co-host of television's *Morning Joe*, recently told President Bill Clinton, "You're a low-talker. Soft. You have to lean in to listen."

Listening

[Love's] first task [is] to listen.

—PAUL TILLICH, *Love, Power, and Justice*

There's almost no female desire like the desire to be heard. Nearly every relationship study documents women's longing for men's full attention, engagement, and empathy. "Love is listening," women explain, a way of saying, "I love you." If so, legions of women must feel love-deprived; men's refusal to listen is one of their chief complaints. Mike Torchia, a personal trainer who has had affairs with more than forty married women, told *Newsweek* that he's in such demand because husbands tune out. "It's very important," he said, "for a trainer to be a good listener."

For lovers it may be crucial. The traditional guides underscore the importance of listening "attentively" to women and discerning subtexts. Attention, claim several philosophers, is the paramount "demand of love." What we seek most in romantic passion is to be the sole focus of another's interest, our unique self perceived and appreciated. A woman blooms under a man's total concentration, and returns the favor, haloing him in superlatives. Brian, the young banker, told me he once listened to a date for forty-five minutes, only to have her say he was the best conversationalist she had ever known.

The role of listener, however, isn't simple, especially in high-stakes romantic exchanges. Psychoanalyst Eric Fromm compares listening to poetry interpretation, an intuitive and creative art. Rather than a passive, laid-back enterprise, it's as demanding as talk. A man has to be fully present, his mind cleared of distractions, and his brain and emotions engaged. A hint of insincerity and a woman's superior bullshit detector will find him out. In addition, he must supply spirited feedback—responsive facial expressions, eye contact, "go on" signals such as "mms" and yeses—and divine the wishes beneath the words. Some sex gods were sublime listeners. Hermes possessed insight into the hidden meanings of speech, and Shiva had supernaturally attuned ears that heard the truths "beyond ordinary perception." Even Pan, the horndog of the Greek pantheon and disciple of Dionysus, listened astutely. His long pointed ears denoted both his animal nature and his gift of prophecy and interpretation. The Greeks considered him the patron of theatrical criticism.

Women's fantasy lovers listen like divinities; they're focused, empathetic, sincere, and emotive, and they read beneath the lines. When Annie of Laura Dave's *First Husband* drifts into a restaurant bar after a nasty breakup, she runs into a chef who listens to her as if there were no other news in town. "So," Griffin says, grazing her cheek with his finger, "care to elaborate?" She does, and becomes so smitten afterward that she marries him and moves to Nowhere, Massachusetts. Throughout their marriage, he's a priest-cum-shrink who grasps her every word and covert desire, and encourages her to take a job in London, where her ex lurks next door. In less than a week, she bails and returns to Griffin.

Harlequin-style ladykillers usually come more alpha-sized. They're hard-shell heroes with soft centers who psych out heroines and feel their pain. Gabe St. James of JoAnn Ross's *One Summer* is a testosterone-fueled marine with a therapy chip. As soon as he meets veterinarian Charity Tiernan, he senses something is wrong and invites her to dinner, where he elicits her story. Studying her with "slow, silent interest," he listens to her wedding fiasco and affirms and commiserates. "Thank you for listening," she says as the clothes come off, while he murmurs, "Feel free to share all you want."

Listening is a ladykiller stealth weapon. Charles Maurice de Talleyrand, Napoleon's prime minister and a leading European politician, was regarded as a "King of Conversation." He also reigned supreme with women. At salons where success depended on talk, the *précieuses* were drawn to him like birds "fascinated by the eye of a snake." But as he told his harem of mistresses and Napoleon, it was an aural illusion. His conversational fame, he said, rested less on his wit than his ability to listen. And he was an expert, hearing people out with complete attention, approval, and a perceptive twinkle in his eye.

Benjamin Disraeli, another major statesman—twice prime minister under Queen Victoria—was a favorite of women and had the same talent for listening. One anecdote has a society lady dining with his rival, William Gladstone. Afterward she said that she thought she'd been "in the presence of the cleverest man in all England." The next day, she sat beside Disraeli and realized *she* "was the cleverest woman in all England." An eloquent speaker when he chose, Disraeli believed the best way to beguile women (and there were many, from his besotted wife to mistresses) was with an appreciative ear. Sometimes silence, he quipped, "is the mother of truth"—and desire.

True to the breed, Gary Cooper "was a great listener," as was Warren Beatty, who soaked up women's conversation. "It's like he hangs onto every word," recalled Natalie Wood's sister. "Everything that comes out of your mouth is the utmost importance to him."

Conversational Balm

Soft is the roucoulade, murmuring, cooing of love.
—OVID, *The Art of Love*

The widow is distraught. She has thrown herself into her husband's tomb and refused food for five days. One night, in this tale from Petronius's *Satyricon*, a Roman soldier on guard hears her cries and descends to the crypt to investigate. In his softest voice, he pours out condolences until she at last comes around. She accepts his food offerings and begins to see the attractions of the living, specifically of the soldier before her. Soon they find a better use for the bier, and spend three nights together in the closed tomb.

Conversation can be at its most seductive in a slow groove. Anthropologists call this phatic speech—the kind that sedates, placates, forges bonds, and supplies romantic comfort food. Male macaque monkeys groom females into a sexy languor before mating with them, just as accomplished ladykillers verbally massage lovers in courtship. Content hardly matters; the object is affiliation, mutual sympathy, and relaxation. It's grease for the amorous wheels, designed to calm, assure, and lull a lady into that lovin' feeling.

Women are particularly partial to grooming talk. Unlike men, say linguists, they speak more for warmth, companionship, and connection. They're really singing a roundelay of social cohesion, observed essayist J. B. Priestley. In the process, they derive a neural payoff that floods pleasure circuits with peace and composure and assuages anxiety.

Men might do well to brush up their phatic. In contrast to a man's, a woman's sexuality is skittish and complex and easily spooked; hers is wired to the "big brain" where primal fears or imperious commands from the neocortex can shut down the works. For women's desire to run free, their minds have to be at rest. "If you're not relaxed, comfortable, warm, and cozy," writes Louann Brizendine, "it's not likely to happen." Few sexual sedatives carry such clout with women as conversational mood music, which anthropologist Helen Fisher traces to our female ancestors who required precoital talk to feel safe.

Soothing speech is a strong elixir. It takes us back to the delights of an infantile state, to the "voluptuous sleepiness" of the maternal embrace, and "the moment of the enchanted voice." Sweet nothings also contain bonding magic. Baby talk between lovers swamps the reward center of the brain with feel-good chemicals and promotes romantic attachment. Richard Burton knew what he was doing when he addressed Elizabeth Taylor as "My Lumps," "Twit Twaddle," and "Toothache."

"Relaxing the Girl" through phatic speech is a classic piece of amorous advice. The *Kāma Sūtra* devoted a whole chapter to the arts of calming discourse, and Ovid directed men to imitate the cooing, caressing language of doves in their love talks with women. Others counseled hypnotic-like techniques—the repetition of soft, suggestive words. Dumuzi uses this device with the goddess Inanna to put her under his sexual sway: "My sister, I would go with you to my garden," he intones. "Inanna I would go with you to my garden / I would go with you to my orchard."

Thomas Mann's "god of love," Felix Krull, speaks fluent phatic and chain-seduces women with his "sympathy" and mastery of the "primordial regions of human intercourse." While a waiter at a resort, he schmoozes a pretty blonde hotel guest by asking the weary girl if she rested well, and "softly" offering to bring up her breakfast: "It's so calm and peaceful in the room, in bed ..."

A similarly suave groomer is Edwardian sex evangelist Herbert Methley of A. S. Byatt's *Children's Book*. When Olive Wellwood, a married author and mother, meets him for an assignation, she stands terrified at the bedroom door. Anticipating her fear, Methley fastens the latch and croons, Of course, you're anxious, "but I mean to make you forget all those thoughts, soon, very soon now." "Don't think, stop thinking," he whispers, "now is the time to stop thinking, my dear, my darling." After which, she experiences a seismic orgasm.

In mass-market romances, men supply a continual loop of erotic Muzak. The Texas heartbreaker of Lisa Kleypas's *Smooth Talking Stranger* sweet-talks the heroine into bed, and John Wright, the African American Romeo of Sandra Jackson-Opoku's *Hot Johnny*, lullabies all his lady friends. "Aw baby girl," he chants to one, "don't cry," "let me lift you up where you belong."

The "Enchanter" of Napoleonic France, François-René Chateaubriand, owed much of his erotic celebrity to his genius for bonding with women. Although a professional wordsmith—a diplomat and author of twenty volumes of prose, including the seminal novels *Atala* and *René*—Chateaubriand was a poor public speaker. Alone with women, however, he was in his element. He immersed himself in their joys and sorrows, listened, drew out confidences, and soothed them in his "rich and sympathetic" voice. After these soulful communions, the greatest ladies fell for him "*suddenly* and *forever*."

Chateaubriand seemed a poor candidate for the Casanova trade. Morose and often "disagreeable," he was five foot four and bandy-legged, and looked like a "hump-back without a hump." He rarely took the initiative; women "came to him." The youngest son of an impoverished, aristocratic Breton family, he returned from exile after the French Revolution to a career in Napoleonic France and an arranged marriage with a titled neighbor, Céleste Buisson.

It was a fractious, unhappy match. Mistresses soon flocked: first, the *salonnière* Pauline de Beaumont who doted on his "caressing" talk, and later the "Queen of the Roses," Madame de Custine, who purchased Henri IV's castle for his pleasure. "He was prepared to make your life a sweet one," said one adorer, "save that he shattered [it]."

Hooked on serial intimacies, Chateaubriand couldn't be faithful, even after he met his great love, Juliette Récamier, a cultured *charmeuse*, hymned as "the loveliest woman of her age." With her he used the same soothe-and-bond philter: "How have you passed the night?" reads a typical letter. "Are you still ill? How I wish I could know all about it! I will come at four o' clock to find out." During their thirty-year relationship, ladies besieged him, not just for his fame, but for his conversation that caressed, comprehended, and wove a web of togetherness and entrancement.

Laughter

Women need four animals: a mink on their back,
a jaguar in the garage, a tiger in the bedroom,
and a jackass to pay for it all.
—OLD JOKE

Two veteran seductresses, Lisa and Carol, are chatting with me over wine spritzers about their old lovers. Lisa brings up a high school flame: "Johnny H!" she says. "He was short and unattractive by traditional standards. My god, though, he was 'The Man.' He was funny with that ability to laugh at himself . . ."

Carol breaks in, "Like Ben! You remember the one I was with for nine years? I wouldn't call *him*," she air-quotes, "'especially attractive.' But *whooẓa*, he had this tremendous sense of humor. Some of the most wonderful times in bed are when you start giggling and laughing over something. And you just lose it."

Lisa slaps her hand on the table. "I think laughter *is* an orgasm."

For women the funny bone is a high-volt erogenous zone. A good sense of humor, say researchers, is "the single most effective tactic men can use to attract women," and a standard request on female dating sites. If a woman laughs at a date's conversation, the greater her desire to see him again, and if she thinks her husband is witty, the more satisfied she is with her marriage. "Make her laugh at something," advised thinkers from the Middle Ages on, "women delight in hearing nothing else."

There's logic in women's desire for mirth: they may get a bigger kick out of verbal humor. In a Stanford University study of humor, researchers found greater activity in the language areas of the female brain than the male brain, as well as higher levels of stimulation in the mesolimbic region, the site of euphoria. Men who amuse women also advertise cognitive fitness. A witty conversationalist exhibits social prowess, self-confidence, adaptability, empathy, energy, and creative intelligence. And he's less likely to bore a lady, short or long term.

Humor, too, is just plain sexy. "What is more seductive," writes philosopher Jean Baudrillard, "than a stroke of wit?" Or wordplay, jokes, and "linguistic zaniness" in general? A corny one-liner like a mistyped hospital note—"Examination of genitalia reveals that he is circus sized"—will go further with the cute doctor than a black Amex. Comedy weakens inhibitions, excites through incongruity and surprise, releases endorphins, and creates intimacy. When we laugh, we shake off culturally imposed shackles and thumb our noses at civilization and its discontents. Comedy, by nature, notes critic Susanne Langer, is transgressive and erotic—"sensual, impious, and even wicked." Laughter wells up, Langer contends, from ancient fertility rites and the celebration of cosmic vitality. Dionysus, the mythic founder of comedy, was accompanied by a troupe of funny-men: satyrs and assorted pranksters. Hermes was an incorrigible joker whose jests "tricked the mind, even of the wise," while his Norse counterpart, Loki, clowned through the Eddas, acquiring two wives and numerous mistresses. They're members of a Trickster brotherhood, fabled for channeling irrational impulses and seducing women with their impious humor. Don Juan, the "*burlador*" (trickster) of Seville, snared women with his outrageous ruses and wit, and in one version of the story, left them "limp with laughter."

Time and again, ladies' men loot hearts with laughter. Will Ladislaw, the sprite-like artist of George Eliot's *Middlemarch*, lures Dorothea away from her husband with his seductive "merriment." After a dreary dispute with the morose Casaubon, Dorothea encounters Will in Rome, who steals her affections with his humor and hilarious account of their first meeting. Mary Stanger, on the other hand, has the prince of fiancés, a devoted, handsome financier in Somerset Maugham's *Up at the Villa*. But the witty Rowley Flint laughs him off the stage. On a moonlit drive through Tuscany, Rowley mocks the stiff banker with such comic panache that Mary giggles uncontrollably and changes plans.

A "hero should make the heroine laugh," commands Leslie Wainger, a Harlequin book editor, "laughter is sexy." Except for a contingent of tortured viscounts and sullen bikers, popular Romeos show women the funny. Reginald Davenport of *The Rake* hooks his lovely estate manager, Lady Alys, with humor, spoofing her recommendation for a new crop: "One of nature's major puzzles," he grins, "is the mangy mangel-wurzel." As Alys cracks up, she thinks "how intimate shared laughter could be."

Shared, too, in many romances is the comic script. Contrary to the cliché of women as humor appreciators and men as generators, the hero and heroine trade sallies as equals in heated erotic exchanges. In Susan Elizabeth Phillips's *Fancy Pants*, the protagonists go toe to toe in a battle of wits. The tart-tongued Francesca Day escapes a porn movie set and bums a ride from a droll pro-golfer, Dallie Beaudine. Throughout the Southern golf circuit, they lob wisecracks and gibes, until they end up parked beside a swamp. He ribs her about gators that feed in the night, she sasses him back, then they're on the trunk of his Riviera, with her foot on the license plate while she cries, "Oh yes . . . Yes. Dallie!"

Casanova, a noted wit, knew well that Venus is the laughter-loving goddess. Trained in improvisational comedy, he regarded humor as his defense against despair and as his entrée to women. An early starter, he charmed his mother at eleven with a racy aperçu. Asked by a guest why *cunnus* (vagina) was masculine and *mantula* (penis) feminine, he replied, "It is because the slave takes his name from his master." As a teenager, he parlayed his humor into the good graces of a Venetian grandee, Alvise Gasparo Malipiero, who installed him in his palazzo and introduced him to his circle of women. Casanova's raillery, however, ran away with him. Seated alone once with his patron's favorite— a voluptuous young adventuress named Teresa Imer—he engaged her in a bit of "innocent gaiety" and sexual peek-a-boo. When Malipiero caught him red-handed, he was caned and banished. But Casanova exited laughing, recycling the story for future comic fodder and seduction.

With twentieth-century British author Roald Dahl, comedy was king, professionally and romantically. Author of *Charlie and the Chocolate Factory* and other classics, the tall, handsome Dahl enamored hordes of women with his antic wit. His humor—bizarre, ribald, and often grotesque—wasn't for the fainthearted. But women reveled in it. They were "crazy for him," and he slept, said friends, "with everybody on the east and west coasts."

In a Dahl short story, "The Visitor," his alter ego has a diary that makes Casanova's read "like a parish magazine." Dahlesque exaggeration aside, Roald's life was not dull. Born to Norwegian parents in Wales and raised by a single mother (his father died prematurely), he was a wild child and wiseacre in constant trouble with authorities. Later, as a fighter ace in World War II, his plane crashed in the desert, where he permanently injured his back. Humor became his anodyne thereafter—and aphrodisiac.

While on assignment as a British agent in America, he was inundated with women. Like his seducer of "The Visitor," he simply talked to them "more wittily than anyone else had ever done before." One conquest, French actress Annabella, remembered how he seduced her at an opening-night party with a black comic tale about a rich man who made gruesome bets. He charmed and trysted with the *gratin*, including such notables as Ginger Rogers, Clare Booth Luce, and journalist Martha Gellhorn.

In 1952, he met and won over movie star Patricia Neal with his madcap humor. She was entranced, but their marriage, which lasted thirty years, was rocky. They did not get on, and the Furies struck: a son contracted hydrocephalitis in a freak accident; a daughter died at seven; Neal had a stroke in 1962; and Dahl endured a slew of torturous medical procedures. He was not faithful. In 1972, he met the jazzy, imaginative Felicity Crosland, divorced Neal, and married "Liccy" in 1983. They lived in his country home, "Gipsy House," until he died at seventy-four, side-splittingly funny and endlessly fascinating.

Today, reports a *New York Post* feature, comedians are the rock stars of the hour, attended by "chucklefucker" groupies wherever they perform. Many are slapstick buffoons and few are pinups. Standup comic David Spade is short and weasel-faced, but he has a romantic history worthy of Casanova. Another blade, James Corden, the rotund star of BBC comedy shows, said, "My weight was never a concern" with women; I "could always make them laugh, so they tended to overlook my physical imperfections." The proverb "A maid that laughs is half-taken" still holds. "Finding someone funny," writes a British columnist, "is the first step to rolling in bed with them. It's easier to get rich than it is to be truly, charismatically funny."

Mental Intercourse

The act of engaging in intelligent and
interesting conversation.

— *Urban Dictionary*

Clare in *The Time Traveler's Wife* has a husband who seduced her for twenty years before they met. Henry DeTamble possesses a paranormal faculty that permits him to hitch rides on the space-time continuum, and woo his wife-to-be from age six on. In perhaps the longest foreplay in literature, he courts Clare at every season of her life with razzle-dazzle conversation in three languages. He talks to her eloquently and wittily about the wisdom of the ages (he owns four thousand books) and tells ripping tales of his adventures.

Next to comedy, and often mingled with it, is conversation that shimmers with intellectual and narrative excitement. The mind is an engine of enchantment; well-turned ideas, learning, and stories pulsate with sex. The female preference for smart, entertaining men is nothing new, but a recent study shows that women want conversational proof. Stimulating talk, they say online and in person, is "always a turn-on."

Brilliant dialogue, claims Geoffrey Miller, may be an ingrained courtship strategy. In his "ornamental brain" theory of evolution, alpha females chose suitors who put on the fanciest cerebral show, who flaunted the highest G factor (general intelligence) and largest vocabulary, and told the punchiest narratives. For the flames to really fly, men and women participated together in a reciprocal exchange of stories and ideas.

Learning and narrative ability are profoundly seductive. Although braniacs can be tedious bores, men who spin knowledge with verbal aplomb can charm the pants off women. "All that information streaming back and forth," writes author Francine Prose, is like some sexual "bodily fluid." According to philosopher Guy Sircello, we feel "intellectual brilliance," when it's finely expressed, in "our most erogenous parts." The same with narrative drama. Stories, say literary critics, are, in essence, "discourse[s] of desire" that duplicate lovemaking in structure and theme and stir us at profound erotic depths.

Amorists through the ages have recognized this cerebral spell. Ovid believed love was fueled by intelligent, eloquent conversation. A man, he decreed, should acquire culture, learn two great languages, and avoid boring a lady. To charm women, instructs the *Kāma Sūtra*, men must master sixty-four branches of knowledge and excel in the art of storytelling. In one exemplum, the author envisions a suitor leading his lover to the rooftop, where he conducts a "pleasant conversation" that ranges from astronomy to spicy love stories. Honoré de Balzac served notice to men in the nineteenth century: unless a lover provides cultured, scintillating talk, a woman will despise him as a creature "destitute of mental vigor."

Trilby, the eponymous peasant girl and model of George du Maurier's novel, doesn't love the taciturn Svengali who co-opts her but the artist Little Billee, who talks like "the gods in Olympus"—high culture mixed with lively anecdotes.

Jonathan Franzen's philosophy professor, Ron, plies his learning for less benign purposes. His highbrow riffs in "Breakup Stories" have granted him his life's ambition: "to insert his penis in the vaginas of the greatest possible number of women." Even after he meets his intellectual match, Lidia, he can't resist exercising his brain-to-brain seductions on other women.

Romance novels play out differently. Here in female fantasyland, heroes fall for their conversational and mental equals and remain true. Dr. Lynn Wyman of Jane Hiller's *Female Intelligence* is a renowned linguist, a conversational black belt with a mission: to teach men to talk. But her client with a sexist-language disorder proves every bit her peer. Brandon Brock, a mental giant and CEO of a global company, completes the cure and meets her verbally one-on-one, regaling her with stories, parading his IQ, and seducing her at last into marrying him.

Real ladies' men would please the most exacting romance reader. The medieval French scholar Abelard was not only the "preeminent philosopher and theologian of the twelfth-century," he was also charismatic—amusing, handsome, and the idol of women. Scholars thronged from all over Europe to Paris to hear his joke-filled, dazzling lectures, and the female population longed for a "place in [his bed]." In an era of lax clerical chastity, Abelard seemed to have availed himself. "I feared," he wrote, "no rebuff from any woman I might choose to honor with my love."

The woman he honored was the niece of the canon of Notre Dame Cathedral, an intellectual wunderkind named Heloise whom he seduced during tutorials and long debates in her study. Their historic romance, however, went afoul. Heloise became pregnant, they married, and the canon's kinsmen found out and castrated Abelard. Heloise was forced to abandon the child and retire to a convent, and Abelard, to enter a monastery. For the rest of their lives they continued their radiant conversations through hundreds of letters in Latin, but Heloise never reconciled herself. She "remained absolutely and unconditionally in love with him, spiritually and physically."

Next to love, conversation was Casanova's "greatest talent." Regarded as the "most entertaining man in Europe of his time," he was a crack storyteller and conversant on a staggering range of subjects, from horticulture to medicine and metaphysics. He couldn't conceive of speechless romantic passion. "Without words," he wrote, "the pleasure of love is lessened by at least two-thirds." And the women he picked knew how to use them as well, if not better, than he. With one inamorata he debated La Fontaine's epigrams; with another, transcendental philosophy; and with Henriette, his conversational superior, Cicero, opera, and the meaning of happiness.

Ivan Turgenev might never have enthralled women as he did without his "beautiful faculty of talk." In the novel *Rudin*, he draws a portrait of himself in action, sowing heartbreak through his conversation. At a house party, the "irregular"-featured Dmitry Rudin regales guests about his German student days with such colorful word pictures, keen ideas, and bold flourishes that the seventeen-year-old daughter (as happened to Turgenev) falls catastrophically in love. Rudin, he writes, "possessed what is almost the highest secret—the music of eloquence. By striking certain heart strings he could set all the others obscurely quivering and ringing."

This was the "secret" of Turgenev's conquest of Pauline Viardot. An opera diva and seductress, Viardot was an exceptional woman—a superb singer, composer, writer, and an exhilarating conversationalist. When he first heard her sing in St. Petersburg in 1843, he was thunderstruck. Each night he joined her other suitors on a bearskin rug and told such vivacious, vividly spun tales that she returned his passion. Their affair—filled with luminous conversation and conducted under the nose of her "almost silent" husband—lasted four decades.

Handled seductively, learning alone can be "erotic in its urgency and intensity." Philosopher Michel Serres believes that "the quintessential ladies' man is a man of ideas." It depends, though, on the delivery. Big Thinkers, like the ungainly Bertrand Russell and Jean-Paul Sartre, intoxicated women because they made ideas sing. Sartre was the most baffling case. Only five feet tall, he had a gargoylish face with a blind eye, yet he was "smart and ardent and very funny," and charmed his many mistresses by "talk[ing] all night." "Seduction," he said, "*is* fascinating speech."

Eighteenth-century *philosophe* Denis Diderot had an unbeatable combination: beauty, a monumental mind, and a "golden tongue." And he was the very devil with women. A man of letters, he was coeditor of the massive *Encyclopédie*, a twenty-year project that encompassed every conceivable topic, including art, math, politics, religion, science, and even fantasy travel. To talk to him was like being born along "a fresh and limpid river whose banks were adorned with rich estates and beautiful houses."

From the time Diderot left home at sixteen to make his way in Paris, his life was an incessant round of romances. Blond, buff, and gorgeous, he was "loquacious [and] expansive," and up to his neck in intrigues—with actresses, a neighbor's wife, a flirtatious book dealer, and scores more. At twenty-eight, however, his famous powers of reason failed him, and he married the wrong woman, a "ravishingly beautiful," pious lace-and-linen dealer. Their incompatibility soon became evident, and he took his pleasures elsewhere, picking more like-minded women: writer Madeleine de Puisieux and his soul mate of twenty years, Sophie Volland, a bespectacled, lively *savante*.

He courted them both, but especially Sophie, with delicious intellectual fare. His letters to her—written as though he "were standing beside her"—showcase his cerebral brand of seduction. He spreads before her the "fruits of the mind" like a banquet: from dissections of farm picnics to digressions on metaphysics and love.

Although Diderot's philandering days ceased with Sophie, women continued to pursue him. The *salonnière* Madame Necker reportedly was "in love with him," and Catherine the Great found him so delightful that she bought his library, paid him to manage it, and invited him to Russia on the condition that he talk to her each day. No stranger to conversational virtuosi, Catherine reckoned "Diderot among the most extraordinary men who ever existed."

The Poetry Potion

[Poetry is] love's best weapon . . . more amorous than love.

—MICHEL DE MONTAIGNE, "On Some Verses of Virgil"

He's the mascot of the undatables. Cyrano de Bergerac with his huge "tusk" of a nose has such an ugly mug that he's a laughingstock and romantic reject. But he has a gift denied to lesser men; he's a verbal prodigy who can duel in rhymed quatrains and compose soaring love lyrics. Afraid that his looks revolt his cherished Roxanne, he feeds his poetry to the dim-witted Christian, and she marries the handsome cadet. After Christian dies, Roxanne retires to a convent where Cyrano visits her for years. At last, fatally wounded, he tells her the truth; she realizes it's *his* "wild, endearing" poetry that has made her "drunk with love," and he dies in her adoring arms.

Poetry is linguistic seduction on steroids. "Lavish fine words" on women, Ovid exhorted. "There's magic in poetry; its power / can pull down the bloody moon." Why the erotic wallop, nobody quite knows. One suggestion is the similarity between poetic expression and passion; they share the same emotional intensity and visceral impact on the body. "I know it's poetry," said Emily Dickinson, when I feel "as if the top of my head were taken off." In thermal imaging experiments, love poetry actually produces a "parched tongue" and "fevered brow"—what Andrew Marvell called "instant fires in every pore." It can cause, writes critic Jon Stallworthy, "an exaltation comparable to making love."

The legacy of prehistory may also account for the libidinal punch of poetry. As cultural historian Mircea Eliade observed, the shaman's aphrodisiacal chants are "the universal sources of lyric poetry," and according to Joseph Campbell and others, they are part of our mythic inheritance. Early mating rites, too, may have included prosody contests. Geoffrey Miller argues that Pleistocene man needed his best language for courtship, which was poetry. No other mode of speech exercises such charm or measures fitness so well. Meter, rhyme, and the right words in the right order impose a stiff mental challenge and broadcast verbal expertise.

Across cultures, women crave poetry. One woman in a survey said her steamiest memory was the day her husband gave her semi-risqué poems with blanks in the rhyme scheme to fill in. Psychology professor Richard Wiseman, who studied sixty-five hundred subjects worldwide, ranked poetry as the third most persuasive tool for men in romance. Women agree; in dating posts and how-tos, they're unanimous. Leave us a "luscious love note," they write, or recite a verse, "even if it's bad." Unsurprisingly, poets report twice as many sexual partners as other men.

Why women have such an erotic relish for poetry is unclear. Biology may be partially responsible. Women are more verbal and emotionally expressive and apt to use both brain hemispheres, just as poetry does. They also like linguistically driven romantic foreplay. Poetry is the ideal vehicle. When we expend energy on language, we're paid back in energy that, explains psychologist Ilana Simons, can "spur a love bond." Poems also combine neural surprise with the "bewitchment of magical speech," which bypasses reason and targets the instinctual, sensual self. At the same time, women have been culturally conditioned for eons to expect and desire love lyrics from men.

As far back as ancient Egypt, suitors wooed women with hieroglyphic love poems, and in fourth-century BC Sumer, priests beckoned priestesses to the ritual marriage bed in trochaic stanzas. Athenian youths learned "skill in composing and reciting" verse as part of their courtship training, and eleventh-century Japanese aristocrats wrote thirty-one-syllable haikus to lovers before and after trysts. "The first device" in courtship, declared medieval Arabic scholars, was a poetic overture. To entice women, men should "quote a verse of poetry, or dispatch an allegory, or rhyme a riddle, or propose an enigma, or use heightened language." With courtly love, poetry became ensconced in the male romantic repertoire in the West, where it has endured from Elizabethan rhymsters to twenty-first-century rappers.

Dramatic heroes traditionally versify ladies into love with them. Christy Mahon of John Millington Synge's *Playboy of the Western World* seduces an Irish village and the reigning belle with his "poet's talking," and the Don Juan of Derek Walcott's *Joker of Seville* is a poet who talks metrical rings around his prey. In the movie *Before Sunrise*, Jesse commemorates his night with Celine by reciting W. H. Auden's "As I Walked Out One Evening" to her beneath a statue in Vienna at dawn. She doesn't forget. Nine years later, she sees Jesse again by chance and leaves her boyfriend for him.

Alexander Portnoy, the frustrated klutz of Philip Roth's *Portnoy's Complaint*, gets one thing right: he reads Yeats' "Leda and the Swan" to his girlfriend and sends her into estrogen storm. The aphrodisiac of poetry can bowl over the unlikeliest couples; in A. S. Byatt's *Possession*, two cynical, mismatched scholars become infatuated as they study a cache of erotic poems together. Marge Piercy's antihero Phil, of *Small Changes*, is a druggie and a dropout, but he transfixes women with his "dancing cloud of words" and rescues Miriam from her prosaic husband. When Phil reenters her life, she regains her will to live: "She had her poet back."

A man can be as lame and surly as Lord Byron, but let him encant some "music of the soul" to a woman and she'll dissolve.

Or pen lyrics of her own. Niccolò Martelli, the "notorious Don Juan" of Renaissance Italy, exchanged verses with poet Tullia d'Aragona, and becharmed Florentine signoras with his sonnets. A modern poetic "lothario," balladeer Leonard Cohen often tailors lyrics for specific girlfriends, some of whom, like Joni Mitchell and Anjani Thomas, are singer-composers themselves.

Actor Richard Burton called this form of seduction "poetic love." "I had a tried and true system," he said. "I gave [them] poetry." One of the finest actors of the twentieth century and gifted with an ambrosial voice and innate "lyricism of spirit," he was a legendary lover. Although not the handsomest of men (with a pockmarked face and stocky build), he withered women, sleeping with nearly everyone in Hollywood. He had only to recite some "wonderful poetry" to Marilyn Monroe for her to smother him in kisses and take him to the prop room. Claire Bloom, his mistress of five years, remembered lying in bed while he sat beside her and reeled off poems "late into the night" with "his beautiful voice." Despite subsequent lovers, she called Burton "the only man to whom I have fervently given all of myself."

He had the same effect times ten on Elizabeth Taylor, then the reigning sex goddess of film. Throughout their decade-long union, he showered her with verse and serenaded her on Broadway with Andrew Marvell's erotic "To His Coy Mistress" and D. H. Lawrence's "The Snake." His letters to her brim with poetry—occasionally his own—on desire, "death," and "liquor." Among other excesses, liquor both destroyed their "marriage of the century" and ended his life at fifty-nine. Still, he was a spellbinder who ruined women for other men. "Imagine having Richard Burton's voice in your ear while you are making love," exulted Taylor. "Everything just melted away. He whispered poetry—we kissed . . . Happiness!"

The prose-poetry of the everyday speech can also enthrall.

Desmond MacCarthy, a minor member of the 1920s Bloomsbury group, was "tongue-enchanted," his talk flowing like
free verse. Known as the "delectable Desmond," he spoke in a
"stroking, meandering voice," with the flair of a "troubadour."
He accomplished little as a writer (only four essay collections),
but Virginia Woolf thought him "the most gifted" of them all.
Her female contemporaries went further: to them, he was an
entrancer.

He wasn't loved for his looks. He had "smallish genitals,"
missing teeth, and the face of a "bald, battered Roman emperor."
Yet one woman after another succumbed to his incandescent
conversation. He liked "the company of pretty women" and
easily seduced them—notably the glamorous chatelaine of a
Greek Island, and the litterateur, Mollie Warre-Cornish, whom
he married in 1906.

Monogamy, however, proved difficult. Admirers hovered
around. The charismatic Lady Cynthia Asquith, one of his "distractions," said that talking to him was like "dancing on a floor
hung with chains." Unable to part with him, his wife endured
his romantic capers for decades. Then at age forty MacCarthy
met American artist Betsy Reyneau, and his marriage collapsed.
MacCarthy's and Reyneau's passionate affair lasted twenty
years, sustained in part by his lyrical letters. When she moved to
New York during World War II, he wrote, Let's imagine we're
in a Manhattan restaurant, surrounded by "bewildered people"
who can't conceive why we see "a world of delight in each
other." "Absurd?" he asked. "Not from the inside."

WHITHER SEDUCTIVE CONVERSATION? Cultural critics fear the
art has nearly vanished with the onslaught of i-communication
and passive entertainment. We're living in a postverbal age of

wordless love. The typical romantic couple in movies, writes film critic David Denby, is now boringly "inarticulate." Reality shows stream with nonversation and birdbrain banter between the sexes. Little wonder. Men no longer have to verbally court women in a world of the "seven-minute seduction," sexts, and mute hookups. Amid this impasse, relationship coaches flog "communication"—dull dialogues in mutual comprehension—but ignore artful, sexy conversation.

Amorous conversation, though, is the left ventricle of desire. It pumps and preserves passion and keeps the blood up. Romantic love is never a sure thing and needs life support. Good talk—an unspoken/spoken erotic duet—soothes, charms, delights, informs, and thrills. Robert Louis Stevenson thought men and women should converse "like rival mesmerists." Be a "talkable man," he urged—summon drama, "giddy and inspiring" words, and transport her to "new worlds of thought." In the film *Sade*, the marquis is more direct. Advising a greenhorn suitor, he says, "Talk to her first. Women grow randy through the ear." Only the fluent deserve the fair.

CHAPTER 6

Torching Up Love

—

*[Without art] none of Medea's herbs can
keep a passion from dying.*

—OVID, *The Art of Love*

Sam is a magnate who runs a retail conglomerate and can have
his pick of ladies. He's fetching to women, and still handsome at
fifty-five: short and svelte, with a thick shock of black hair and
elfin eyes in a rugged Mediterranean face. Tonight I'm his guest
at a charity gala, seated beside him and across from his wife,
Lynn. They exchange a "private joke" look, and Lynn, an un-
Botoxed blonde in plain black velvet, winks back.

Over the appetizer, I ask Sam about them: "Tell me your
secret. You and Lynn seem to be so—like this!—after what?
Thirty years."

Sam puts down his spoon, glances at Lynn, and talks almost
nonstop through dinner. "My only advice to my son, Josh," he
begins, "was 'marry a woman who wakes up happy, and if she
doesn't, it's your responsibility to make sure she does.'"

"How so?"

"Well, first," he says, lowering his voice a notch, "you've got
to reliably—reliably—take a woman to a place she's never been

before. Also, I like to give her little surprises, like the Key West Fantasy Fest trip last year."

"But there must be more," I prod. "Staying excited by each other is pretty rare."

"Yes, well!" He flings an arm over the back of my chair. "We share a lot of interests. We laugh. Then there's this other thing: she's a lawyer, you know, an old school feminist, and holds her own. We tussle over stuff. Plus, now this is strange: I'm a 'glass half full' person, extroverted, and Lynn's the reverse—a mystery woman in some ways—and that's challenging, interesting. Besides we're not the rest-easy type—always on the move. Right now, I've gotten interested in the Silk Road; long story short, learning Mandarin. Lynn's off on Roman history."

He swivels suddenly. Lynn is giving him the "less talk, please" eye. He blows her a kiss, shrugs, and says, as he turns back to his chocolate bombe, "It's courtship every day! You have to keep it going."

Almost any man can make a woman fall in love with him; the hard part is retaining it. The odds aren't favorable. Romantic love—much as we like to believe otherwise—is fickle, unstable, and highly degradable. After the first euphoric rush, desire declines, eroding over time into quiet companionate love at best, boredom at worst. Under these circumstances, women may become even more restive than men. They burn out faster in relationships, initiate 60 percent of breakups, and according to some theorists, are more inclined to stray. Since the dawn of history, lovers have dreamed of stemming this tide and preserving the first passion.

Scientists have discovered a tiny group of couples, like Lynn and Sam, who've managed to hold the glow. When psychologists viewed their brains with an fMRI scanner, they found the same payoff in the reward circuitry that new lovers experience, along with extra activity in the attachment and pair-bonding centers. But, cautions neuroscientist Stephanie Ortigue, these studies tell us only so much; the understanding of long-lived love is still "frustratingly elusive." Scientifically speaking, we seem no more enlightened than the ancient Hindu *Kāma Sūtra*, which attributed enduring passion to "bewitchment techniques."

There is, however, a long philosophic tradition devoted to the maintenance of desire. "The art of love," instructs Havelock Ellis, "is even more the art of retaining love than of arousing it," and he cites dozens of works since antiquity on the subject. As he and others underscore, this is advanced seduction. It requires dedication and creativity and the entire gamut of erotic spells, from charisma and character to physical and psychological lures. Women must do their part, of course, but men bear the chief responsibility. They're obligated, stress amorists, to take the initiative and invest more "mating effort" to keep love alive.

Great lovers are perpetual suitors. Instead of settling back after the "catch," they intensify courtship. As the drift to ennui impinges, they scale up praise, humor, great sex, and conversation and raise the soothe quotient with intimacy and shared interests. They keep erotic tension humming. Passionate love is a charged dynamic—nothing inert about it—that demands an experienced hand at the controls, an artist who maintains a sexy flux of calm and rapture, habit and novelty, presence and absence, pleasure and pain, intimacy and mystery, concord and discord, yes and no. Ladies' men don't do dull. They combine accelerated love charms with an alternating buzz of opposites and infinitely faceted personalities. They lead a dance, to *that* woman's tune, as if the music never ended.

Fun/Festivity

How much fun are you to live with?
—DR. PHIL

Every morning when Gustin steps out of his "Top Transport" Town Car, the cabbies at the Darien, Connecticut, train station say, "Here comes Hollywood." It's easy to see why. With his close-cropped white hair, pencil mustache, starched white camp shirt, and leonine carriage, he looks like a middle-aged Creole version of Errol Flynn. "These guys," he chuckles (some of whom work for his car service), "can't understand how come I'm an old man and I can get women." He understates the case; Gustin is a love rocket. Amicably separated from his wife, he has more female adulation at sixty-seven than he knows what to do with: a live-in girlfriend of three years, a devotee who calls daily from the Caribbean, and comely singles in bars and nightclubs.

One hot June morning, he invites me into his parked Lincoln, turns on the AC, and tries to explain his "certain something" with women. "I'm from Trinidad," he says in his silky island upspeak. "God didn't give us money, but he gave us happiness." That, he thinks, is the key to it all, besides "class," "character, of course," and "supergood sex." "You see," he says, "you have to get a woman to feel relaxed, and the way to do it? Laughter, laughter, laughter. If I quarrel with my lady it always ends in laughter, and we hug each other up."

Gustin also swears by festivity. "In Trinidad we party *all* year. You have a good time, the blood starts flowing, the music puts a rhythm into your body." And the women can let go and get their wild on. He met his wife that way, seduced others, and once incensed a husband so much at Carnival that he can't go home again. "He says he'll kill me whenever I come back."

In the meantime, he's living to the hilt. The last time he went to the dentist, he realized he'd slept with everyone in the office except the male doctor. "The women talk," he figures, "they want to find out if it's true—whether they'll enjoy it too." Rip-it-down joy: that's his love mantra. As he drives off to pick up a passenger, he rolls down the window and throws me a thumbs-up: "Crank it!" he calls. "To life!"

Passion is fun-dependent; without play, gaiety, and carnival license, it fades to gray. Commitment conspires against us; custom and dailiness insidiously sap desire and induce ennui. Therapists, for that reason, tell couples to work on playfulness—kid around, take date nights, and vacations to holiday resorts. Howard Markman, a psychologist who runs a breakup-prevention program at the University of Denver, found that the amount of fun in a relationship predicted its success.

Fun, though, is easier said than done. A consumer-capitalist ethos of overwork and purchased, passive entertainment militates against celebration. There's also an art to festivity. For fullest enjoyment, it's episodic and alternates with everyday reality. (Imagine a year-round Mardi Gras.) And a flair for gaiety is crucial; eros is "addicted to play" and insists on unbound merriment, nonsense, song, and dance. Ladies' men not only maintain a rhythm between carnival and the nine-to-five; they are masters of revels.

Homo festivus has a special draw for women. The "Perfect Man," writes Erica Jong, *must* have "a sense of playfulness." This may be related to women's tendency toward hypervigilance in desire (via the judgmental neocortex) and their current stress overload. In studies, women report significantly higher tension than men over the last five years, and cite stress as a major reason for disinterest in sex. Critic Laura Kipnis speculates that women often have affairs just to flee the sociocultural pressure and have some "fun." Joyous revelry provides the perfect sex holiday for the mind: reward receptors light up, and opiate-like chemicals flow free.

Men who put fiesta into the love bond may strike an adaptive chord in the female libido. Besides disinhibition, joy, and emotional discharge, festivity gives women a read on a man. Playfulness, as psychologists Geoffrey Miller and Kay Redfield Jamison observe, is an excellent fitness indicator, denoting youth, creativity, flexibility, intelligence, optimism, and nonaggression. Prehistoric men were prone to violence toward stepchildren and refractory mates, and modern hotheads still can be. Shared frolic diffuses aggression and assures women they're in safe company. Larking together is an "affinitive display" that binds a couple and creates a secure play space to unwind, goof, and celebrate.

Mythic archetypes may have left an imprint too. Sex gods were "liberators." At their rites, early mankind imitated the deities and cut loose. They shed rules, rank, and prohibitions and mimed the prodigal exuberance of nature. The Sumerians threw a New Year's free-for-all after the commemoration of the sacred marriage of fertility gods Dumuzi and Inanna; and in ancient Egypt, women waved images of genitals, talked dirty, and danced in the streets in honor of Osiris, the creative spirit. Dionysus was the "deliverer" and joy-bringer who released everything that had been penned up, and led women to wanton mountaintop revels.

Scholars of eros recommend "some fun" to keep passion fresh. The *Kāma Sūtra* spends almost as much space on the arts of festivity as sexual positions, and Castiglione's *Courtier* advises Renaissance lovers to supply "magnificent banquets" and gaiety for romantic success. Modern thinkers agree: Ethel Person, author of *Dreams of Love and Fateful Encounters*, ranks playfulness and the delights of regression as a precondition for lasting desire, and British psychiatrist Adam Phillips suggests that "the cruelest thing one can do to one's partner is to be good at fidelity but bad at celebration."

If Charles Bovary and other dour husbands hadn't dispensed this form of cruelty, we'd have fewer adultery novels. It's Dr. Bovary's tedious gravity that drives Emma up a wall and into the arms of the roué Rodolphe. Fittingly, Rodolphe seduces Emma at an agricultural fair where the carnival atmosphere suspends social constraints. "Why cry out against the passions?" coos Rodolphe. Let's overturn "conventions of society." As the judge announces the prize hog, Emma enlaces her fingers with Rodolphe's.

Carol Edgarian's novel *Three Stages of Amazement* updates the mirthless cuckold to the twenty-first century. Charlie Pepper, a driven surgeon and robotics entrepreneur, pursues a bicoastal career with such frenetic resolve that he forgets festivity and leaves his wife, Lena, to a dismal grind of freelance deadlines and child care. That is, until an old beau, the sportive Alessandro, resurfaces and lures her into an AWOL escapade. When the stunned Charlie confronts her, Lena replies, "You were good, smart. Steady. Loving. Kind," but "we want to laugh. We want to laugh."

Popular romances fantasize beyond flings with playmates. In these novels heroines demand committed partners who keep the party going. Colt Rafferty of Emily March's *Hummingbird Lake* is more than a safety engineer with a PhD; he's a celebrator, and just what the doctor ordered for traumatized pediatrician Sage Anderson. As they become a couple and marry, he teaches her how to play. He appears in jeans and a Santa suit, carrying a pillowcase filled with a Slinky, Silly Putty, and bottles of Napa wine, and barrels off with her at the finale on a Gold Wing motorcycle as she lets out a "joyous laugh."

History has short-shrifted Roman politician and general Mark Antony; he's viewed as Cleopatra's puppet, a bungler, and "gigantic adolescent." Antony, however, was a formidable public figure as well as a ladies' man who sank deep hooks into women. His looks helped; he was tall, muscled, and heartbreak handsome, with a corona of thick curls and a "tunic tucked high on his rolling hips." He was, besides, a seductive blend of a lord of misrule and a lord of the realm.

A born leader of men, Antony commanded brilliant campaigns and rose through the political ranks to become governor of the Eastern Roman Empire under the triumvirate after his defeat of Julius Caesar's assassins. At the same time, he was an unapologetic party animal who traveled with a caravan of musicians, actors, and mountebanks and drank deep of hedonistic excess. He carried golden drinking cups before him in processions as though they were religious relics, and entered Ephesus as the new Dionysus, accompanied by bacchants, satyrs, and pans.

Women flung themselves at him. Besides mistresses, Antony had five wives, none of whom wearied of him. His third wife, Fulvia (who treasured his practical jokes), made war on his behalf, and after she died in the attempt, he married his rival's sister, Octavia. She, too, remained fond of him, interceding with her brother and sending Antony troops, despite his defection to Cleopatra.

Antony's encounter with Cleopatra at Tarsus in 42 BC was a meeting of two force fields. Dressed in the robes of Isis, she was his mythic counterpart, a ruler who mixed politics and festivity better than he. While they plotted the formation of a Roman-

Egyptian dynasty, they founded the "Society of Inimitable Livers," dedicated to the celebratory arts. Together they nearly achieved their dynastic ambition. But after the naval defeat at Actium in 30 BC, they went down in divine form. Before their joint suicides, Antony hosted an extravagant feast, with entertainment, music, and the best wines and cuisine. That evening, they say, inhabitants heard the "marvelous sound of music" and chants of bacchanals as the god Dionysus and his entourage left the city.

If Antony's carnival spirit captivated women, it worked tenfold for Romeos of the 1950s. When "ladies" were girdled and gloved and conditioned to "good girl" asexuality, men who tore off the restraints and brought on the revels held an irresistible appeal. David Niven, British film star of over a hundred movies, was one of the most appealing. A delectable meld of English gentleman and randy cutup, he endeared women in droves—many long-term. Said one of his conquests, everyone was "crazy about him."

As soon as he arrived in Hollywood in 1934, he began laughing women into bed, from newcomers like Marilyn Monroe to Rita Hayworth, Merle Oberon, and Grace Kelly. A carnival king, he was a ham, prankster, risqué raconteur, and fabulous party-giver. Although twice married, once to his great love, who died at twenty-eight in an accident, he was a chronic womanizer. Nevertheless, women forgave him everything when he strode in with his saucy smile. He was "total fun," recalled lovers, with a humor "as delicious as French pastry." Women looked at him, they said, "as if it was God turning up." In a way, it was—the god dearest to women—the "joyful one" who bursts bonds and ushers in play and jubilation.

Another British bon vivant, Kingsley Amis, had the same limb-loosening effect on the female fifties generation. Teacher, poet, and author of *Lucky Jim* and other comic novels, he was an enticing hybrid of literary lion and Liber, the Roman god of fertility and festival. With Amis, women "seemed to have no verbal or sexual inhibitions at all." He was a lark—playful, irreverent, and fall-down funny.

His first wife, Hilary Bardwell, remembered being disenchanted with him at first. He had "yellow and snarly" teeth, a rotten haircut, wretched clothes, and no money or distinction. But he was a freer-upper; he "made everyone laugh." He also made free with the ladies. After his marriage to Bardwell in 1948, he philandered with a vengeance, once charming guests at a party into the garden for a quickie.

Yet she was too smitten with him to leave. She gamely sat out his 1959 teaching stint in America, where he turned Princeton into an academic Woodstock a decade in advance—boozy picnics, hijinks, and liaisons with faculty wives. One ascribed his sex appeal to his liberating sense of the ridiculous—"the most powerful seduction of all." For him, she elaborated, "America with her straight-laced Puritans, was one big laugh-in."

After fifteen years, his wife divorced Amis, and he married novelist Elizabeth Jane Howard, who stood by him throughout his downward cycle into drink and dissipation. At the end, "Hilly" took him to live with her and her third husband, Lord Kilmarnock. There, she tended him lovingly until he died, knowing "his weaknesses" and "ador[ing] him anyway."

We now have carnival license everywhere we turn: X-rated entertainment, clothing-optional resorts, orgiastic club nights, and Las Vegas. But there's mounting evidence of a national fun-seepage. Author Pamela Haag writes of the rise of semi-happy, "melancholy marriages," and critic Barbara Ehrenreich thinks we've lost the arts of festivity and entered a "drab and joyless" era. But eros always unchains the pleasure principle, the archaic instincts, and has the last laugh. In sexual selection, it really *is* the survival of the fizziest. The couple that plays together stays together.

Novelty, Curiosity

Keep it New or it's Through.

—ADAGE

Professor Jack Harris is on spring break and back for a second interview. This time he's talking about his marriage. "There's almost nothing a woman could do now," he says, swinging his legs onto an ottoman, "to get me into bed." His voice has the same Tidewater tinge, but his looks have changed subtly since his last visit. He has a designer stubble and new dress style: a lavender-striped shirt, black cords, and a bracelet. He spins it around his wrist and explains, "From Japan when I visited the in-laws. A month ago, you'd never see me wearing something like this. Unpredictability: that has to be one of the top qualities of a great lover."

Since his marriage eight years ago, he's made a habit of subverting habit. "You have to be proactive," he says. "Surprise—spontaneity—is one of the best ways to keep things alive. My wife never knows what she'll get when she comes home. Sometimes I'll do flowers or sashimi, change plans, or spring a new idea on her, like a sabbatical in Zaire. If you ask her, she'll say that's part of the allure and attraction. Still," he goes on, "I married for the security." Then he clasps his hands behind his head professorially: "Boredom, though—never," he exclaims. "A ladies' man is someone—here goes!—who continues to seduce and fall in love, and have that reciprocated over the life course."

Romantic love requires dependability and security, but there can be too much of a good thing. Total predictability—same old, same old—can drain desire. To keep passion juiced, experienced lovers inject the familiar with novelty, change, and mystery. The unexpected, say scientists, gooses the brain, throwing pleasure switches and unleashing dopamine and norepinephrine, neurotransmitters associated with energy and elation. Such jolts may be vital for sustained ardor. New and exciting things, claim love experts, preserve "the climate of romance" and ward off the toxic effects of tolerance. The unforeseen can make the heart grow fonder.

According to folk wisdom, men are the erotic novelty hounds with an innate lust for variety. That view may be changing. Psychologists Cindy Meston and David Buss found that women may be just as avid for the new and different. Darwin believed that novelty seeking, "change for the sake of change, acted like a charm on female[s]" and was a driving force in sexual selection. This prompted men, conjectures Geoffrey Miller, to devise novel and surprising courtship maneuvers. Prehistoric suitors included delightful marvels and mysteries in their amorous arsenal, Miller surmises, as a way of holding women's attention and securing longer relationships with more offspring. Romance, perhaps inherently for women, includes mystique, novelty, and surprise.

Secrecy and surprise are standard tools of the seducer's trade. Johannes of Kierkegaard's *Diary of a Seducer* structures his campaign for the guileless Cordelia on the startle-and-swoon principle: "If one just knows how to surprise," he gloats, "one always wins the game." Curiosity can be so erotic, writes Roland Barthes, that it's almost "equivalent to love"; we're exalted by those who puzzle and intrigue us.

These seductions only potentiate for the long haul. Honoré de Balzac warned husbands that if they didn't supply variety, surprise, and curiosity, someone else would. Mate poachers, he advised, come "arrayed in all the graces of novelty and all the charms of mystery." Without some enigma and novelty in a relationship, writes psychiatrist Michael Liebowitz, a woman will likely contract "old boyfriend syndrome" and take her love down memory lane. As amorist thinkers caution, female affections can fluctuate; a man must preempt ennui with "perpetual freshness."

The first female love objects weren't designed for predictability or boredom. Dionysus, the "mysterious and paradoxical" deity, vanished in incomprehensible ways and reappeared in spellbinding apotheoses. Shiva personified mysteries and arrived without warning in dozens of strange forms, while the Norse fertility god, Odin, was nothing if not a man of surprises. The object of an all-female ecstatic cult, he trafficked in the occult and paid random calls as an old wizard, eagle, squirrel, or peasant.

Lovers of this cast in literature are rarely husband material. They're compulsive seducers, like Tomas of Milan Kundera's *Unbearable Lightness of Being*, whose strategy of choice is mystery and amazement. He pops up outside a woman's apartment window as a window washer and enters and leaves bedrooms like an incubus. Gareth van Meer in Marisha Pessl's *Special Topics in Calamity Physics* is a more sophisticated maestro of marvels. Ostensibly an eminent political science professor, this "Pajama Playboy" operates a clandestine political ring and cloaks himself in conundrums and disguises. Women literally beat down his door. "Having a secret," he tells his daughter. "There is nothing more delirious to the human mind."

As to be expected, romance readers have no use for these reprobates; their heroes are both "one-woman" men and fonts of incessant novelty. A core theme of women's erotic fiction, writes editor Lonnie Barbach, is the "unexpected or unknown" within established relationships. Romance novels specialize in mystery men with conjurers' packs of surprises—double agents, exiled lairds, and incognito reporters—but they're domesticated and devoted exclusively to the heroine.

No one does it better than Sir Percy Blakeney—a uxorious spouse and "the Scarlet Pimpernel," the mastermind of an underground rescue mission during the French Revolution. When he shocks his wife with his true identity, Lady Blakeney exalts: her "mysterious hero" is now "one and the same" as her beloved husband.

The swashbuckling Cam Rohan of Lisa Kleypas's *Mine Till Midnight* is a novelty junkie's dream. A half gypsy with a diamond earring, he runs a private gambling parlor, materializes as if by magic in drawing rooms, and spirits the heroine, Amelia, to sex under the stars. True love, though, corrals him, and he gives his wife the best of both worlds. Settled with him in her family manse, Amelia sighs rapturously, "How could anyone have a normal everyday life with you?"

Casanova, famous for his staying power in female hearts, realized that love is "three quarters curiosity." While "everavailable" to those he loved, he took care to supply women with novelties and question marks. "*Coups de théâtre* are my passion," he wrote, "joyful surprises," such as the gift of a portrait concealed in a jewel with a secret hinge, or exotic costumes produced for two marchesi before a ball, or the sudden arrival of a theater troupe by boat at a party. A natural dramatist, he relished mystery and camouflage, and once piqued his mistress, a lascivious nun, by crashing a convent fête masked and disguised as Pierrot.

The eighteenth-century diplomat and war hero duc de Richelieu owed his "fantastic renown" with women to more than charm, charisma, and boudoir skills. He was a captivating mix of genie and grand seigneur. And he kept lovers infatuated with him. A cadre of former mistresses joined forces to free him from the Bastille in 1718; an old flame successfully campaigned for his promotion at court years later; and his wife of six years thanked him as she died for the permission to love him.

Loving Richelieu was far from tranquil. This "dashing little duke" liked to mystify and astound. During one intrigue, he tunneled into a lover's bedroom through the fireplace, and in another, he dressed in a nun's habit and rendezvoused with a mistress at her convent. But his most famous caper involved his affair with the daughter of the regent whom he had plotted to overthrow. When the regent caught Richelieu and sentenced him to death, Princess Charlotte forced her father to pardon him—for a price. In exchange, she promised to marry the loathsome Duke of Modena and live in exile with him in rural Italy.

Unfazed, Richelieu disguised himself as a ragged book vendor and traveled to Modena. There he infiltrated the palace, revealed himself to the astounded Charlotte, and dallied with her each afternoon while the duke hunted. One day the duke returned early, saw the "derelict" with his wife, and suspecting nothing, asked for news from Paris.

"And that rascal the duc de Richelieu?"

"Oh, he's a gay dog," replied the peddler. "They say he made a wager that he'd come to your palace in spite of you and try some extraordinary adventure."

At this, the duke roared with laughter: "I defy him! But you're such an entertaining fellow, come back whenever you please."

Richelieu obliged, and lingered for weeks until his admirers lured him back to Paris. The princess never recovered. Each day she repaired to a private "chapel," where she wept before an altar she had built to worship him, adorned with souvenirs and a lock of his hair "surmounted by a crown of interlocked hearts."

Viennese Belle Époque painter Gustav Klimt was as sensual and enigmatic as his famous erotic masterpieces, *The Kiss, Danaë,* and others. A staid society painter and bourgeois bachelor who lived with his mother and sisters, he was a ladies' man swathed in secrets. Beneath his blue smock he wore nothing, and he had a sub rosa relationship with couturier Emilie Flöge for twenty-seven years. She was the mystery lady of *The Kiss,* and his lifelong companion and adorer.

She was not his only adorer. The wealthy wives he painted, like Adele Bloch-Bauer of *Judith and the Head of Holofernes,* often became lovers, and his models comprised a small seraglio who—reputedly—had fourteen of his children. Klimt's attraction had much to do with his creative genius, strong libido, and celebration of female sexuality. But he had another appeal as well: he was a mage of riddles and surprises.

Remembering her obsession with Klimt, seductress Alma Mahler said that she was "taken" by his inscrutability and floored by his impromptu kiss in the middle of St. Mark's Square. He characteristically arrived unannounced at a spa to visit Emilie in 1912 and sent her four hundred cryptic postcards. And women who visited his studio received a tour from Ali Baba. On the outside they saw a flower-bordered gemütlich cottage studio; on the inside, an eye-popping "wonder-room"—brilliant gold-leaf canvases on easels, Japanese and Chinese gowns, African stools, and a black-and-white-striped sofa strewn with textiles and newspapers—and models lounging around in their underwear. Klimt liked to claim that he was "not a particularly interesting person," but it was only one of his *trompe l'oeils* calculated to obfuscate, entice, and surprise.

Cut and Thrust

———

[Love is] a refined and delicate form of combat.

—HAVELOCK ELLIS, *Psychology of Sex*

Amanda and Adam are a poster couple for eternal romance. They're still jazzed by each other. They fix intimate suppers in pajamas, laugh, canoodle, romp, and exchange surprise gifts just for the hell of it. Their pet nicknames are Pinkie and Pinky. But they're no Hallmarky old marrieds. They're rival lawyers and strenuous, loud-mouthed combatants in the movie *Adam's Rib*, played by Katharine Hepburn and Spencer Tracy.

That's the source of their sizzle—the tension of concord and fireworks. And the fireworks almost burn the house down. As Amanda defends her client (a wife who shot and injured her husband and his mistress) with increasing success against her husband, the heat escalates. Adam taunts her and threatens to feed her in little pieces to the jury, and she gives tit for tat. By the time Amanda wins the case, Adam has moved out, and a predatory neighbor, armed with champagne, has moved in on his wife.

When Adam catches them in an embrace, the fur flies: insults ricochet, doors slam, furniture crashes. Then on the brink of divorce, they make up. Each humorously meets the other half-way, and they drive off to the country, where they leap into bed as the camera cuts to "The End."

Couples who never utter a harsh word and live in seamless harmony for decades are sweethearts of the love industry. Therapists and coaches evangelize concord in relationships: curb anger and jealousy, they counsel, and replace conflict with rational dialogue and affectionate concern. Companionate calm, however, carries a cost—romantic stagnation. Partnerships, although havens of trust and peace, need periodic shake-ups. Aggression, fear, and power struggles underlie passionate love, and skilled lovers take them head-on and transmute them. Instead of gagging adverse emotions, they convert them to erotic excitement through a delicate play of combat and truce, pain and pleasure. Love, for ladies' men, is an ongoing duel and duet.

Logically, women should run the other way from romantic turmoil. Due to their brain's hypersensitivity to fear and stress, they have an instinctive "aversion to conflict." But women seem strangely partial to love quarrels. "Conflict," writes the female editor of an anthology, *Let's Call the Whole Thing Off*, is "love's secret ingredient, the drop of vermouth without which the martini would cloy."

Cindy Meston and David Buss confirmed this proclivity; anxiety and jealousy, they discovered, can whet female desire. Women, they also found, often relish a good fight since it releases adrenaline and other stimulants and helps them emotionally connect with men before sex. Power, too, enters in. If the "battle of the sexes" is, at base, a struggle for a balance of power, quarrels can be a strike for parity in a world of gender inequality. Elizabeth Taylor once said her fights with Richard Burton exhilarated her because they made her "feel like an intellectual equal."

Scholars of romantic love routinely recommend spats, jealousy, and nips of distress to keep passion on its toes. Quarrels, writes philosopher Robert Solomon, "are a sign of strength in love"; they not only test commitment but also preserve autonomy, vital tension, and sexual desire. They can serve as periodic bacchanals, explains Ethel Person, airing suppressed grievances and permitting desire to endure. Like opposition, jealousy has its aphrodisiacal uses. Triangulation, say historians, can jolt amour, triggering the stimulants of fear, possession, and competition.

Conflict and pain, however, come with caution flares. Sensitivities differ; what revs one relationship unravels another. Some women have low thresholds for discord and cringe under attack. Great lovers read these differences and avert "true cruelty." It's easy to skid into anarchic rage. The trick, says Adam Phillips, is to maintain "the right amount of misunderstanding," to alternate hostility with harmony and follow contretemps with the sweets of reunion and repose.

The mythic model of eternal desire, while not placid, avoids the hate zone. Inanna and Dumuzi begin their love affair with a fight, which Dumuzi suavely defuses: "Queen of the Palace let us talk it over," he entreats, and "From the starting of the quarrel / Came the lovers' desire." The first Hindu couple, love gods Shiva and Parvati, forever feud and reconcile. Incarnations of the playful war of the sexes, they constantly bicker, jockey for advantage, fan up jealousy, and make love.

In literature, lovers are less adept at handling the demon of discord. Eric, the aspiring tennis pro of Lionel Shriver's *Double Fault*, marries the top-seeded Willy, and at first all goes well. Willy's lecherous coach gins up their passion, and the newlyweds displace aggression into competitive play and win-win sexual tussles. Then Eric begins to outrank her on the courts, and Willy injures her knee, skewing the power balance and unkenneling the hounds of hell. Their fights spin out of control, and the marriage ends.

Popular romances see love combats in a rosier light. Heroes take the heroine's measure and convert jealous threats and angsty brawls into hot-sheets renewals of desire. Gerard, the Marquess of Grayson, of Sylvia Day's *The Stranger I Married*, is an erotic golden glove. Ensconced in an open marriage with Lady Pelham, he mounts an offensive to monopolize her. With jibes, digs, and taunts, he goads her into disputes and leaves for mysterious nights on the town. Finally mid quarrel, he calls her out: "Look how aroused you are, even in your fury and distress." As he thumb-strokes her nipples and she submits to his embrace and monogamy, he promises not to bore her: "I have just enough of the rapscallion left in me," he vows, "to want you to suffer a bit, just as I will be suffering."

As a rule, real ladies' men transcend strife with love and go light on pain, cycling back and forth between discord and concord. Pianist Franz Liszt handled his sensitive mistress of five years, Countess Marie d'Agoult, with a delicate touch. He staunched quarrels with amorous reassurances, and while on tour, he wrote her florid love letters strewn with random nicks— evasions and hints of admirers. When they parted, he cushioned the blow; he was the "sad and deeply distressed" party.

Women who tangled with Gabriele D'Annunzio needed thicker skins. He could be combative and cruel (nasty letters or infidelities), but this "prodigy of love" lavished incomparable rewards. He hymned inamoratas as divinities and discarded them so gently they continued to love him. "Even if all the women of Don Giovanni's dreams were to pass through my bed," he told an ex, "they would leave me with a longing and fierce desire for you."

For his partner of nine years, actress Eleonora Duse, he amped up the drama. He staged blazing fights, flirted with her rivals, and once lost her in a labyrinth of cacti in Cairo until she cried in desperation. After this "game," he clasped her in a voluptuous embrace and delivered a night of "incalculable profundity and of infinite sweetness." "I hate D'Annunzio, and yet I adore him," exclaimed Duse.

Debonair *New Yorker* cartoonist and Casanova Charles Addams had the rare distinction of never making an enemy in his life. Often mistaken for Walter Matthau with his long face and bulbous nose, he nonetheless charmed legions of women into a lifelong passion for him. His taste in women was top-drawer: Greta Garbo, Joan Fontaine, and Jackie Kennedy, to name a few. A "gentle man," he was kind, fun, witty, genuine, and wonderful in bed. Lovers said they accepted his many infidelities because time with him, no matter how short, was priceless.

Addams, however, had a dark, aggressive side—an inner haunted house like his cartoon mansion. The duality both heightened his fascination and drew out the Morticia in women. Barbara Skelton, a British novelist and "femme fatale," spoiled for a fight the moment she met him, once baiting him into a naked bout of fisticuffs. Another Barbara, his second wife, went ballistic. She attacked him with an African spear, smashed the headlights of his 1928 Mercedes, and cut all the left sleeves out of his jackets. Yet after these brawls, Addams always placated her and restored the peace. The union lasted two years, but Barbara's affection persisted. She reappeared in his life in her sixties and couldn't speak of him after his death without crying.

"It was impossible," said his third wife, "Tee" Miller, "to stay mad at him." Before their marriage in 1980, they had a furious altercation about seals in Long Island Sound and parted angrily. The next day the postman arrived at her door with an unsigned painting of the seal he'd seen. None of Addams's lovers, including film star Joan Fontaine, forgot him, and at his funeral the room was packed with "all the ladies who doted on him."

A great seducer can sometimes ratchet the tension and still secure passion, but he has to choose carefully. "God's own mad lover" Jack London had a deadeye for his kind of woman. The turn-of-the-century American adventurer and author of *Call of the Wild* (among other works), London had a cataclysmic effect on women. It was "his fate," he said, "to be able to win love easily." A muscled roughneck, he had a face to launch a thousand fantasies—huge blue, dark-lashed eyes and a sensual mouth set in classic Phidian features.

But his allure for women went beyond pretty. He was an intriguing compound: a dominant alpha male and at the same time a sensitive poet and champion of talented, smart, and independent women. His adventures began early and always with strong proto-feminists who were his equal in the ring: Maggie, the only female "Oyster Pirate" in San Francisco; an intellectual socialite; an actress; a writer; and math teacher Bess Madden, with whom he contracted a "scientific marriage." Throughout their three years together, he openly philandered, picking mistresses in vintage London mode. When star-struck candidates arrived at his California home, he handed them boxing gloves and fencing foils and subjected them to a "fierce but fun combat."

At twenty-six he met his match, Charmian Kittredge, who swaggered into his life and outrode, outshot, and outfought him. The first time she beat him at fencing, "he grabbed her and kissed her." He hailed her as his "Mate Woman," divorced Bess, and married Charmian in 1905. Their union was a four-teen-year soap opera: torrid breakups and makeups, stray flings, and exotic second honeymoons with his "Dearest love woman." Just before London's premature death from kidney disease at forty, Charmian gave up in exhaustion and moved to the sleeping porch. But London was hard to dislodge. Although she had numerous affairs afterward (one with Houdini), she kept a nude photo of her "Mate Man," taped on the windowsill at the back of her desk.

Couples, of course, vary in what they can stand, and most struggle valiantly in the trenches for harmony. Everyone fears *Who's Afraid of Virginia Woolf?* mayhem. Passionate love, though, comes with baggage—rage, fear, and angst. Ideal lov-

"Adonis of the drawing room," Prince Clemens von Metternich

"The most remarkable lover of his time," Gabriele D'Annunzio

"Genius" and ladies' man Aldous Huxley

Elizabethan "darling," Sir Walter Raleigh

"Golden Tiger," Prince Grigory Potemkin

Pianist and heartthrob Franz Liszt, who ignited a "Lisztmania" throughout nineteenth-century Europe

French romantic writer and "enchanter" François-René Chateaubriand

"Great lover"
Carl Jung

Charmer, author,
and casanova,
Roald Dahl

Rock star "Mick the Magic Jagger"

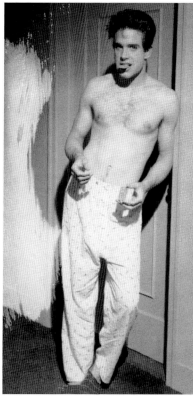

Warren Beatty in high seduction mode

Woman slayer and American author Jack London flaunting his body beautiful

Actor David Niven laughing a conquest into bed

The indecently magnetic French actor Gérard Depardieu

ers turn this around. Always accounting for individual differences, they confront these demonic drives and transform them, through a negative-positive mix, into a high-grade aphrodisiac, one without an expiration date.

Inexhaustible Selfhood

When self-improvement stops, love stops.
—ROBERT SOLOMON, *About Love*

The love match seems inconceivable: an attractive, ambitious blonde in her twenties and a jobless man fifteen years her senior. But as author Christiane Bird recounts it, he was unspeakably magnetic. The first night she met him at a writers' conference, she followed him through the snow to an empty brownstone he was house-sitting, and lived with him on and off for three years.

The question she asks herself is why. Besides her rescue complex, the fun, and good sex, she boils it down to the man. He was the forever-interesting type—complicated, insightful, entertaining, curious, and knowledgeable about "everything." In comparison, other men seemed cardboard cutouts. This is what women want, Bird decides. "Someone who will enlarge our world, expand life's possibilities, and make us more than the sum of our parts." "Sometimes," she concludes, "Mr. Wrong is Mr. Right."

For lasting passion, an inexhaustible, expansive identity is the penultimate spell. Desire is a glutton and craves everything— continual enrichment, complexity, and enlargement. "There is no end," declares historian Roberto Unger, "to what people want of another." Men who eternally enthrall are manifold. They're "like a mine," wrote Christopher Isherwood. "You go deeper and deeper. There are passages, caves, whole strata."

Contrary to Darwinist dogma, women aren't content with mere material assets; they seek inner assets—men who are multifaceted, convoluted, and on the stretch. Experts suggest several reasons. First, a growth-fueled, polysided mate prevents consumer boredom, providing constant mental stimulation. Second, he's less likely to thwart female development. Given women's systematic stunting throughout culture, this is a strong lure. No wonder women in surveys consistently voice a desire for partners committed to change and mutual growth, and speak of leaving stick-in-the-muds who stifle them. Complained one adulterous wife, "I mean my husband isn't running around worried about my growth as a human being, so I am."

Love at its best, say students of romantic psychology, is a drive for psychic health. Eros, the life force, pushes us to outdo ourselves—to expand, individuate, and transcend limits. Humanist psychiatrist Abraham Maslow distinguished this positive "B love" from the "D" variety, which is mired in neurotic stasis and need. Women are increasingly disinclined to settle for "D"s. As Erica Jong writes, a positive, dynamic relationship is "always in a state of metamorphosis"; "the perfect man transforms the perfect woman."

The sex gods were works in progress—proliferous, complex, and many in one. The multi-aspected Shiva was in a permanent state of transformation, dancing the endless Dance of Life, and Dionysus grew into one of the most contradictory and abundant deities in the pantheon. The phallic Hermes, meanwhile, expanded over the centuries to become a master of every trade: thief, orator, seducer, litterateur, accountant, inventor, and guide through the underworld. In their worship of these gods, women expanded as well, casting off patriarchal fetters and ascending to the ranks of the divine.

Jan Kjærstad's postmodern *Seducer* reconfigures Don Juan

along these old mythic lines. Rather than a misogynistic rake, Jonas Wergeland is a futuristic love god who has "everything" and treasures women, boosting each of his lovers to the top of their professions. As all twenty-three women bloom under his influence, he evolves from geologist, musician, architect, adventurer, athlete, and intellectual, to "television's greatest talent" and host of "Thinking Big." His inspiration is reciprocal; women's passion for him, especially his wife's, make him "unbeatable"

Ladies' men of Wergeland's caliber aren't usual literary fare. "No simple Lothario," Thomas Chippering of Tim O'Brien's *Tomcat in Love*, is "complicated." He's a linguistic scholar, a decorated soldier, and polymath who is on a personal-growth crusade. Women find him "attractive beyond words," thrill over his plural charms, and drag him to bed. But it's a tale told by an idiot. Chippering, the narrator, is delusional—a sexoholic and predator—who spirals into madness and reduces his wife to a psychiatric nurse.

Not so in women's popular fantasies. As romance critics point out, the new hero is a multidimensional "Omega Man" who "grow[s] with the heroine" and reveals ever-"new aspects of himself." In Laura Kinsale's *Flowers from the Storm*, Christian, the Duke of Jervaulx, is inner plentitude personified: an aesthete, athlete, lover, and brilliant mathematician. When he's shot in a duel and loses his power of speech, he marries a prim Quaker, Maddy Timms, and together they embark on parallel psychological journeys. As Christian learns to speak, solve more difficult equations, and access his softer side, Maddy integrates her repressed sensuality and matures into a cultivated, open-minded adult. "You make me better," they tell each other at the denouement as they recommit to their joint development.

In reality, ladies' men—however actualized and growth-directed—don't always confer personality upgrades on women. Yet some do. The multi-gifted duc de Richelieu nourished Émilie du Châtelet's intellectual genius; Denis Diderot inspired Madeleine de Puisieux's six books; and Franz Liszt, despite his defections, rescued Countess Marie d'Agoult from the sterile life of society hostess and turned her into an esteemed author, "Daniel Stern." Mamah Cheney, who lived with Frank Lloyd Wright during his most prolific phase, broke the "Angel of the House" mold, taught languages at Leipzig University, and translated the work of feminist Ellen Key.

Casanova, a man of parts, became a priest, lawyer, scientist, violinist, novelist, businessman, and memoirist. In the process, he helped promote many lovers; he redeemed a "ruined" countess with social and financial support; launched Angiola Calori's career as an opera singer; and encouraged Henriette's learning and her defiance of eighteenth-century gender constraints.

The American Victorian writer Harold Frederic epitomized the German concept of *Bildung*—the constant unfolding of one's potential. A ceaseless evolver, he was a colossal personality who "took women by storm." Author of ten novels and two volumes of nonfiction, he wrote one of the finest studies of seduction in literature, *The Damnation of Theron Ware*, starring a vanguard "Venus." He appreciated women, aided the growth of his loved ones, and knew how to fascinate them.

For a ladies' man he was a huge and unhandsome specimen. "Big-bellied" with thick lips and a walrus mustache, he looked like a giant "cucumber" in his signature long green overcoat. He grew up in Utica, New York, but worked in London as the British correspondent for the *New York Times* from age twenty-eight until he died. Although he told highly colored tales about his background—desperate poverty and such intellectual neglect that he learned to read from soap boxes—his past was more prosaic. He came from a middle-class home with a devoted mother, received a regular education, married a conventional hometown girl, and rose to be editor of the *Albany Evening Standard* at twenty-six. But there was nothing prosaic about the man. Frederic was a presence: baroque, myriad-minded, and larger than life.

From the moment he arrived in London, talented women converged. While drifting apart from his wife, who retreated to the suburbs with their five children, he cultivated accomplished ladies in town, including three "attractive young" poets. One rhapsodized, Frederic is "a man of power," a "barbaric king well worth the taming." He was not, however, the tamable kind; he flew under the radar, living covert lives at men's clubs, on backstreet labyrinths, and in the arms of a second "wife," Kate Lyon.

Lyon, an American expat who wore a pince-nez and oozed "sex at every pore," shared a secret household with him for eight years and had three of his children. Her passion for him never flagged. A one-man continuing education program, Frederic studied rare plants, book-binding, philately, photography, politics, music theory, haute cuisine, and theology. His complexity deepened. Contradictory and mercurial, he wore bohemian Chinese shirts but belonged to the anti-bohemian movement, and was both vain and insecure, snobbish and democratic. In contrast to Frederic's estranged, reclusive wife, Lyon flourished, becoming a gifted intellectual hostess and short-story writer.

Frederic's early death at forty-two was just as mysterious and complicated as the man himself. There were so many conflicting accounts—death-bed resurrections with trips to bars and hovering faith healers—that Kate Lyon was tried and acquitted for manslaughter. Afterward, she remained single, but thrived (ghostwriting for Stephen Crane at one point) and retired on her royalty checks to Chicago, where she died at eighty. The

British thought Harold Frederic "the frankest man in two hemi-spheres," but the women drawn into his penumbra knew better. He was as complex, as multifarious as they get, not to mention captivating.

The year of Harold Frederic's death coincided with the ascent of another leviathan on the British literary horizon— H. G. Wells. In 1898, the thirty-two-year-old Wells had just published three scientific romances, among them *The War of the Worlds*, and was on the brink of writing over a hundred books of fiction and nonfiction on an encyclopedic range of topics. He was also on the brink of a career as a "great amorist." Although he coyly denied it in his autobiography, he was a heavyweight ladies' man, loved forever by a fleet of superior women.

To see him on old BBC tapes is not to believe it. Wells was short and tubby, with a center-parted slick-down, and a high, squeaky voice. Sensitive to his physical deficiencies, he com-pensated with a cerebral "sexual system" of his own. Dynamic and lively, he had an omni-curious mind and could talk to women about everything.

For a man of his rational bent (a zoologist by training and logician by temperament), he was surprisingly romantic about women. He sought "lover-shadows," twin personae, who were intelligent, free-souled pioneers. After a first, ill-suited marriage to his cousin, Wells accrued an honor roll of women. A partial exception was his second wife, "Jane," his former biology stu-dent and mother of his two sons, who wrote minor short stories, kept house, and looked askance at his affairs.

In each case, Wells claimed, women seduced him—achievers like writer-journalist Dorothy Richardson; scholar Amber Reeves, who had his daughter; and Elizabeth von Arnim, a best-selling author. All went on to further accomplishments and held him dear. Richardson wrote at least sixteen books; Reeves, three novels; and von Armin, twenty, including *The Enchanted April*, adapted five times on stage and screen.

As Wells grew in prominence and intellectual breadth, gifted women gave him no rest. His most famous liaison with writer Rebecca West lasted ten years, during which she gave birth to their son and wrote acclaimed pieces for *The New Yorker*. Despite West's cavils about Wells's destructive effect on her work, she published two novels under his aegis, and admitted that being with him was like "seeing Nureyev dance or hearing Tito Gobbi sing."

With age, Wells gravitated to global politics and lobbied for world peace, predicting atomic warfare. He took up religion, world history, art and design, cinema, racial inequality, and eugenics. Beside him was always a retinue of brilliant women: birth-control activist Margaret Sanger, war correspondent Martha Gellhorn, and his "chief mistress," Moura Budberg, linguist and Russian secret agent. Wells thought that if any man had had his amorous opportunities, he would have acted accordingly. But he wasn't just any man; he was a boundless, multiple personality who drew exceptional women and drove them to excel with him. As Margaret Sanger—still excited by him years later—said, "To be equal to his company, you must pull yourself up [and] keep alive every second."

All told, personhood is the fizz in the love philter. A vacuous Mr. Big can assemble the ingredients and follow the steps for eternal passion—from conversation and festivity to a difficulty-delight master mix—but it will go down like Nyquil. The ladies' man himself—his inner wealth of fascinations—is the big magic, and so potent he doesn't need everything. He can add and subtract charms, forget seasonings, and brew to suit his strengths. He can be a temperamental chef—capricious and combustible.

But he has the formula few possess—the sorcerer's secret to the female heart. Great seducers grasp what women desire at the quick of their beings. They ennui-proof their identities, and practice a love artistry that's time-tested and time-resistant and customized for each woman. They're continual romancers who keep romance crackling. As the dreamboat tells the heroine in the movie *The Wedding Date*: It's just "about giving you what you need." "Holy crap!" she says. "You're worth every penny."

CHAPTER 7

The Great Seducer Now

—

I say to you, make yourself a lady's man
as much as you can.
—William Makepeace Thackeray, *Sketches and Travels*

If men knew all that women think,
they would be twenty times more audacious.
—Alphonse Karr, *Les Guêpes*

I'm in my living room with five "hot choosers"—two married, two divorced, and one single—who love men and have always had their pick. They're here to discuss the great seducer. "Don Juan! Casanova!" exclaims Anne, a psychoanalyst in her forties with a blonde chignon and chunky silver rings. "None of those labels work. Can't we just talk about the men who besot us?"

She has our attention. The group leans in around the coffee table: Karen, a racehorsey, retired financier; Zoe, a Eurasian twenty-seven-year-old art dealer; Trina, a petite documentary filmmaker swathed in a paisley shawl; and Roxie, the senior member of the klatch, a journalist in round red glasses and a gray bob.

Karen speaks first. "I can't talk generally—only about my

own experience. It wasn't money, first off. But it was a high bar. I wouldn't say Mac was the most attractive man. Except he had this certain presence."

Trina tosses the end of her shawl over her shoulder and breaks in: "'Star Quality,' that glow!"

"Exactly," Karen resumes. "And you know, Mac was just adventurous, unusual, and fun! He'd say, 'Let's go down to Aria [a nightclub] and play.' And he loved to communicate; I really like that in a man. He also made sure I knew he cared; he was totally connected to me. I had a fabulous ten years with him."

"I had a Pierre once," says Roxie, swinging her red glasses by the stems. "He was very short, burly, almost gorilla-esque. But he was just *wow*! My mother didn't care this much for me. That total caring is very sexy. I would go for focus, concentration, and intensity. Ladies' men, I imagine, have the ability to focus on a woman so that she feels re-defined in a very good way."

Zoe punches her knee in agreement. "Yes! I knew this guy in a band who reminds me of Russell Brand. You couldn't trust him to take out the garbage or take a shower every day. But he makes you feel so special—as if you're the only person in the room he really wants to hear from. He appreciates women."

Anne adds with an analyst's nod. "A man who loves women, makes women love *him*. One of the men I dated like that had two sisters and a mother he adored. And those kind of guys love women's bodies."

Trina hugs her shawl and lets out a long contralto laugh. "Listen, sex has to be the most important thing. Anything else you can get from a friend. I just followed my clitoris across the world."

Karen and Roxie both frown. "But you can have sex without falling in love with someone," protests Karen.

"Right," chimes in Roxie. "I like conversation, the communication, the contact, the humor."

"Listen," Trina cranes forward. "Only we know what went on behind closed doors and can speak about the men who made us feel fabulous. Twelve years ago, I was involved with this man who brought an extraordinary amount of fire. He was one of my 'fire-signs.' Every day was an event—book, ideas, and excitement. It was a phenomenal relationship. He gave me such an incredible template. Nobody can rob me of that! And how great I felt about myself and—."

"They make you feel," Anne breaks in, "sexually capable of anything. That you're totally desirable."

"In truth," Trina sweeps the circle of women with a charged look, "you'd do anything for a man like that."

Zoe sinks back on the sofa and sighs, "I'd love to meet these men."

The Romantic Landscape

"How's chances?" as the Irving Berlin ballad goes. What sort of erotic climate is Zoe stepping into? At a glance, it doesn't look like a season for romance; in fact, writes Maryanne Fisher in *Psychology Today*, there *is* none on the dating scene. Gone are the old rituals and rules, and in their place reign confusion, anomie, superficiality, and cynicism. "The love experience," say trend-trackers like sexual theorist Feona Attwood, has "flattened and fragmented." Rather than grand amours, we have "cold heat," desire without passion, and plural, light attachments. Although an advance for sexual liberation, casual coupling, hookups, and turnstile partners have shriveled eros.

A hypersexualized culture hasn't put us in the mood for love either. An excess of the explicit, show-and-tell nudity, and boudoir graphics has paradoxically neutralized desire. We're numbed by wall-to-wall cleavages, buns, crotch shots, and coital live feeds. "Sexual boredom," states Judith Seifer, former president of the American Association of Sex Educators, Counselors, and Therapists, "is the most pandemic dysfunction in this country."

The Internet has opened up a pantopia of erotic possibilities, but it has also discouraged romance. We're more into Facebook than face time with significant others, and can always find a bigger, better deal in cyberspace where endless options beckon. Love is "liquid"; ties are frailer; we can e-snub or press "Delete." Online porn has also taken some of the bloom off the rose. *Scientific American Mind* reports that moderate use can cause "dissatisfaction with a partner's sexual performance and appearance" and plant doubts about a relationship. The commodity culture has further eroded romantic love. Desire has insidiously migrated to the mall, where it's been trivialized and merchandized by beauty czars and enmeshed in a "web of consumer spending."

Meanwhile, desire itself seems to be dwindling. Critic Camille Paglia believes "a sexual malaise [has] sunk over the country." Nothing is sexy anymore; we've sprung an erotic energy leak, with the genders in a state of terminal indifference and apathy. The sixties' sexual optimism, note cultural commentators, including Maureen Dowd, has curdled into bitterness and disillusion, and ushered in an age of irony and discontent, and lukewarm, melancholy marriages.

Estranged Men

Nobody seems happy with the current lovescape, and rarely have men and women been less happy with each other. Many men aren't feeling the love right now. In an unprecedented cultural shift, women have undermined male dominance, advancing in business, in education, and in public and private life. Amid this dislocation, many men's egos and libidos have taken a hit. Feeling increasingly demoralized and emasculated by this change in traditional roles, men report erectile dysfunction at ever earlier ages, often as young as eighteen.

Anger has also crept into men's relations with women. Unhinged by the loss of historic prerogatives and power and uncertain how to adapt, some men have reverted to chauvinism. "The men of my generation are angry, howling nasty," inveighs *New York Times* correspondent Charlie LeDuff, and aren't about to "waste time trying" to "understand women." In a recent retrosexist outbreak at Yale, men chanted obscenities at freshman women and rated them in an email blast according to the number of beers it would take to have sex with them. Tucker Max's misogynistic hump-and-dump adventures with "sluts," *I Hope They Serve Beer in Hell*, has sold over 1.5 million copies. In TV and movies, notes *New Yorker* writer Anthony Lane, "sexual politics are going backward fast."

Another contingent of men has retreated from the fray by taking shelter from romantic engagement in man caves with their buddies. Director Judd Apatow has created a popular genre, the "bromance" movie, out of this trend: guys who've opted out of the whole love business to bond with each other and horse around with guitars, video games, and easy pieces.

Machismo is making a feeble last stand too, with men anxious to salvage the shreds of masculine identity. Pickup artists feign warrior cojones and roll out paramilitary maneuvers to seize prey in bars for quickie takedowns. Culture-wide, men feel romantically beleaguered, regarding women with a wary, jaundiced eye and clenched fists.

Estranged Women

Women are equally at odds with men. The biggest surprise for researchers in one survey of over two thousand women was the female anger toward men. For every misogynistic Tucker Max, there's a man-basher, cat-calling "ass-pirate" and sporting T-shirts that read, "Boys are stupid. Throw rocks at them!" Two scholarly books have chronicled a rise in misandry (antipathy to men), and attack jokes fill the Internet: "What is that insensitive bit at the end of the penis called?" "The man." Or: "What do clitoris, anniversary, and a toilet have in common?" "Men always miss them."

If men are riled and unnerved by the gender quake, women are bitterly disappointed by it. The sexual and feminist revolutions of a half century ago were supposed to have ushered in a love fest—fem-centric sexuality, parity, and romantic happiness—especially as women rose in the world. When it didn't work out that way, and the male backlash kicked in, generations of women felt cheated.

Women's libidos have been just as quashed as men's by all this. Two-thirds of women opted for anything but sex in a 2010 study, and female sexual dysfunction persists in large numbers. "Women's sex lives," says New York University psychology professor Leonore Tiefer, "are often a struggle, a disappointment, an archipelago of regret."

Nor are relationships paying off as hoped. Since 1972, women have become steadily unhappier according to several 2009 studies, a trend caused in part, claims *Huffington Post* writer Lisa Solod Warren, by men's failures to pass muster. Spouses and boyfriends aren't "evil," per se, she writes, they're "obtuse" and "clueless," despite "women's every effort to wake them up." Napping on the job has consequences. Women's infidelity is rising, and the most commonly cited reasons are boredom and neglect. "Women," said one seasoned cicisbeo (lover of wives), "just want to be loved."

Not just loved, but loved extravagantly. Improbably, in the midst of erotic famine and dismay with men, women have never asked so much of romantic partners. Journalist Jillian Straus and others document the sky-high expectations of contemporary women, while romance novels parade battalions of superlative lovers—complete-package Casanovas. The voices of reason advise settling for a Mr. Almost Perfect and simpatico pal, but as Zoe, the art dealer, says, "Why would I settle? I can earn my own money. I'm looking to meet someone who blows my socks off." Women with options, report researchers, aren't satisfied with "solid, good, nice men" any longer; they seek passion and excitement, too, in "hedonic" unions with equals.

Imagining a Neo-Ladies' Man

So what would a "hedonic" man look like if Zoe could locate him in this unpromising scene? Although each woman has her own mate print and preferences, ladies' men have remained remarkably similar through the ages. A 2012 survey of romantic values concludes that "women's needs haven't changed one bit"; what enthralled a queen of ancient Sparta and an eighteenth-century *salonnière* still enthralls the banker, product manager, and college dean today. With a few tweaks; every era favors a signature set of charms.

The twenty-first century, with its tectonic upheavals, is changing—ever so slightly—the face of the ladies' man. Driven and overtaxed themselves, women will unlikely embrace high-maintenance men like the overwrought, labile Gabriele D'Annunzio and the alcoholic Kingsley Amis. "Too needy" is one of the top-five deal-breakers for women in a new study, and both Karen and Trina of my focus group had discarded lovers when they became clingy or flunked AA.

Money and status, minor lures in any age, are losing further ground with women. Reflecting a common sentiment, none of the "hot choosers" at my gathering cared about either. The brighter the woman, found a University of Michigan study, the less swayed she is by a man's wallet size, and in a University of Louisville survey, three-fourths of women would choose a teacher with short workdays over a surgeon with eight times his salary.

Some charms, though, will carry more weight with women. One may be looks. As popular romances dramatize, the "female gaze" has been liberated in recent decades. Women notice beautiful men with nice bulges and are less tolerant of Pillsbury Doughboys. A *Psychology Today* feature notes that the more attractive and self-sufficient the woman, the more she values a man's appearance. As a result, male cosmetic surgery is climbing and men admit, "it's really to do with women." Karen, Roxie, Anne, Trina, and Zoe all mentioned "the chemistry of good looks," but as soon as they spoke about specific lovers, their tune changed; their favorites were consistently unhandsome and "sub-average." Supporting the homely seducer phenomenon, psychiatrist Michael Pertschuk discovered in a large-scale study that women tend to like a loved one's appearance, regardless of stated ideals.

Sexual virtuosity will also loom large in the new ladies' man profile. Stanford professor Shelby Martin, who has studied the "orgasm gap," believes women lag behind men largely through male ignorance and ineptitude. Another factor is female naiveté, which is changing fast. *Huffington Post* contributor Gail Konop Baker writes that as women's power in the workplace grows, their "inner vixen is coming out and saying HELLO." These vixens will demand their due. Mass-market romances, with their man stallions and detailed orgasmic romps, have anticipated this desire for years. No great seducer has ever failed women, but now he must be at concert pitch to keep up with today's pleasure-claimers. Every guest at my klatch put a premium on sex with a capital *S*.

Women, too, will ask for an extra dose of romantic zeal in a postmodern ladykiller. Despite the privilege of the sexual initiative, "women want men's urgency." The great lovers my group discussed were regular Aly Khans, surging in like Roxie's Pierre. Neuroscientists Ogi Ogas and Sai Gaddam determined in their 2011 investigation that women long to be vehemently desired and pursued. Journalist Laura Sessions Stepp made the same finding in her sample of young women. Weary of putting the make on men, they yearned for suitors like romance heroes who scoop up heroines and say, "There's something about you I'm finding impossible to stay away from." According to sexual psychologist Marta Meana, assertive, fervid male ardor is critical to the female libido. "Strike one" against Ashton Kutcher's character in the movie *A Lot Like Love* (and what keeps the heroine from committing for seven years) is that he doesn't "make the first move."

Fun and novelty in a technoculture of overstimulation will

be another priority. Where the media saturates us with nonstop amusement, and ubiquity has dulled appetites and spirits, women are going to want, as Karen the financier says, "entertainment value." Seventy-five percent of women in the 2012 "romance" survey complained of boredom with dates or partners. Cultural historian Paul Hollander writes that in his study of thousands of twenty-first-century personals, "the most unexpected" discovery was the desire for fun, ranking first in importance from Alabama to California. We're ravenous for unplugged, engaged enjoyment. Anne, the psychoanalyst at my gathering, tied this to the secret of lasting excitement: "Habit kills," she says. "Marvelous lovers keep things interesting, and desire grows and intensifies in that way."

With ladykillers, "macho," to quote Zsa Zsa Gabor, has never proved "mucho." And tomorrow's Casanovas will have moved beyond machismo and strengthened androgynous appeals. The authors of *The Future of Men* anticipate a swing toward "M-ness," masculinity that combines the best of traditional manliness, such as courage and honor, with positive female traits—expressivity, nurturance, and communication.

Such "M" heroes have long been a fantasy in romance novels—SEALS with the sensitivity of psychics—and have lately become women's preferred picks in dating and mating. Zoe reserved her highest praise for a friend whose mother "raised him like a girl" without making him one. "It just turned into an appreciation of women and the finer things," she says. Adds Karen, "The feminine side of Mac was so much of his charm; he could relate to me; it was an equalizer."

If gender equality is a given in modern relationships, the ladies' man will have to be a "worthy sparring partner," as Stepp's subjects requested—a man whose character, IQ, and conversation match or outmatch a woman's. Female medical students in another study sought men at least at their level who, said one, know "art, history, philosophy, and literature." "If you're successful," Karen chips in, "you screen men differently in order to keep the parity thing going."

Like romance heroines, today's smart, ambitious women want peers for lovers. In personals and polls, intelligence is one of the most desired traits, and everywhere women clamor for conversation. With good talk on the wane in a tech-addled age, the colloquial arts will become increasingly seductive. Roxie, the journalist of my discussion group, said she liked conversation better than sex.

As women's horizons and growth opportunities expand, they'll prize multifaceted, self-potentiators, the H. G. Wells of the world, and be less thrilled with seducers like Porfirio Rubirosa, whose growth stopped at the polo ground. On dating sites, observes Hollander, male "Renaissance characters abound"; men boast of lifelong learning and a Leonardian breath of interests, from sculpture, philosophy, and Matisse to reggae.

They're targeting a current feminine wish. The medical-school women wanted a man who would "grow at the same rate," and the female ideal in *The Future of Men* was a "growing type of man" who was "well-rounded." Anne the analyst defines ladies' men as "people who are crazy for growth, and want to stay interesting, to shift their lives and ours."

A great seducer's most powerful spell now, though, may be the simplest: attention. Roxie calls "concentration" and "focus" the essence of the ladykiller. Amid the population explosion and cyberverse, we compete with billions to be noticed, and after a millisecond, we vanish without a trace. Instead of watching the one we're with, we're often watching texts, laptops, game consoles, and flat screens, sometimes all at once, with timers pinging and pots boiling. Everyone is multitasked to distraction. A major female grievance is men's fixation on smartphones and virtual images.

"Falling in love," however, is foremost a "phenomenon of attention." Every romance hero puts the heroine in his cross-hairs and singles out her "specialness" for adoration. Attention is the food of love, and researchers Cindy Meston and David Buss found that "attention-deficit" propels many women into random sex. To be looked at, perceived in her uniqueness, can hit a woman like a voltaic charge.

"The snap of the ladies' man," writes poet Molly Peacock in an email, "is the feeling of really being seen. It's the man's ability to zero in, erase your sense of invisibility, as if you were a camouflaged animal in a forest being found." "Such a man," she continues, "can be downright ugly, but if he's lovely, trim, and expresses something vulnerable about himself, it's simply a knockout recipe for falling in love. You're hooked, you're sunk, you have to struggle for your last bit of social sanity before you plunge."

A Neo-Ladies' Man: The Reality

Women are poised to plunge. "In our post-feminist age," asks British journalist Glenda Cooper, "what's so wrong about the seducer; the very word conjures up high-octane sensuality and pleasure." The "eternal seducer" is "God's gift to women," concurs Marina Warner, "only giving them what they want." Actress Sienna Miller quips, "I've met a few Casanovas that I like and some that I haven't, and I hope to meet a few more."

One of the Casanovas Miller refers to is Jude Law, her phi-landering ex-fiancé. Since ladies' men, in reality, often can't resist exercising their talents abroad, how's a liberated woman to cope? For starters, if she wants her man to herself, as the majority do, she has enough seductive chops nowadays to secure him, like Minette Helvétius and Pauline Viardot before her. On the other hand, libertine lovers may license a woman's own roving libido, and give her space to sample the goods. Or their magical presence may be worth it. "If Liszt," said one admirer, "would only love me for a single hour that would be joy enough for life." Novelist Jane Smiley explains, "Some men are so delightful, so engaged that time with them is valuable no matter what."

At this point, love-life coaches and counselors cry foul: therapy exists to serve social harmony, and these fantastic ladies' men—actual and imagined—only exacerbate the erotic crisis, setting women up for disappointment, further alienating men, and destroying homes. Recent research, however, shows that high amorous aspirations lead to higher-quality relationships. It pays to wish.

Most men, philosopher Ortega y Gasset acknowledged sadly, "never succeed in being loved by anyone," while a select group are universally adored. What is the secret? he asked. Honoré de Balzac compared the average man to "an orang-outang trying to play the violin," and thought the answer lay in the example of erotic geniuses. As philosophy has its Descartes and war its Napoleons, he wrote, "love has its great men although they be unrecognized."

These geniuses may be unrecognized, but I discovered that they're far from extinct. The men I interviewed landed on my doorstep without any deliberate search, and would have doubled in number if I'd had time to follow up leads. They're undoubtedly a shadow society, but they're more plentiful than believed, even in this romantic slump, and available for inspiration.

Taking Balzac's advice, I go to a Paganini of amour for a

realistic read on how keen men will be for his inspiration. Bryce Green, the Scottish couturier I had visited in SoHo, greets me with a peck on each cheek, his sandy, frizzled mane spilling over a mandarin tuxedo collar.

"You've come to the right place," he says, loping across the studio in faded jeans and green cowboy boots. "The *men* I hear about!"

"Not red-hot lovers, I'm guessing. Unlike you . . ."

"Completely," he begins. "I don't look like their husbands or boyfriends or behave like them. I don't know how to play it cool. I have Scottish blood in my veins—fire. But I know how to play it charming."

"Lord, women must be all over you."

"Well, yes," he demurs, tapping a tracing wheel on his thigh. "But I'm much happier taking the initiative, romancing a woman and making her feel loved and appreciated. That's what women like, I think—somebody who puts it out there and gives them unconditional love. Humor is huge too. And stimulation."

"Back to these other men," I pursue. "Don't they want to pick up on this stuff?"

"Well," he considers, "men are in a crisis. There's a lot of insecurity, fear, and a serious lack of charm. I hate generalities, but British and European men are more in touch with their feminine side. And being respectful, kind, and romantic doesn't fit in with the 'jock' idea of masculinity."

"You'd say then, that men aren't looking to you for enlightenment?"

"Absolutely not!" he exclaims as we part on Broome Street.

That same day, Rick, the fire captain whom Vivien Leigh once compared to Rhett Butler, calls up and vehemently disagrees. "Sure, there are men that aren't mentally or physically fit for seduction," he says, "phonies, cowards, porn-addicts, body-count guys, drunks, and moguls who buy women—but the rest? Hey, everyone wants to learn to love and be loved."

Selling Men on the Ladies' Man

Could Rick be right—that beneath the armor of swagger and cool—men are just as anxious as women for connection and a grand passion? Although men's magazines would rather run household tips than love-and-relationship stories, new research has shown that men are closet romantics. They fall in love at first sight more often and fare worse emotionally after breakups than women do. Men prefer romantic over sexual images and yearn equally for children and marriage. Eighty-four percent of men under thirty-five believe they will stay married to the same person forever. Love, wrote Garrison Keillor, "is the mainspring of our lives."

With traditional definitions of masculinity in tatters, the ladies' man might be a fresh model of male identity. The Dionysian man hasn't had a starring role in the Western masculine pantheon, but his pedigree goes to the heart of manhood. Dionysus personified male sexual energy and traced his ancestry to the phallic gods of remote antiquity. If, claim cultural scholars, "we need a new myth of love" for our century, we also need a new guiding myth of the lover that's vital, holistic, and virile. "Sexual behavior," romantic success with women, writes psychiatrist Willard Gaylin, "is the ultimate expression" of manhood.

Enamoring and keeping a woman enamored isn't for boys or sissies. The arts of love demand finesse, brains, ego strength, imagination, and mettle. Romantic love is a "hazardous business," replete with peril and risk. Poet Robert Bly defines the "lover" as a manly paragon who navigates the dangerous terrain of desire with "strong warrior energy." To therapists Robert Moore and Douglas Gillette, the lover constitutes one of the four major archetypes of masculinity, an image of the life force and joyous sensuality that men ignore at their peril. "Archetypes," these therapists warn, "cannot be banished or washed away; men must integrate them."

The Making of a Ladies' Man

The integration of the "lover," Bly explains, has been a male initiation rite throughout history. During the Renaissance, he points out, a young man was trained in well-bred lovemaking, developing his inner seducer "from seed to flower." The concept today is virtually unknown. Men get their erotic education from porn, locker rooms, cursory sex-ed classes, the media, and couples' therapy bromides, none of which address lovecraft.

Perhaps desirability is unteachable, but educators in the past believed a man could improve his chances through cultivation. Aspasia, the hetaerae of third-century BC Greece and erotic philosopher, ran a school for instructing men in the amorous arts. Her teaching, known as "The Aspasian Path," emphasized continuous self-culture, along with "charming language," "honest praise," and an "element of enchantment." Later in seventeenth-century Paris, the courtesan Ninon de Lenclos opened an academy to turn out love-savvy cavaliers. "It takes a hundred times more skill to make love," she catechized, "than to command an army."

Aldous Huxley, author of the dystopian *Brave New World*, also wrote a utopian counterpart, *Island*, where men on the mythical Pala learn to become supernatural lovers. Schooled in

"Special Techniques," which enhance female pleasure, they are masters of "the art of loving" and have "the richest erotic and sentimental vocabulary in Southeast Asia." Men are freed from the narrow confines of masculinity and develop into full unique human beings who are "two hundred percent male" and "almost fifty percent sensitive-feminine." Couples make love like Shiva with his goddess in ecstatic unions with the cosmos.

Huxley dreamed large; he was a great lover in his day. Nevertheless, educators unanimously plead for better instruction in romantic love; one of the newest disciplines is "mating intelligence." If men would spend just "one-tenth" of the time on love they give to work, decreed Dutch sexologist Dr. Theodoor Hendrik van de Velde in the twentieth century, we could re-enchant relationships. How, though, to proceed? The majority of men, says sex researcher Timothy Perper, are at entry level. In a series of tests, he found that nearly all his male subjects were "oblivious" about the "art of seduction"—not to mention the crucial art of ongoing seduction, necessary for durable unions. At the end of the movie *Blue Valentine*, a brutal chronicle of marital breakup, the bereft husband cries, "Tell me what you want! I'll do it! I'll do it!"

The Making of a Neo–Ladies' Man

Suppose such a thing were possible: the training of ladies' men? What would the process look like? First, we would need to cull candidates, selecting men who love women and aren't afraid of change. Next we would have to remove roadblocks; men approach the ladies' man burdened with issues— misinformation, biases, and contradictory emotions. While they high-five a Casanova, they also resent his lion's share of the erotic spoils. As the "libertine" in a Stephen Jeffrey play says, "The gentlemen will be envious."

Besides envy, there are prejudices to dispel. Since great seducers menace the social order, men are taught early on that they're deviants and enemies of the state. Favorites of women are also effeminate in some circles, a stigma that goes back to ancient Greece, where real men extricated themselves "from the domain of the feminine." They're "foppish dreamers," writes sociologist Anthony Giddens, "who have succumbed to female power." A neo–ladies' man will have to get beyond all this—the jealousy and indoctrination—and prepare for cultural headwinds. Philosophy professor Irving Singer drives it home: Casanovas "have generally been scorned by men."

Level One

How other men regard Hugh Jackman, the Wolverine of the *X-Men* franchise, and "one of the sexiest men alive," can only be guessed. He may be a Hollywood fabrication, but he could set an agenda for a student ladykiller. A self-proclaimed romantic who actively courts his wife of sixteen years with tango nights, anniversary surprises (three hundred roses tied to a hundred helium balloons), and public tributes, he's both a nice guy and polysided fascinator. Women love him "for his selves," wrote theater critic Ben Brantley of his one-man show. "He contains, if not multitudes, then a teeming crowd of twos." He's bi-everything: he-man and song-and-dance man; roughneck and gentleman; best boyfriend and best girlfriend.

It's as a romancer, though, that he reduces women to "puddle[s] of desire." In movies like *Kate & Leopold* and in interviews, he's a passionate suitor who deploys the seducer's full complement of physical and psychological charms. He looks and moves like an Adonis, and woos women with dance, music, praise, intimacy, and attentive conversation on "all kinds of topics."

Asked about his MO, he says it's a learned process. He cites the manners and chivalry he acquired at home, his gym workouts, dramatic training, and serendipitously, etiquette lessons. During his preparation for *Leopold*, a tutor drilled him twice a day in the bygone discipline of pleasing: graceful gestures and social poise—"truly listening," being "present and intelligent," and doing it all with honesty and sincerity.

Sociologist Marlene Powell, a student of contemporary sexuality, believes Jackman's method may be a first step for would-be ladies' men. Etiquette, she writes in an email, can foster seductive charm. She lists chapter titles from a 1901 etiquette book—"Courtship and Its Demands," "Anniversaries and How to Celebrate Them," and "The Language of the Hand"—and concludes that "at least some of the people in the past learned and practiced the art of seduction and romance." We can "reinstate some of this," she suggests, the same way.

But as the flute master in the Japanese folktale tells his pupil who has spent years in technical instruction, "Something missing." That's the *whoosh* of charisma. (When I saw Hugh Jackman on Broadway, I found no *aaah* there; only a perfect assembly-line ladies' man.) Can we *teach* "the charge, the bolt, the buzz" of the great seducer?

Trina, the independent filmmaker at my soiree, insists you can't: "Disney scouts used to go to playgrounds," she says, "and they'd always pick out the one boy with 'it.'" Psychologist Jack Harris agrees. "Look," he says, "you line up a kindergarten class, and *bam!*" he claps. "You know the kid with charisma. This stuff is innate, I'm sorry." Powell is of another opinion:

"Erotic charisma," she argues, can be acquired with systematic positive reinforcement, confidence building, and impression management.

Level Two

Kurt, the German photographer and woman-charmer I had met before, has another take on sexual charisma altogether, one that recalls Joseph Campbell's hero's journey or the shaman's internal ordeal where he acquires "psychological voltage" and reemerges with "irresistible magnetic mana."

"It isn't something you can learn, only unlearn," Kurt says gnomically.

We're in a Village tapas bar after the opening of his new exhibit, a multimedia installation attended by an arty mob and four generations of his girlfriends. He spears a *chopito* and elucidates. "It's about letting go of the ego, all those old stories about yourself, and plugging into a higher power, a force, whatever you want to call it. And this," he adds with a low chuckle, "is very, *very* sexy."

"How does this work exactly?"

"Okay," he puts down his fork, takes a swig of Rioja, and rakes his fingers through his tousled bangs. "The story about myself isn't pretty. Until my twenties," he says, "I was rejected by every girl. I felt ugly, horrible really. Then I came to New York and began my spiritual development.

"It was extremely intense. For eight years, I worked with a therapist and finally reached the source of my pain; my mother was awful, she . . . Anyway, I broke down in tears. I had to let go of that past, that illusory self."

"Then," he resumes after we dispatch the mini-paellas and frittatas, "my therapist turned to me and said, 'Kurt, you have to see that women are really attracted to you.' And that was the big change. Now with women I sort of follow an inner voice that tells me what to do. And it's always the right thing. I'm just myself," he shrugs.

"All right," he concedes, flicking me a puckish look. "I understand women; I'm a gay man in a straight man's body," he grins. "I'm very passionate; I love to see a girl have a good time; I'm probably the funniest German I know. And dancing is almost better than sex. But every man is a ladies' man; we simply lose connection with that side of us. Charisma is being yourself. Not doubting who you are. You have to work at it, though."

Kurt's way of working at it isn't for everyone. Perhaps there *is* no single route to becoming a ladies' man. A great lover's signature is his singularity, his "ineffable specialness." Standardized instruction may not be for Casanovas, after all. To over-think him is to produce Stepford seducers. Roland Barthes's advice on erotic education may still be the best: "Just leave it alone," he writes, "like those obliging natures who show you the path, but don't insist on accompanying you on your way."

Future Prospects

Nobody is forecasting a resurgence of ladies' men anytime soon. Jack Harris reminds me that great seducers may "always be a minority, an extreme typology." But so were female marines and African American surgeons a century ago; you can never tell. What women want in love, they sometimes get. As biobehavorist Mary Batten explains, women are the natural choosers in mating, unless subverted by deceit or usurped by force; it's just a matter of recouping their lost powers of choice and seduction. Even doctrinaire evolutionist David Buss admits, "When women start preferring to have sex with men who walked on their hands, in a very short time half the human race would be upsidedown." Geoffrey Miller imagines a future where women will prefer something more ambitious: men who "deliver the greatest rapture."

On a birthday visit to Paris I run into one of those female-designed rapture artists and get a glimpse of tomorrow. Meandering through the Left Bank, I duck into a costume-jewelry store the size of a walk-in closet. There's a glass display counter and two walls festooned with art-piece necklaces—bright Lucite chokers, tulle-and-turquoise rivières, chains, beads, and mobile-inspired pendants. As I survey earrings in the case, I hear a custardy voice directed to me from behind. "Ah, this is it! Formidable."

I turn around, and it's as though I've touched a live socket. Everyone says that when they meet him, even when he wasn't famous. Gérard Depardieu, his motorcycle helmet under one arm and his girlfriend Clémentine Igou beside him, is giving me his celebrated half smile and a sparkling eye-lock.

France's most illustrious actor and film star (of *Cyrano de Bergerac*, *The Count of Monte Christo*, and over 150 other movies), Depardieu is the reverse image of a classic French lover. Bearish and rough-hewn with a boxer's crooked nose, he looks more like a bouncer at a lowlife bar than a *tombeur*—a renowned ladykiller. He has had six celebrity relationships with the most glamorous, talented women of his generation, including Chanel icon Carole Bouquet (an eight-year affair), and has been accused of "almost indecent magnetism."

Right now, he's training it on me. As delicately as though he were handling lace coral, he holds up a metal medallion composed of four dissymmetric ovals ending in a small, skewed zero.

At first, he speaks in French: "It's exquisite, you see. Unusual, off-beat."

Then when I try to reply, he switches to English and asks where I'm from. "Yes, I adore New York!" Suddenly he's laughing and gesticulating, and I understand why he once said "joie de vivre" was his "something special."

"I lived at what?" he recounts, "Seventy-Sixth and Madison [this was during the filming of *Green Card*], and above me there was—Oh, a famous painter! He was mad, crazy, fabulous!"

With a balletic sweep of an arm, he includes Clémentine in the conversation, who talks about her two years on Tenth Street. At the end, we shake hands and I tell him, "You are a great artist." To my surprise, he colors and fixes me with a look of infinite sweetness. "Thank you," he says simply, and heads out the door after praising the collection to the shop owners. (Yes, I bought the necklace.)

French actress Miou-Miou isn't the only one to observe that "Gérard knows how to seduce women." But few know how he became so "lovable" (to quote costar Andie MacDowell) and charismatic. He wasn't born to it. Depardieu is the product of good fortune, innate élan, and a succession of female mentors.

He grew up in a poverty-stricken, taciturn family in the drab town of Châteauroux, with a mother who told him she tried to abort him and thought him a dunce. He had a severe speech impediment and obstreperous temperament. At thirteen, he dropped out of school and seemed headed for a career of petty crime. He hung out with toughs, fenced stolen goods, and lived a bare-knuckled life of cheap thrills and street violence. Although so timid he could hardly speak to girls, he was befriended in his teens by two prostitutes who became his "sexual tutors."

His fate as a small-town scofflaw might have been sealed had he not visited a friend in Paris one weekend. He sat in on an acting class and became hooked. Under an inspired teacher, he learned to free his impacted emotions, access his inner "delicacy and sensibility," and to speak fluently through an experimental course in audio-psychotherapy. He acquired a "whole new language of music, poetry, intuition, and the emotions."

But he still couldn't talk to women. A fellow acting student, Elisabeth Guignot, a psychologist and cultured *femme du monde*, changed all that. They fell in love, and in a reverse Pygmalion story, she taught him the elements of charm, conversation, intimacy, style, culture, and taste. During their twenty-five-year marriage, she "guided him into the language and sensibilities of women."

She was only the first in a long line of female guides who instructed him in everything from generosity and courage to authenticity—such notables as filmmaker Agnès Varda, author Marguerite Duras, and actors Jeanne Moreau and Catherine Deneuve. "I always turned toward these women," he said, "who could lead me, step by step."

After *Green Card* in 1991 and a *Time* interview in which he allegedly confessed to a rape at age nine, women at large denounced him as a macho thug. Feminist film critic Molly Haskell went to France to investigate and came away with a different view. She concluded that he had been manipulated by press agents and misunderstood in the translation process, and sat in on one of his movie sets to see the man for herself. "He was all there, playful, grinning; there were no barriers between us. He grinned at me," she wrote, "and I grinned back. Possibly I blushed . . . Depardieu is the new world, regeneration, hope, attraction, Eros."

The eighteenth-century Erasmus Darwin called "Eros the masterpiece of creation," and his grandson Charles thought the lover at least equal to the warrior: "The power to charm the female," he wrote, "is in some cases, more important than the power to conquer other males in battle." Yet the ladies' man has been largely ignored by mainstream historians and thrown to the wolves of popular stereotypes and prejudice.

Scholars who have taken him seriously side with the Darwins. The great seducer, they say, is a potent phenotype, rooted in eons of myth and fable and lodged in the deepest recesses of women's fantasies. He's what Ortega y Gasset termed "the interesting man," an erotic superspecies who radiates fascination and enraptures women—many women—for a lifetime. His arts, advised two amorist authorities, shouldn't be the province of a clique of roving ladykillers. Van de Velde and Havelock Ellis urged men to harvest the ladykiller's parts for the sake of ordinary unions. Every man, they wrote, should be "Don Juan to his wife over and over again"; "the adulterer's art should be the husband's art."

Few may be called to be Casanovas. The ladies' man, though, shouldn't bring more pressure to bear on distressed men, more impossible sexual standards to meet, more stage fright. Instead, the great seducer and his arts can be a male liberation movement, a release from the stranglehold of games, bogies, inertia, and ignorance, and a recovery of erotic empowerment, passion, and joy. The parameters are wide, exclude money and beauty, and permit a man to flaunt his strengths within a broad spectrum of love charms.

The gender standoff and sexual blight may persist for a host of reasons and exceed the ladykiller's best efforts, even if his ranks increase. But he's a privileged window onto women's profoundest erotic desires. Therapists and scientists can't tell us how to orchestrate ardor or perpetuate it. Yet what could be more coveted throughout time than passionate love? For many, it's "the culmination of life," "the supreme thing in the world." Whatever their flaws, great seducers are the *primo uomos* of romantic passion; they glom onto women's erotic wishes and fulfill and surpass them.

The dying patriarch in the movie *Meet Joe Black* tells his daughter to hold out for one of these men, a passion artist who sweeps her off her feet and makes her "sing with rapture." "Expect the lightning," he says.

Five months after my Casanova roundtable, I get an email from Zoe, the young art dealer determined to wait for a lady-killer who would blow her socks off: "OMG, I found him!" she writes. "Blaise loves me and from the beginning he told me that I was smart and beautiful and how lucky he was to have me. He made me laugh. He's one of the most interesting people I've ever met. Plus, he's adorable. :)"

No online algorithms, no sensible considerations, no promises of rank, riches, compatibility, or safety can make a woman fall madly in love with a man. He can't bribe, bully, or talk her into it. As French philosopher Georges Bataille makes clear, "The seductive, the marvelous, the ravishing wins every time." And cracks Bette Midler, "If you know what women want, you can rule."

Acknowledgments

No search for that mystery man, the great seducer, can be done alone. In my case, a corps of guides, good angels, and wise heads came to my aid and made this book possible. Thanks go first to the generosity of the men and women (disguised throughout) I interviewed. Their articulate voices, stories, and insights lit the path and brought the ladies' man alive.

I'm also indebted to New York University's Liberal Studies Program where I was able to explore the seducer figure in history and literature with my students in a Cultural Foundations course. There I had the good luck to find Walter J. Miller, a ladies' man himself, who read and critiqued an early précis of the book.

Others who helped sharpen my ideas along the way were Professors Marlene Powell, Robert E. Harrist Jr., Michael Parker, John Clubbe, and Joan Blythe. Equally helpful were Professor István Deák, Gloria Deák, Drs. Sylvia Karasu, Peter Buckley, Maxine Antell, Scott Goldsmith, and Monica Peacocke. Instrumental, too, were Marc Daniels, Kate Hurney, Bob Braverman, Joni Evans, Barbara Stern, Sheila Kohler, Kathryn Staley, Catherine Hiller, John Pritchard, and Molly Peacock.

I'm grateful, in addition, to the scholars in Prague who opened archives and shared extensive, little-known information about Casanova: Dr. Paolo Sabbatini, Miloš Čuřík, Maria Tarantova, and Marcela Gottliebová.

Then there were friends and acquaintances who steered me to ladies' men—past and present—and provided valuable input: Theodora Simons, Bette and Francis Mooney, Carol Curtis, Selva Ozelli, Hannah Solomon, Sylvia Chavkin, Finn MacEoin, Michael Rosker, Neide Hucks, Delores Cook, Jenni Kirby, Helen Rogers, Jean-Jacques Célérier, and many people who dropped hints in passing.

Primarily I'm grateful for a wicked-smart, inspired editor, Amy Cherry, whose vision charted the course and whose sharp editorial eye kept me on the straight and narrow. Thanks, too, to Laura Romain for her countless services throughout; to crack copy editor Mary Babcock; to the Norton art department; and to my extraordinary agent, Lynn Nesbit. Special appreciation, as well, to IT maven Frank Vasquez and permissions assistant Kristen Lefevre.

Above all, I'm speechlessly thankful to my family, who weathered the research and writing process and were my life support, first readers, and finest critics: my daughter Phoebe and husband Philip, the book's exemplar and inspiration.

$\mathcal{N}otes$

INTRODUCTION

1 "A man without": Anthony Bonner, *A Handbook of the Troubadours*, ed.
F. R. P. Akehurst and Judith M. Davis (Berkeley: University of California
Press, 1995), 77.

1 "Almost all women": Simone de Beauvoir, *The Second Sex*, trans. Constance
Borde and Sheila Malovany-Chevallier (New York: Vintage Books, 2009),
685.

3 concept of an individual "love map": See John Money, *Love Maps* (Buffalo,
NY: Prometheus Books, 1986), xv, 19, passim.

3 2004 cross-cultural DNA study: "A History of Sex," *Economist*, September
23, 2004.

3 seem to have similar: Ibid.

3 recent critic: Peter Conrad, "The Libertine's Progress," in Jonathan Miller,
ed., *Don Giovanni: Myths of Seduction and Betrayal* (New York: Schocken
Books, 1990), 92.

4 "Forbear, foul ravisher!": Ben Jonson, *Volpone; or, the Fox* (Boston: Phillips,
Sampson, 1857), act 3, scene 6, lines 267–268, 291.

4 "unspeakable type": Juliet Mitchell, "Preface," in Sarah Wright, *Tales of
Seduction: The Figure of Don Juan in Spanish Culture* (New York: Tauris
Academic Studies, 2007), 10.

4 Rougemont thinks: Denis de Rougemont, "Don Juan," in Isidor Schneider,
ed., *The World of Love* (New York: George Braziller, 1964), vol. 1, 480–481.

5 "I'm into having sex": 50 Cent, "In Da Club," www.azlyrics.com/
lyrics/50cent/indaclub.html (accessed May 9, 2012).

5 "The professional seducer": Giacomo Casanova, *History of My Life*, trans.

Willard R. Trask (Baltimore: Johns Hopkins University Press, 1997), vol. 12, chapt. 5, p. 111.

6   "as if they were": Judith Summers, *Casanova's Women: The Great Seducer and the Women He Loved* (New York: Bloomsbury, 2006), 2.

6   At twenty-four: Casanova, *History of My Life*, vol. 3, chap. 2, p. 33.

6   without "a moment of": Ibid., chap. 4, p. 59.

6   When her relatives: Ibid., chap. 5, p. 76.

7   "most honorable man": Ibid., vol. 9, chap. 4, p. 86.

7   "being born for": Ibid., vol. 1, Preface, p. 32.

7   "I don't seduce": Albert Camus, *Notebooks, 1951–1959*, trans. Ryan Bloom (Chicago: Ivan R. Dee, 2008), 11.

8   "clinical picture": Gail S. Reed, Review, "*The Quadrille of Gender: Casanova's Memoirs*," *Psychoanalytic Quarterly* 61 (1992), 101.

8   Spanish doctor: The doctor was Gonzalo Rodríguez Lafore. See discussion in Sarah Wright, *Tales of Seduction: The Figure of Don Juan in Spanish Culture* (New York: Tauris Academic Studies, 2007), 56–57.

8   "mother complex": Otto Rank, *The Don Juan Legend*, trans. David G. Winter (Princeton, NJ: Princeton University Press, 1975), 22, 18.

8   targeted his narcissism: For a brief summary, see "A Field Guide to narcissism," *Psychology Today*, December 9, 2005.

8   Feiffer's antihero: Jules Feiffer, *Harry, the Rat with Women* (Seattle: Fantagraphics Books, 2007), 119, 93.

8   problem with ladies' men: See Gregory Pacana, "The Casanova Disorder," *Philadelphia Mental Health Examiner*, October 14, 2010.

8   "eroticism deformed": Dr. Gregorio Marañon quoted in Lawrence Osborne, *The Poisoned Embrace: A Brief History of Sexual Pessimism* (New York: Pantheon Books, 1993), 161.

8   by the name of sexual addiction: See Donald G. McNeil Jr., "An Apology with Echoes of Twelve Steps," *New York Times*, February 23, 2010. See Peter Trachtenberg's seminal *Casanova Complex: Compulsive Lovers and Their Women* (New York: Poseidon Press, 1988).

9   romantic con men: See Martha Stout, *The Sociopath Next Door* (New York: Broadway Books, 2005).

9   "I couldn't say no": "Locked Up Lothario," *Smoking Gun*, March 15, 2010, www.thesmokinggun.com.

9   they belong to another category: See Christopher Peterson, *A Primer in Positive Psychology* (New York: Oxford University Press, 2006), 236–244.

9   Most share some: See, especially, Abraham H. Maslow, *Toward a Psychology of Being* (New York: Van Nostrand Reinhold, 1968), 157; and "Normality," in Burness E. More and Bernard D. Fine, eds., *Psychiatric Terms and Concepts* (New Haven, CT: American Psychoanalytic Association and Yale University Press, 1990), 127–129.

10   "complete harmony": Lydia Flem, *Casanova: The Man Who Really Loved Women*, trans. Catherine Temerson (New York: Farrar, Straus and Giroux, 1997), 74.

10   *homme du monde:* Rodney Bolt, *The Librettist of Venice: The Remarkable Life of Lorenzo Da Ponte* (New York: Bloomsbury, 2006), 108.

10   Woman after woman: Ibid., 69.

11   "serial romantic": Ibid., 82.

11   "'I love you'": Quoted in ibid., 82.

11   "sweetheart": Quoted in ibid., 221.

11   "coffee, cakes": Ibid., 165.

11   A veritable "Phoenix": See ibid., chap. 9, "That True Phoenix," 158.

11   "sighed for him": Quoted in ibid., 285.

12   "Displays of power": Ruben Bolling, "Tom the Dancing Bug," *Salon*, March 25, 2004, salon.com.

12   "Surely": Quoted in Matt Ridley, *The Red Queen: Sex and Evolution of Human Nature* (New York: HarperCollins, 1993), 267.

12   Buss sums them up: David M. Buss, *The Evolution of Desire: Strategies of Human Mating* (New York: Basic Books, 1994), 19–48.

13   "A high-status male": Donald Symons, *The Evolution of Human Sexuality* (New York: Oxford University Press, 1979), 193.

13   Women, say neo-Darwinians: Buss, *Evolution of Desire*, 32, 33.

13   "good, loyal domestic type": Richard Dawkins, *The Selfish Gene* (New York: Oxford University Press, 1989), 154.

13   "For women the world over": Quoted in Mary Batten, *Sexual Strategies: How Females Choose Their Mates* (New York: Putnam, 1992), 62.

14   "from a biological standpoint": Joann Ellison Rogers, *Sex: A Natural History* (New York: Henry Holt, 2001), 391.

14   "The woman who had not slept": Quoted in Philippe Jullian, *D'Annunzio*, trans. Stephen Hardman (New York: Viking, 1971), 245.

14   "ugly," with "unhealthy teeth": Quoted in Anthony Rhodes, *The Poet as Superman: D'Annunzio* (London: Weidenfeld and Nicolson, 1957), 20, 133.

15   "Look, look, since": Quoted in Jullian, *D'Annunzio*, 122.

15   Russian marchesa: Gerald Griffin, *Gabriele D'Annunzio: The Warrior Bard* (New York: Kennikat Press, 1970), 47.

15   "in vain to forget": Ibid., 47.

15   "I have a need": Quoted in John Woodhouse, *Gabriele D'Annunzio: Defiant Archangel* (New York: Oxford University Press, 1998), 61.

15   "green mouths of the sirens": Quoted in Jullian, *D'Annunzio*, 121.

15   "sorcerer": Quoted in Tom Antongini, *D'Annunzio* (Boston: Little, Brown, 1936), 71.

15   "the most remarkable lover": Quoted in Rhodes, *Poet as Superman*, 20.

15   "a ladies' man": Antongini, *D'Annunzio*, 59.

16   "Women aren't attracted": David de Angelo, email, "Why a Wussy Can't Attract Women," *Double Your Dating*, ddeangelo@doubleyourdating.com, February 28, 2007, 2:34:13 EST.

16   "Makeover Team": Seduce & Conquer, www.seduceandconquer.com/ guys/ (accessed March 2, 2007).

17   Unless you're a "tribal leader": Mystery, *The Mystery Method: How to Get Beautiful Women into Bed* (New York: St. Martin's Press, 2007), 8.

17   Swagger into a bar: Ibid., 21.

17   This entails a broadside: Neil Strauss, *The Game: Penetrating the Secret Society of Pickup Artists* (New York: Regan Books, 2005), 137.

17   Often with the help: Ibid., 42; and "Player Guide: *Rolling Stone* Article about Speed Seduction," by Eric Hedegaad in 3/5/98 Rolling Stone, www .pickupguide.com/layguide/r.article.htm (accessed May 14, 2012).

17   It's as effective: Paraphrased from Mystery, who writes that it's "a quick, sharp correction, like a dog in training." *Mystery Method*, 172.

17   "Venusian Artist" isolates: Ibid., 25.

17   Later, he calls: Ibid., 205.

17   "slammed her hard": Quoted in Strauss, *Game*, 71.

17   PUA learns: Mystery, *Mystery Method*, 25; and "The Tao of Steve," www .script-o-rama.com/movie_scripts/t/tao-of-steve-transcript.html (accessed April 24, 2010).

17   Seducers stay cool: Tony Clink, *The Layguide: How to Seduce Women More Beautiful Than You Ever Dreamed Possible* (New York: Citadel Press/ Kensington, 2004), 17.

17   Gamer convert: Strauss, *Game*, 12.

18   Real-world enchanters: Ibid., 211.

18   "Golden Prince": See book title, Gordon Young, *Golden Prince: The Remarkable Life of Prince Aly Khan* (London: Robert Hale, 1955).

18   "You weren't in the swim": Leonard Slater, *Aly: A Biography* (New York: Random House, 1964), 7.

18   "threw away the rule book": Ibid., 7.

18   Unspectacular in dress: Ibid., 59.

19   "Darling": Quoted in ibid., 91.

19   "charming, very special way": Quoted in ibid., 240.

19   "queen": Quoted in ibid., 239.

19   "madly, deeply": Quoted in ibid., 6.

19   As soon as he saw Rita Hayworth: Ibid., 152.

19   "C3 locations": Mystery, *Mystery Method*, 205.

19   "He made women feel": Quoted in Slater, *Aly*, 138.

19   "sentimental guy": Quoted in Edward Douglas, *Jack: The Great Seducer* (New York: HarperCollins, 2004), 314.

20   "Just What the Love": Veronica Harley, "Just What the Love Dr. Ordered: Best Relationship Books," April 15, 2010, http://shopping.aol.com.

20 Gottman's "love laboratory": John Gottman, *Why Marriages Succeed or Fail* (New York: Fireside Books/Simon & Schuster, 1994), 185.

20 Through careful self-monitoring: Ibid. 176.

20 Rephrase her complaints: Ibid. 207.

20 "like you would": Quoted in Philip C. McGraw, "Dr. Phil: So Much Intimacy Based on Imagination," *O, The Oprah Magazine*, October 1, 2006.

21 Foreplay looms large: Eve Salinger, *The Complete Idiot's Guide to Pleasing Your Woman* (New York: Alpha Books, 2005), 186.

21 "quite simply, irresistible": Quoted in Benita Eisler, *Byron: Child of Passion, Fool of Fame* (New York: Vintage Books, 1999), 266.

21 "Once seen": Quoted in Fiona MacCarthy, *Byron: Life and Legend* (New York: Farrar, Straus and Giroux, 2002), 271, 144.

22 "What on earth": Quoted in Andrew Maurois, *Byron*, trans. Hamish Miles (New York: P. Appleton, 1930), 296.

22 "His laugh is": Marguerite Blessington, *A Journal of Conversations with Lord Byron, With a Sketch of the Life of the Author* (Boston: G. W. Cotterel, 1839), 23.

23 "loveable man": Quoted in Maurois, *Byron*, 374.

23 "agony of regret": Quoted in MacCarthy, *Byron*, 268.

23 "How beautiful he was": Quoted in Maurois, *Byron*, 557–558.

23 Modernist painter Willem de Kooning: Mark Stevens and Annalyn Swan, *de Kooning: An American Master* (New York: Alfred A. Knopf, 2007), 75.

23 "let women come to him": Ibid., 116.

23 "I wanted to punch him": Quoted in Anthony Summers and Robbyn Swan, *Sinatra: The Life* (New York: Vintage Books, 2005), 161.

23 "amazing lover": Quoted in Douglas, *Jack*, 246.

24 "Sexiest Man Alive" issue: *People*, November 18, 2008.

25 He not only had: David Bret, *Satan's Angel* (London: Robson Books, 2000), 253.

25 boorish seventeenth-century Lord Rochester: Modigliani quoted in Nigel Cawthorne, *Sex Lives of the Great Artists* (London: Prion, 1998), 154.

CHAPTER 1: CHARISMA: LIGHTNING IN A BOTTLE

31 "He had like a halo": Quoted in Jurgen Hesse, "From Champion Majorette to Frank Sinatra Date," *Vancouver Sun*, August 31, 1970.

32 Within seconds, we feel it: See "The X-Factors of Success," *Psychology Today*, May 1, 2005. Scientists note that you can "spot it [charisma] within seconds." Also see Mark Greer, "The Science of Savoir Faire," *American Psychological Association* 36, no. 1 (January 2005).

32 Normally associated with: For a summary of the research in this field, see Jessica Winter, "How to Light Up a Room," *O, The Oprah Magazine*, October 2010; and http://cbea.nmsu.edu/~dboje/teaching/338/charisma.htm (accessed February 18, 2011).

32 Many experts, however, caution: Ernest Becker, *The Denial of Death* (New York: Free Press Paperbacks/Simon & Schuster, 1973), 136.

32 Schiffer observes: See Irvine Schiffer, *Charisma: A Psychoanalytic Look at Mass Society* (New York: Free Press/Macmillan, 1973), 43–48.

32 Roach thinks: Joseph Roach, *It* (Ann Arbor: University of Michigan Press, 2007), 8–12.

32 Mythologists stress the impact: Charles Lindholm, *Charisma* (Cambridge, MA: Basil Blackwell, 1990), 158.

32 "one of the more contentious": "Charisma," in Adam Kuper and Jessica Kuper, eds., *The Social Science Encyclopedia* (New York: Routledge, 1996), www.bookrags.com/charisma (accessed May 14, 2012).

33 Paul: Marisa Belger, "For Richer or For Poorer," in Hilary Black, ed., *The Secret Currency of Love* (New York: Harper, 2010), 31.

33 When he asked her: Ibid., 34.

33 *Joie de vivre* packs: See *Psychology Today*, May 1, 2005; this is one of the five components of charisma.

33 "It's not the men": Quoted in Peter Haining, ed., *The Essential Seducer* (London: Robert Hale, 1994), 49.

33 "the thrust of the sap": Quoted in Len Oakes, *Prophetic Charisma: The Psychology of Revolutionary Religious Personalities* (Syracuse, NY: Syracuse University Press, 1997), 29.

33 When we're passionately in love: Michael R. Liebowitz, *The Chemistry of Love* (Boston: Little, Brown, 1983), 96.

33 "splendid triggering": José Ortega y Gasset, *On Love: Aspects of a Single Theme*, trans. Toby Talbot (New York: New American Library, 1957), 108.

33 "Exuberance is seductive": Quoted in Kay Redfield Jamison, *Exuberance: The Passion for Life* (New York: Vintage Books, 2004), 210.

34 Greek Dionysus: Carl Kerényi, *Dionysos: Archetypal Image of Indestructible Life* (Bollingen Series, vol. 65), trans. Ralph Manheim (Princeton, NJ: Princeton University Press, 1976), xxxvi.

34 "the exultant god": Walter F. Otto, *Dionysus: Myth and Cult*, trans. Robert B. Palmer (Bloomington: Indiana University Press, 1965), 78, 103.

34 "In no love story": Quoted in Helen Handley, ed., *The Lover's Quotation Book* (New York: Barnes and Noble, 2000), 22.

34 "he was so much alive": Geoffrey Chaucer, "The Wife of Bath's Tale," in *The Canterbury Tales*, trans. Nevill Coghill (New York: Penguin, 2003), 259.

34 "exuberant joy": Bernard Williams, "Don Juan as an Idea, in Lydia Goehr and Daniel Herwitz, eds., *The Don Giovanni Moment* (New York: Columbia University Press, 2006), 111.

34 "animated and high-spirited": Theodor Fontane, *Effi Briest*, trans. Hugh Rorrison and Helen Chambers (1895; New York: Penguin, 2000), 77.

34 Heroes of women's popular romances: See, for example, Lisa Kleypas's

"big, sexy tomcat," Jack Travis of *Smooth Talking Stranger*, whose erotic cocktail is a combination of "vitality, confidence, and masculinity" (New York: St. Martin's Paperbacks, 2009), 46.

34 Nineteenth-century French Romantic poet: Charlotte Haldane, *Alfred: The Passionate Life of Alfred de Musset* (New York: Roy, 1960), 45.

34 Deploying an élan assault: Ibid. 47.

34 Lord Palmerston: Margaret Nicholas, ed., *The World's Greatest Lovers* (London: Octopus Books, 1985), 39.

35 "exactly like his work": Quoted in William G. Hyland, *George Gershwin: A New Biography* (Westport, CT: Praeger, 2003), 215.

35 "a joyous delight": Quoted in Howard Pollack, *George Gershwin: His Life and Work* (Berkeley: University of California Press, 2006), 205.

35 "his exuberant vitality": Quoted in ibid., 112, 205.

35 "I *was* crazy": Quoted in ibid., 115.

35 He never married: Hyland, *George Gershwin*, 115.

36 "He loved every aspect": Quoted in ibid., 116.

36 "All love begins": André Maurois, "The Art of Loving," in *The Art of Living*, trans. James Whitall (New York: Harper and Row, 1959), 17.

36 "Emotional intensity": Lindholm, *Charisma*, 20.

37 "I turned the heads": Quoted in Peter Trachtenberg, *The Casanova Complex: Compulsive Lovers and Their Women* (New York: Poseidon Press, 1988), 32.

37 Romantic love is: Robert C. Solomon, *About Love: Reinventing Romance for Our Times* (New York: Touchstone/Simon & Schuster, 1988), 23.

37 philosophers say: William Gass, "Throw the Emptiness out of Your Arms: Rilke's Doctrine of Nonpossessive Love," in Robert C. Solomon and Kathleen M. Higgins, eds., *The Philosophy of (Erotic) Love* (Lawrence: University of Kansas Press, 1991), 463.

37 Under a functional magnetic resonance imaging scan: See Helen Fisher, "The Drive to Love: The Neural Mechanism for Mate Selection," in Robert J. Sternberg and Karen Weis, eds., *The New Psychology of Love* (New Haven, CT: Yale University Press, 2006), 91.

37 It's so close: See Elaine Hatfield, "Passionate and Compassionate Love," in Robert J. Sternberg and Michael L. Barnes, eds., *The Psychology of Love* (New Haven, CT: Yale University Press, 1988), 199–205.

37 His appearances were: Otto, *Dionysus*, 74.

37 "God, how slow": Colette, *The Other One*, trans. Elizabeth Tait and Roger Senhouse (New York: New American Library, 1960), 130.

37 To qualify for: Sarah Wendell and Candy Tan, *Beyond Heaving Bosoms: The Smart Bitches' Guide to Romance Novels* (New York: Fireside Books/Simon & Schuster, 2009), 70.

37 Tightly wound and "aggressively ardent": Ernest Newman, *The Man Liszt* (New York: Charles Scribner's, 1935), 40, 14.

38   "His personal magnetism": Quoted in Lucy Hughes-Hallett, *Heroes: A History of Hero Worship* (New York: Anchor Books, 2005), 36.

38   culture that enshrined moderation: Plutarch, *The Rise and Fall of Athens*, trans. Ian Scott-Kilvert (New York: Penguin, 1960), 246.

38   "second Dionysus": Hughes-Hallett, *Heroes*, 14.

38   He fled to the enemy: E. F. Benson, *The Life of Alcibiades* (London: Ernest Benn, 1928), 109.

38   king's wife numbered among them: Plutarch, *Rise and the Fall*, 267.

39   "The subject of this treatise: *The Complete Kāma Sūtra*, trans. Alain Daniélou (Rochester, VT: Park Street Press, 1994), 111.

39   Women in Trenton: See Janet Evanovich, *Ten Big Ones* (New York: St. Martin's Paperbacks, 2004), 290–291.

39   fierceromance blogspot: Carly Carson, "Heros in Romantic Fiction," June 16, 2009, http://fierceromance.blogspot.com; and Evanovich, *Ten Big Ones*, 390.

39   sex drive lies on a continuum: For the best treatment of this, see John Money, *Love and Love Sickness: The Science of Sex: Gender Differences and Pair Bonding* (Baltimore: Johns Hopkins University Press, 1980), 78–100, 118.

39   "sensuality": Quoted in Otto Rank, *The Don Juan Legend*, trans. David G. Winter (Princeton, NJ: Princeton University Press, 1975), 18.

39   Throughout deep history: For a discussion of the "magical effect" of sexual indulgence and phallic images, see George Ryley Scott, *Phallic Worship: A History of Sex and Sexual Rites* (London: Senate/Random House UK, 1966), 42–45.

40   Women's dream lovers: A surprise for newcomers to the romance genre is the amount of explicit sex. Sarah Wendell and Candy Tan discuss this under the heading, "The Hero's Wang of Mighty Lovin'," in *Beyond Heaving Bosoms*, 83.

40   "walking orgasm": E. C. Sheehy, "Midnight Plane to Georgia," in *Bad Boys Southern Style* (New York: Brava/Kensington, 2006), 125.

40   "It's bath time": Ibid., 167.

40   "Don Juan Khan": Leonard Slater, *Aly: A Biography* (New York: Random House, 1964), 6.

40   "charm in neon": Definition of charisma from "Fast Forces of Attraction," *Psychology Today*, January 2008.

40   Trained as a boy: Ibid., 4.

40   But he added: In an interview, he said that "class," a desire to make women happy, and "a rose at a special moment" were his secrets to being a great lover. Quoted in a reprint of an interview with Porfirio Rubirosa in *El Universal*, 1955: "Porfirio Rubirosa: What Women Need," *Repeating Islands*, June 6, 2010, http://repeatingislands.com/2010/06/21/porfirio-rubirosa-what-women-need.

41   "Rubi is so virile": Quoted in Shawn Levy, *The Last Playboy: The High Life of Porfirio Rubirosa* (New York: HarperCollins, 2005), 160.

41 "hero of the boudoir": Quoted in H. Noel Williams, *The Fascinating duc de Richelieu: Louis Francois Armand du Plessis* (New York: Charles Scribner's, 1910), 51.

41 "Profligate," adorable, and hypersexed: Cliff Howe, "duc de Richelieu," in *Lovers and Libertines* (New York: Ace Books, 1958), 7.

41 "unbridled animal magnetism": Ibid., 9.

41 "could ruin a woman": Williams, *Fascinating duc de Richelieu*, 51.

41 Women were "wild": Howe, "duc de Richelieu," 7.

41 "clothed as Amazons": Quoted in Williams, *Fascinating duc de Richlieu*, 51, 50.

42 "Destructive, damnable": Thomas Otway, *The Orphan: or, the Unhappy Marriage* (London: W. Feales, 1735), act 3, scene 1.

42 "a honey-dripping chick magnet": Marc Shapiro, *Ashton Kutcher: The Life and Loves of the King of Punk'd* (New York: Pocket Books, 2004), 4.

42 "love[s] the company of women": Ibid., 5.

42 "treat women right": Quoted in ibid., 23.

42 tradition is ancient: This refers to Jonathan's love for David in the Old Testament, 2 Samuel 1:26.

42 Mirror neurons light up: See discussion of Pentland's work in Winter, "How to Light Up a Room."

43 Unlike the macho deities: Otto, *Dionysus*, 172.

43 Chekov's rake: Anton Chekov, "The Lady with Lapdog," in *Lady with Lapdog and Other Stories*, trans. David Magarshack (New York: Penguin, 1964), 265.

43 "like[s] women": W. Somerset Maugham, *Up at the Villa* (New York: Vintage Books, 1940), 57.

43 "Women are more important": Jennifer Crusie, *Bet Me* (New York: St. Martin's Paperbacks, 2004), 213.

43 "madly in love": Lydia Flem, *Casanova: The Man Who Really Loved Women*, trans. Catherine Temerson (New York: Farrar, Straus and Giroux, 1997), 80.

43 "he loved women": Simon Sebag Montefiore, *Potemkin: Catherine the Great's Imperial Partner* (New York: Vintage, 2005), 183.

44 "sweetly endearing appreciation": Quoted in Suzanne Finstad, *Warren Beatty: A Private Man* (New York: Three Rivers Press, 2005), 86.

44 "He's just wonderful": Quoted in ibid., 293.

44 "sweet man": Quoted in James Lincoln Collier, *Duke Ellington* (New York: Macmillan/McGraw-Hill, 1991), 10.

44 "Spoiled rotten": Quoted in John Edward Hasse, *Beyond Category: The Life and Genius of Duke Ellington* (New York: Da Capo Press, 1993), 22, 256.

44 "absolutely adored him": Ibid., 257.

44 "as flowers": Quoted in ibid., 257.

44 "Is this the beautiful department?": Quoted in ibid., 257.

44 "Does your contract": Quoted in "The Duke," in Irving Wallace et al., *The Intimate Sex Lives of Famous People* (New York: Delacorte Press, 1981), 262.

44   "charismatic presence": Don George, *Sweet Man: The Real Duke Ellington* (New York: Putnam's, 1981), 109.

45   "The more feminine": "The Evolution of Homosexuality: Gender Bending. Genes That Make Some People Gay Make Their Brothers and Sisters Fecund," *Economist*, October 23, 2008, 97.

45   gender ambiguity: See Roach, *It*, 4, 11.

45   "*is* the charismatic personality": Camille Paglia, *Sexual Personae: Art and Decadence from Nefertiti to Emily Dickinson* (New York: Vintage, 1990), 441.

45   women differ from men: For a discussion, see Andy Newman, "What Women Want (Maybe)," *New York Times*, June 12, 2008.

45   Other studies show: See "Evolution of Homosexuality," 97; and Lois Rogers, "Feminine Face Is Key to a Woman's Heart, *Sunday Times* (London), December 8, 2002.

46   Sigmund Freud and Carl Jung: See discussion in June Singer, *Androgyny: Toward a New Theory of Sexuality* (Garden City, NY: Anchor Books, 1977), 29–33.

46   "sensual perfection": Quoted in "Androgyny," *Parabola: Myth and the Quest for Meaning*, 3, no. 4 (1997), 27.

46   "great He-She": Quoted in ibid., 24.

46   "divine sensual delight": Alain Daniélou, *Gods of Love and Ecstasy: The Traditions of Shiva* (Rochester, VT: Inner Traditions, 1992), 63.

46   "Man-Woman" Dionysus: He was known as *thelymorphos*, a man with the appearance of a woman. Arthur Evans, *The God of Ecstasy: Sex Roles and the Madness of Dionysos* (New York: St. Martin's Press, 1988), 21.

46   "Woman Whisperer": Maureen Child, *Turn My World Upside Down* (New York: St. Martin's Paperbacks, 2005), 1.

47   Byron's androgyny: Benita Eisler, *Byron: Child of Passion, Fool of Fame* (New York: Vintage Books, 1999), 267.

47   "ravishing androgyny": Quoted in Jeffrey Meyers, *Gary Cooper: American Hero* (New York: William Morrow, 1998), 88.

47   Six foot three: Ibid., 34–35.

47   "fell over themselves": Quoted in ibid., 50.

47   "Gary had crooked": Quoted in Meyers, *Gary Cooper*, 90.

47   explain his "hypnotic" effect: Quoted in ibid., 36.

48   "the perfect balance": Quoted in ibid., 88.

48   "Creative types have": Rusty Rockets, "Sexual Success and the Schizoid Factor," *Science a GoGo*, April 28, 2006, www.scienceagogo.com/news/creativity.shtml.

48   They may lack: See Len Oakes, who quotes Weber about charisma: "It is creative," for "in its pure form charisma . . . may be said to exist only in the process of originating." Oakes, *Prophetic Charisma*, 27.

48   "incredibly close": Quoted in Handley, ed., *Lover's Quotation Book*, 23.

48   "have more sex appeal": The 2008 studies were conducted at Newcastle

upon Tyne and the Open University. "Sex Appeal," Peterman's Eye, January 7, 2009, www.petermanseye.com/curiosities/notables-gossip/467-sex-appeal.

48   Art, he theorizes: See Geoffrey Miller, *The Mating Mind: How Sexual Choice Shaped the Evolution of Human Nature* (New York: Doubleday, 2000), 258–291.

48   "visible signature": Quoted in Rockets, "Sexual Success and the Schizoid Factor."

49   "an archaic prototype": Paglia, *Sexual Personae*, 45.

49   cave paintings: Weston La Barre, "Shamanic Origins of Religion and Medicine," *Journal of Psychedelic Drugs* 11, nos 1–2 (January–June, 1979).

49   "the songs of the night": Otto, *Dionysus*, xvi.

49   "Mick the Magic Jagger": Laura Jackson, *Heart of Stone: The Unauthorized Life of Mick Jagger* (London: Blake, 1997), 58.

49   He puts a sock: Ibid., 49.

50   "her very own Dionysus": Quoted in ibid., 75.

50   "male opposite": Quoted in Marina Warner, "Lucian Freud: The Unblinking Eye," *New York Times Magazine*, December 4, 1989.

50   "the greatest living realist painter": Quoted in ibid.

50   "astonish, disturb": Quoted in ibid.

50   Married twice: "Lucian Freud: The Life," *Independent*, May 30, 2002.

50   Every woman cited: Simon Edge, "Lucian Freud the Lothario," *Daily Express*, August 6, 2009.

50   He quoted poetry: Ibid.

51   Freud the artist: Rowan Pelling, "A Woman of Easel Virtue," *Independent*, April 17, 2005.

51   "felt like being an apple": Quoted in Edge, "Lucian Freud the Lothario."

51   "the most primitive form": Oakes, *Prophetic Charisma*, 26.

51   "Don't Fence Me In": Cole Porter, "Don't Fence Me In," Warner Brothers, 1944.

51   renegade souls: Philip Rieff writes, "A charismatic is he who makes a break with the established order." Philip Rieff, *Charisma: The Gift of Grace, and How It Has Been Taken Away From Us* (New York: Vintage Books, 2007), 160.

51   "irresistible magnetic mana": Quoted in Oakes, *Prophetic Charisma*, 26.

51   an intangible "apartness": Roach, *It*, 8.

52   phallic Hermes: Norman O. Brown, *Hermes the Thief: The Evolution of a Myth* (New York: Vintage Books, 1969), 34.

52   Perpetual wanderer Dionysus: Euripides, "The Bacchae," in *The Bacchae and Other Plays*, trans. Philip Vellacott (New York: Penguin, 1954), 214.

52   "eccentric" rover: Knut Hamsun, *Mysteries*, trans Gerry Bothmer (1891; New York: Farrar, Straus and Giroux, 2006), 3.

52   Even the exemplar: Ibid., 165.

52 "Bombay Casanova" Ormus Cama: Salman Rushdie, *The Ground beneath Her Feet* (New York: Picador USA/Henry Holt, 1999), 190, 177.

53 "own master": Giacomo Casanova, *History of My Life*, trans. Willard R. Trask (Baltimore: Johns Hopkins University Press, 1997), vol. 2, chap. 2, p. 33.

53 "I rebel": Albert Camus, *The Rebel: An Essay on Man in Revolt* (New York: Vintage, 1956), 22.

53 "It's his way": Albert Camus, *The Myth of Sisyphus*, trans. Justin O' Brien (1955; New York: Vintage International, 1983), 74.

53 Women found him: Herbert R. Lottman, *Albert Camus: A Biography* (Corte Madera, CA: Gingko Press, 1997), 125.

53 "managed to keep them": Olivier Todd, *Albert Camus: A Life*, trans. Benjamin Ivry (New York: Carroll and Graf, 1997), 413.

53 Fabled lover, iconoclast: Sara Wheeler, *Too Close to the Sun: The Life and Times of Denys Finch Hatton* (London: Jonathan Cape, 2006), 203.

53 "like a centripetal force": Quoted in ibid., 32.

54 "at least eight women": Ibid., 22.

54 Finch Hatton "belonged": Errol Trzebinski, *Silence Will Speak* (Chicago: University of Chicago Press, 1977), 156.

54 "As for charm": Beryl Markham, *West with the Night* (New York: Farrar, Straus, and Giroux, 1942), 120.

54 invention wasn't original: Trzebinski, *Silence Will Speak*, 156.

54 "like a meteor": Quoted in ibid., 156.

54 "The flaw that punctuates": Hillary Johnson, "The Flaw That Punctuates Perfection," *Los Angeles Times*, November 30, 2001.

55 Roach traces: Roach, *It*, 17.

55 "straddling characteristics": Schiffer, *Charisma*, 30.

55 "The things I find": Erica Jong, "The Perfect Man," in *What Do Women Want* (New York: Jeremy P. Tarcher/Penguin, 1998), 173.

55 Bader probes: See Michael J. Bader, *Arousal: The Secret Logic of Sexual Fantasies* (New York: Thomas Dunne Books/St. Martin's Press, 2002), 140.

55 "a way to get inside": Johnson, "Flaw That Punctuates Perfection."

55 "disease of God": Quoted in Oakes, *Prophetic Charisma*, 26.

56 emotionally or physically damaged man: Mary Jo Putney, "Welcome to the Dark Side," in Jayne Ann Krentz, ed., *Dangerous Men and Adventurous Women of the Romance: Romance Writers on the Appeal of the Romance* (Philadelphia: University of Pennsylvania Press, 1992), 101.

56 Readers can find: See "Wounded Heroes," Listmania, www.amazon.com/Wounded-Heroes/lm/1W95CIQLARZYP (accessed October 23, 2009).

56 "delicate prongs": Rebecca Silver, "Fearful Symmetry," in Lonnie Barach, ed., *Erotic Interludes* (New York: HarperPerennial, 1986), 225.

56 Hardy Cates: See Lisa Kleypas's two novels about Hardy Cates: *Sugar Daddy*

(New York: St. Martin's Paperbacks, 2007) and *Blue-Eyed Devil* (New York: St. Martin's Paperbacks, 2008).

56   "divine defect": Edward Craig, *Routledge Encyclopedia of Philosophy: Questions to Sociobiology* (New York: Routledge, 1998), 60.

56   "Great seducer" Jack Nicholson: Phrase from book title, Edward Douglas's *Jack the Great Seducer* (New York: HarperEntertainment, 2004).

56   "King of Hollywood": Quoted in ibid., 221.

57   "I saw such a wonderful": Quoted in ibid., 268.

57   "old Jack Magic": Quoted in ibid., 6.

57   "gentle giant": Quoted in Ann Pasternak Slater, "Introduction," in Ivan Turgenev, *Fathers and Sons*, ed. Elizabeth Cheresh Allen and Constance Garnett (New York: Modern Library, 2001), xii.

57   Tall and stoop-shouldered: Avraham Yarmolinsky, *Turgenev: The Man, His Art and His Age* (New York: Orion Press, 1959), 41.

57   Ignoring his mother's curses: V. S. Pritchett, *The Gentle Barbarian: The Work and Life of Turgenev* (New York: Ecco Press, 1977), 86.

57   "Christ": Quoted in Yarmolinsky, *Turgenev*, 57.

57   "enigmatic tang": Schiffer, *Charisma*, 44.

58   "much more bizarre": James A. Donovan, "Toward a Model Relating to Empathy, Charisma, and Telepathy," *Journal of Scientific Exploration* 11, no. 4 (1997), 455, 464. Also see full article, 455–471.

58   "to the back burner": Quoted in Mark Greer, "The Science of Savoir Faire," January 2005; and Carlin Flora, "The X-Factors of Success," *Psychology Today*, May/June 2005.

58   "forbidden impulses": Becker, *Denial of Death*, 135.

59   Can men en masse: Rieff, *Charisma*, 105.

59   Biologist Amotz Zahavi and others: Zahavi contends that higher-ranking women pick men who are honest advertisers in courtship. For good summaries of his view, see Joann Ellison Rodgers, *Sex: A Natural History* (New York: W. H. Freeman/Times Books/Henry Holt, 2001), 221–223; and "Deceit versus Honest Signaling," www.animalbehavioronline.com (accessed May 14, 2012).

For studies that show charisma can't be faked, see researcher Nada Gada's work discussed in Greer, "Science of Savoir Faire," and psychologist Howard S. Friedman's affective communication test, which measures charisma. Friedman concludes, "Truly charismatic people are authentic." Winter, "How to Light up a Room."

CHAPTER 2: CHARACTER: THE GOODS

60   "Character alone is worthy": Andreas Capellanus, *The Art of Courtly Love*, trans. John Jay Parry (New York: Columbia University Press, 1960), 35.

61   "Good moral character": Geoffrey Miller, *The Mating Mind: How Sexual*

Choice Shaped the Evolution of Human Nature (New York: Doubleday, 2000), 293.

61 Claude Adrien Helvétius: Jules Bertaut, *Égéries du xviiie siècle* (Paris: Librarie Plon, 1928), 147.

61 "Apollo": Quoted in "Introduction" in C. A. Helvétius, *De L'esprit or Essays on the Mind and Its Several Faculties* (London: J. M. Richardson, 1809), vi.

62 "Look like this man": Quoted in Bertaut, *Égéries*, 148.

62 "joined more delicacy": Quoted in ibid., 149.

62 "greatest happiness": Quoted in Darrin M. McMahon, *Happiness: A History* (New York: Grove Press, 2006), 217.

62 Unalloyed virtue: For this insight and study, see Helen Fisher, *Why Him? Why Her?* (New York: Henry Holt, 2010), 206.

62 Medieval amorists: Capellanus, *Art of Courtly Love*, 35. Here Capellanus writes, "'Beauty alone never pleases if it lacks goodness,' and it is excellence of character alone which blesses a man with true nobility."

62 "Honesty [and] virtue": Robert Burton, *The Anatomy of Melancholy*, ed. Floyd Dell and Paul Jordan-Smith (New York: Tudor, 1927), 631.

62 "No love without goodness": Baldesar Castiglione, *The Book of the Courtier*, trans. Charles S. Singleton (Garden City, NY: Anchor Books, 1959), 335.

62 Solomon believes: See Robert C. Solomon, *About Love: Reinventing Romance for Our Times* (New York: Touchstone Books/Simon & Schuster, 1989), 240–246.

62 women seem to be of two minds: This is a contentious issue, with a number of contradictory studies. For the female preference for male kindness and sincerity, for nice guys, see David M. Buss, *The Evolution of Desire: Strategies of Human Mating* (New York: Basic Books/HarperCollins, 1994), 44–45; and for the contrary view, see Mason Inman, "Bad Guys Really Do Get the Most Girls," *New Scientist*, June 18, 2008.

62 "that old-fashioned quality": Erica Jong, "The Perfect Man," in *What Do Women Want?* (New York: Jeremy P. Tarcher/Penguin, 1998), 172.

63 polarized choice: See Edward Horgan, "Exceeding the Threshold: Why Women Prefer Bad Boys," *Exposé: Writing from the Harvard Community* (2011), 1–14, expose.fas.harvard.edu/issues/issues_2011/horgan.html (accessed January 26, 2012).

63 Miller speculates: Geoffrey Miller, "Virtues of Good Breeding," in Miller, *Mating Mind*, 339. Also see 292–340.

63 "You enjoy helping those": Steven Pinker, *How the Mind Works* (New York: W. W. Norton, 1997), 400.

63 "giver of good things": Norman O. Brown, *Hermes the Thief: The Evolution of a Myth* (New York: Vintage Books, 1947), 23.

63 "too reckless" Cuchulain: Norma Lorre Goodrich, *Medieval Myths* (New York: Meridian Books/Penguin, 1961), 186.

63 Female readers always rate: According to a recent poll conducted by the

Orange Prize for Fiction, 1,900 women voted for "Mr. Darcy as the man they would most like to go on a date with." Cherry Potter, "Why Do We Still Fall for Mr. Darcy?" *Guardian*, September 29, 2004.

63 "You showed me": Jane Austen, *Pride and Prejudice* (New York: Middleton Classics, 2009), 317.

64 "with kindness": Quoted in Lydia Flem, *Casanova: The Man Who Really Loved Women*, trans. Catherine Temerson (New York: Farrar, Straus and Giroux, 1997), 217.

64 "sweetness of character": Charlotte Haldane, *Alfred: The Passionate Life of Alfred de Musset* (New York: Roy, 1961), 67.

64 "extraordinary, good person": Quoted in Suzanne Finstad, *Warren Beatty: A Private Man* (New York: Three Rivers Press, 2005), 350.

64 "fornication and bastardy": Peter Guralnick, *Dream Boogie: The Triumph of Sam Cooke* (New York: Back Bay Books, 2005), 229.

64 "woman's man": Ibid., 496.

64 "genuineness": Quoted in ibid., 101, 142.

65 He had erotic crackle: Ibid., 210.

65 "never crass, never vulgar": Ibid., 195.

65 "Lady, you shot me": Quoted in ibid., 619.

65 "a real gentlemen": Quoted in ibid., 361, 275.

66 "needn't be such a saint": George Gershwin, "Boy Wanted," WB Music, 1924.

66 "will tame": Ovid, *The Art of Love*, trans. Rolfe Humphries (Bloomington: Indiana University Press, 1957), 137.

66 "All true desire": Robert Bly, *Iron John: A Book about Men* (New York: Addison-Wesley, 1990), 132.

66 Women, in a recent study: Cited in Mark Tyrrell, "Fortune Favours the Brave (and So Does Dating)," Uncommon Knowledge, www.uncommon -knowledge.co.uk/dating.html (accessed March 17, 2011).

67 Men, too, have special terrors: For more on this, see Wolfgang Lederer, *The Fear of Women* (New York: Grune and Stratton, 1968); and Karen Horney, "The Dread of Women," in Harold Kelman, ed., *Feminine Psychology* (New York: W. W. Norton, 1967), 133–146.

67 As the Romans said: Ovid, *Art of Love*, 124.

67 Another explanation is more erotic: Social anthropologist Fernando Henriques claims that one of the purposes of male contests for brides was to arouse women. See his *Love in Action: The Sociology of Sex* (New York: E. P. Dutton, 1960), 156–163.

67 Sumerian "Fearless One": Quoted in Diane Wolkstein, "Inanna and Dumuzi," in *The First Love Stories: From Isis and Osiris to Tristan and Iseult* (New York: HarperPerennial/HarperCollins, 1991), 52; and "Dumuzi (Tammuz): Lord of Love and Fertility, the Divine Bridegroom," www.gatewaystobabylon .com/gods/lords/lordumuzi.htm (accessed 3/27/2009).

67   "How bold this bacchant": Euripides, "The Bacchae," in *The Bacchae and Other Plays*, trans. Philip Vellacott (New York: Penguin, 1954), 207.

68   "I am not afraid": Giacomo Casanova, *History of My Life*, trans. Willard R. Trask (Baltimore: Johns Hopkins University Press, 1997), vol. 2, chap. 2, p. 33.

68   "The same energy": Quoted in "Juan Belmonte," in Irving Wallace et al., *The Intimate Sex Lives of Famous People* (New York: Delacorte Press, 1981), 524.

69   paladin in full-tilt revolt: Frank McLynn, *Robert Louis Stevenson: A Biography* (New York: Random House, 1993), 94.

69   Despite poverty, "tatterdemalion": Ibid., 97, 101.

69   "Keep your fears": Robert Louis Stevenson, source unknown, quoted in "Quotations Book," http://quotationsbook.com/quote/14862 (accessed May 14, 2012).

69   We are "unhorsed": Robert Louis Stevenson, "On Falling in Love," in Isidor Schneider, ed., *The World of Love* (New York: George Braziller, 1964), vol. 2, 261.

69   "sly Hermes": Quoted in McLynn, *Robert Louis Stevenson*, 27.

70   "Love," wrote Stendhal: Stendhal, *Love*, trans. Gilvert and Suzanne Sale (Harmondswood, UK: Penguin, 1957), 139.

70   "Eroticism is primarily": Georges Bataille, *Eroticism: Death and Sensuality*, trans. Mary Dalwood (San Francisco: City Lights Books, 1986), 31.

71   The loved one: David Holbrook, *Sex and Dehumanization in Art, Thought and Life in Our Time* (New York: Pittman, 1972), 31.

71   Positive Psychology Center: See Christopher Peterson, *A Primer in Positive Psychology* (New York: Oxford University Press, 2006), 145; and T. Byram Karasu, *The Spirit of Happiness: Discovering God's Purpose in Your Life* (New York: Simon & Schuster, 2006), passim.

71   Neumann thinks: Erich Neumann, *The Great Mother: An Analysis of the Archetype* (Bollingen Series vol. 47), trans. Ralph Manheim (Princeton, NJ: Princeton University Press, 1963), 97.

72   they don't get more lovable: Sarah Wendell and Candy Tan, *Beyond Heaving Bosoms: The Smart Bitches' Guide to Romance Novels* (New York: Fireside Books/Simon & Schuster, 2009), 70.

72   "For the Love of God": See "For the Love of God," All About Romance, www.likesbooks.com/religion.html (accessed March 21, 2011).

72   "destiny of mankind": Quoted in Ernest Newman, *The Man Liszt* (New York: Scribner's, 1935), 32.

72   "masterpiece of God": Quoted in ibid., 161.

72   "uncomely" loner: Quoted in Spencer Klaw, *Without Sin: The Life and Death of the Oneida Community* (New York: Penguin, 1993), 12.

73   "extraordinarily attractive to women": Quoted in ibid., 12.

73   "eager to sleep with him": Wallace et al., *Intimate Sex Lives of Famous People*, 553.

73 "claiming spirit": Klaw, *Without Sin*, 12.

73 "idolatrous attachment": Ibid., 11.

73 "Anybody," he explained: Quoted in ibid., 11.

73 "exemplary lover": Ibid., 11.

74 "shone like an angel's": Quoted in ibid., 36.

74 "The desire to know": Cathleen Schine, *Rameau's Niece* (New York: Houghton Mifflin, 1993), 132.

74 Studies show women: See Ewen Callaway, "Nerds Rejoice: Braininess Boosts Likelihood of Sex," *New Scientist*, October 3, 2008.

74 fourth-century sex manual: *The Complete Kāma Sūtra*, trans. Alain Daniélou (Rochester VT: Park Street Press, 1994), 45.

75 "distinction of mind": Ovid, *Art of Love*, 133.

75 easy to see the parallels: Martha Nussbaum, "The Speech of Alcibiades: A Reading of Plato's Symposium," in Robert C. Solomon and Kathleen M. Higgins, eds., *The Philosophy of (Erotic) Love* (Lawrence: University Press of Kansas, 1991), 302.

75 "reached inside women's": Miller, *Mating Mind*, 237.

75 Dionysus brought civilization: Brown, *Hermes the Thief*, 23.

75 Irish folk hero and sex god: Norma Lorre Goodrich, "Chuchulain," in *Medieval Myths* (New York: Meridian Books, 1966), 183.

75 intellectuals haven't fared well: For a list of movies and novels that portray professors, especially, in this light, see William Deresiewicz, "Love on Campus," *American Scholar*, June 1, 2007.

76 Intellectuals proliferate: In Jane A. Radway's study, "intelligence" is ranked as the most important quality in a hero, see *Reading the Romance: Women, Patriarchy, and Popular Literature* (Chapel Hill: University of North Carolina Press, 1984), 82. For professors as an archetype, see Tami Cowden, "We Need a Hero: A Look at Eight Hero Archetypes," *All About Romance*, May 14, 1999, www.likesbooks.com/eight.html.

76 "He made her think": Nora Roberts, *Vision in White* (New York: Berkley Books/Penguin, 2009), 116.

76 "buns or dick size": Norman Rush, *Mortals* (New York: Vintage, 2004), 213.

76 "Mad Hatter's": Quoted in Caroline Moorehead, *Bertrand Russell: A Life* (New York: Viking, 1992), 303.

76 "several enjoyable evenings": Ibid., 388.

76 "In spite of myself": Quoted in Miranda Seymour, *Ottoline Morrell: Life on the Grand Scale* (New York: Farrar, Straus and Giroux, 1992), 109.

76 "one genius in the family": Quoted in Sybille Bedford, *Aldous Huxley: A Biography* (Chicago: Ivan R. Dee, 1973), 74.

77 "he made": Quoted in ibid., 43.

77 "threw open a whole world": Quoted in ibid., 40.

78 "gigantic grasshopper": Quoted in Nicholas Murray, *Aldous Huxley: A Biography* (New York: Thomas Dunne, 2002), 5.

78   "he was ribald": Quoted in Bedford, *Aldous Huxley*, 74.
78   "Intelligence": Quoted in ibid., 627.
78   "Loving well requires": Daniel Goleman, *Social Intelligence: The New Science of Human Relationships* (New York: Bantam Books, 2006), 190.
78   "one of the best": Quoted in Nick Paumgarten, "The Tycoon: The Making of Mort Zuckerman," *New Yorker*, July 23, 2007, 46.
78   "fun to be around": Ibid., 45.
78   "sheepskin jacket": Quoted in ibid., 55.
78   "gift of intimacy": Quoted in ibid., 55.
78   "the master of love magic": Brown, *Hermes the Thief*, 15, 35.
79   social dexterity is now regarded: For a summary, see John F. Kihlstrom and Nancy Cantor, "Social Intelligence," socrates.berkeley.edu/~kihlstrm/social_intelligence.htm (accessed March 24, 2011). Also see Daniel Goleman's books: *Social Intelligence* and *Emotional Intelligence: Why It Can Matter More Than IQ* (New York: Bantam Books, 1994).
79   None of which is new: See NPR interview with Daniel Goleman, "Is Social Intelligence More Useful Than IQ?" Neal Conan, host, *Talk of the Nation*, October 23, 2006, www.npr.org/templates/story/story.php?storyid=6368484.
79   Two millennia ago: See Ovid, *Art of Love*, 135, 134, 128.
79   Every amorous guide: See especially *Complete Kāma Sūtra*, 319; and Andrea Hopkins, *The Book of Courtly Love: The Passionate Code of the Troubadours* (New York: HarperSanFrancisco, 1994), 43.
79   Miller thinks: See Miller, *Mating Mind*, chap. 9, 292–340.
79   Whether through talent: Finstad, *Warren Beatty*, 38.
79   "fine divination": Havelock Ellis, "Art of Love," in *Studies in the Psychology of Sex* (New York: Random House, 1936), vol. 2, 544.
79   "tacto": José Ortega y Gasset, *On Love: Aspects of a Single Theme*, trans. Toby Talbot (New York: New American Library, 1957), 110.
80   Dionysus soothes: Ovid, *Art of Love*, 122.
80   "I think he's just really": Jennifer Crusie, *Bet Me* (New York: St. Martin's Paperbacks, 2004), 168.
80   Czech lothario Tomas: Milan Kundera, *The Unbearable Lightness of Being*, trans. Michael Henry Heim (New York: Perennial Classics/HarperCollins, 1984), 20.
80   Inconstant as he was: "David Niven," Answers, www.answers.com/topic/david-niven?print=true (accessed October 31, 2008).
80   obscure soldier: "Sir Walter Raleigh (1552–1618)," Luminarium: Anthology of English Literature, www.luminarium.org/renlit/raleghbio.htm (accessed October 31, 2008).
80   He gave her: Robert Lacey, *Sir Walter Ralegh* (London: Phoenix Press, 1973), 43.
81   Prince Clemens von Metternich: Raoul Auernheimer, *Prince Metternich:*

Statesman and Lover, trans. James A. Galston (Binghamton, NY: Alliance Books, 1940), 214.

81 "Adonis of the Drawing Room": Quoted in ibid., 214.

81 "He is pleasing": Quoted in ibid., 19.

81 While still at university: Margaret Nicholas, ed., "Metternich," in *The World's Greatest Lovers* (London: Octopus Books, 1985), 50.

81 "made every woman": Ibid., 50.

81 "cared for all": Ibid., 52.

81 "beautiful naked angel": Ibid., 50.

82 "extremely handsome": Auernheimer, *Prince Metternich*, 25.

82 "*homme à femmes*": Desmond Seward, *Metternich: The First European* (New York: Viking, 1991), 140.

82 dominant figure: "Modern History Sourcebook: Prince Klemens von Metternich: Political Confession of Faith, 1820," Fordham University, www .fordham.edu/halsall/mod/1820metternich.html (accessed February 7, 2009).

82 "Politics and love": Auernheimer, *Prince Metternich*, 224.

82 "Pleasure considered": Honoré de Balzac, *The Physiology of Marriage: Petty Troubles of Married Life*, ed. J. Walker McSpadden (Philadelphia: Avil, 1901), 62.

82 "I would like to invite you": *Vicky Cristina Barcelona*, direc. Woody Allen, Weinstein Company, 2008.

83 To evolutionary diehards: "spandrels" is a term coined by Stephen Jay Gould and Richard Lewontin. See Paul Bloom, *How Pleasure Works: The New Science of Why We Like What We Like* (New York: W. W. Norton, 2010), xiii.

83 "having your pleasure center": Michael R. Liebowitz, *The Chemistry of Love* (Boston: Little, Brown, 1983), 69.

83 "Love is pleasure": Frankie Goes to Hollywood, "The Power of Love," www.elyrics.net/read/f/frankie-goes-to-hollywood-lyrics/the-power-of -love-lyrics.html (accessed May 14, 2012).

83 default position: See Miller, *Mating Mind*, 148–176. "Hot choosers," explains Miller, is the chooser in the mating game who can afford to pick on the basis of pleasure. See ibid., p. 149.

83 school of neo-Freudians: The 1960s neo-Marxists Herbert Marcuse and Norman O. Brown argued for a nonrepressive civilization that reinstated the erotic principles of joy, play, pleasure, and satisfaction within the reality principle. See especially *Eros and Civilization: A Philosophical Inquiry into Freud* (Boston: Beacon, 1955); and Norman O. Brown, *Life against Death: The Psychoanalytical Meaning of History* (Middletown, CT: Wesleyan University Press, 1959).

83 "the delight of mortals": Walter F. Otto, *Dionysus: Myth and Cult*, trans. Robert B. Palmer (Bloomington: Indiana University Press, 1965), 55.

83 "everything that had been": Ibid., 95.

83 "Pleasure" was "the image": Alain Daniélou, *Shiva and Dionysus*, trans. K. F. Hurry (New York: Inner Traditions International, 1984), 57.

84 sex researcher Marta Meana: Cited in Daniel Bergner, "What Do Women Want," *New York Times Magazine*, January 25, 2009.

84 Perhaps this stems: For anxieties, see Cindy M. Weston and David Buss, *Why Women Have Sex: Understanding Sexual Motivations—From Adventure to Revenge (and Everything in Between)* (New York: Times Books/Henry Holt, 2009), 45; Helen Fisher, *The First Sex: The Natural Talents of Women and How They Are Changing the World* (New York: Ballantine Books, 1999), 85–91; and Natalie Angier, *Woman: An Intimate Geography* (New York: Anchor Books, 1999), 756–780, 346–351.

84 "adorably beautiful": See Eloisa James, *Pleasure for Pleasure* (New York: Avon Books, 2006), 43, 286–302.

84 Mary Gordon's novel: See Mary Gordon, *Spending: A Utopian Divertimento* (New York: Simon & Schuster, 1998).

84 *Kāma Sūtra: Complete Kāma Sūtra*, 65.

84 "endeavor to please": Ovid, *Art of Love*, 123.

84 mindset is what counts: Balzac, *Physiology of Marriage*, 68.

84 "pleasure, pleasure, pleasure": Casanova, *History of My Life*, vol. 4, chap. 2, p. 34.

85 "What's wrong": Quoted in Shawn Levy, *The Last Playboy: The High Life of Porfirio Rubirosa* (New York: HarperCollins, 2005), 304.

85 "head and shoulders": William Grimes, "A Jet-Set Don Juan, Right Up to the Final Exit," *New York Times*, September 16, 2005.

85 "the most magnificent penis": Quoted in Levy, *Last Playboy*, 126.

85 "We were like": Quoted in ibid., 178.

85 "I am": Quoted in ibid., 19.

85 "Merry Monarch": Tim Harris, *Restoration: Charles II and His Kingdoms* (New York: Penguin, 2005), 46.

85 "charm[ing] all": Stephen Coote, *Royal Survivor: A Life of Charles II* (London: Sceptre, 1999), 46.

86 "the love of her life": "'The French Mistress': The Interview," The Word Wenches, http://wordwenches.typepad.com/word_wenches/2009/07/fre.html (accessed May 14, 2012).

86 Studies show that Americans: See John Tierney, "Carpe Diem? Maybe Tomorrow," *New York Times*, December 29, 2009; and Lauren Sandler, "The American Nightmare," *Psychology Today*, March/April 2011.

86 "I give women pleasure": *Don Juan DeMarco*, direc. Jeremy Leven, New Line Cinema, American Zoetrope, and Outlaw Productions, 1995.

86 "I am large:" Walt Whitman, "Song of Myself," in *Leaves of Grass* (Boston: Small, Maynard, 1904), sect. 51, 78.

86 "never wrong about such matters": Steven Millhauser, "An Adventure of Don Juan," in *The King in the Tree* (New York: Vintage Books, 2003), 79.

86   "man of many projects": Ibid., 69.

87   "The lover": Jean-Paul Sartre, *Being and Nothingness*, trans. Hazel E. Barnes (New York: Washington Square Press, 1966), 484, 485.

87   Actualized individuals: See W. Keith Campbell, Craig A. Foster, and Eli Finkle, "Does Self-Love Lead to Love for Others? A Story of Narcissistic Game Playing," *Journal of Personality and Social Psychology* 83, no. 2 (2002), 343. These researchers note that "high self-esteem individuals [more actualized people] experience love more passionately than do individuals with low self-esteem."

87   souls that are "overfull": This is a paraphrase of Nietzsche from "Thus Spake Zarathustra": "I love him whose soul is . . . overfull," in *The Portable Nietzsche*, trans. Walter Kaufmann (New York: Penguin Books, 1968), 128.

87   women in surveys express a preference: See John Marshall Townsend, *What Women Want—What Men Want: Why the Sexes Still See Love and Commitment So Differently* (New York: Oxford University Press, 1998), 150.

87   "authentically powerful": Ethel S. Person, *Feeling Strong: The Achievement of Authentic Power* (New York: William Morrow/HarperCollins, 2002), xvii.

87   "He has five": Quoted in Maureen Dowd, "The Carla Effect," *New York Times*, June 22, 2008.

87   Ancestral women: Miller, *Mating Mind*, 211, 213. He explains this cerebral lure via an ornamental mind theory; see p. 153.

88   Dionysus was the lord: Otto, *Dionysus*, 49; and Carl Kerenyi, *Dionysus: Archetypal Image of Indestructible Life* (Bollingen Series vol. 65), trans. Ralph Manheim (Princeton, NJ: Princeton University Press, 176), xxxiv.

88   Grace, a poor girl: Alice Munro, "Passion," in *Runaway* (New York: Vintage Books/Random House, 2004), 174, 168.

88   "There were so many layers": Jennifer Crusie, *The Cinderella Deal* (New York: Bantam Books, 2010), 208.

88   Known as the "siren": Georgina Masson, *Courtesans of the Italian Renaissance* (New York: St. Martin's Press, 1975), 62.

89   "comparable to a gem": Carl Jung, *Aspects of the Feminine* (Bollingen Series vol. 20), trans. R. F. C. Hull (Princeton, NJ: Princeton University Press, 1983), 47.

89   Vibrant and brilliant: Walter Isaacson, *Benjamin Franklin: An American Life* (New York: Simon & Schuster, 2003), 2.

89   Franklin was: Claude-Anne Lopez, "Why He Was a Babe-Magnet," *Time*, July 7, 2003, 64. Also see Isaacson, *Benjamin Franklin*, on the subject of his "sexual appetite" and womanizing, 72, 68–72.

90   "gaiety" and "gallantry": Quoted in Isaacson, *Benjamin Franklin*, 362.

90   "capture her and keep her": Quoted in Carl Van Doren, *Benjamin Franklin* (New York: Viking, 1938), 651.

90   "very bad": Quoted in Sydney George Fisher, *The True Benjamin Franklin* (Philadelphia: Lippincott, 1899), 329.

90 "disgusted": Quoted in ibid., 329.
91 "Character is power": Booker T. Washington, from "Quotes on Character from Various Sources," Character Above All, PBS, www.pbs.org/newshour/character/quotes/ (accessed February 2, 2012).
91 His "character": Casanova, *History of My Life*, vol. 1, preface, 31, 32.
91 He freely admits: Ibid., vol. 9, chap. 4, p. 86, and vol. 1, preface, 30.
91 With his acute insight: Judith Summers, *Casanova's Women: The Great Seducer and the Women He Loved* (New York: Bloomsbury, 2006), 2.
91 "sweet and affable": Quoted in Vincent Cronin, *Catherine: Empress of All the Russias* (New York: William Morrow, 1978), 197.
91 "If you want": Ovid, *Art of Love*, 133.
92 "You must not": Quoted in Morton M. Hunt, *The Natural History of Love* (New York: Alfred A. Knopf, 1959), 32.
92 "The man": Ellis, "Art of Love," 530–531.
92 "violence of the soul": Solomon, *About Love*, 23.
93 "hot choosers": Miller, *Mating Mind*, 149.
93 "Seduction is destiny": Jean Baudrillard, *Seduction*, trans. Brian Singer (New York: St. Martin's Press, 1990), 180.

CHAPTER 3: LASSOING LOVE: THE SENSES

97 "Love is the poetry": Honoré de Balzac, *The Physiology of Marriage: Petty Troubles of Married Life*, ed. J. Walker McSpadden (Philadelphia: Avil, 1901), 61.
98 "the physical part": Quoted in Morton H. Hunt, *The Natural History of Love* (New York: Alfred A. Knopf, 1959), 256. The entire quote is from the comte de Buffon: "There is nothing good in love but the physical part."
99 "Appearances belong to": Jean Baudrillard, *Seduction*, trans. Brian Singer (New York: St. Martin's Press, 1990), 10.
99 They voted him: See *Esquire* poll of 10,000 women; in "The *Esquire* Survey of the American Woman," *Esquire*, May 2010, 77; and a poll that canvassed three dating websites: Date.com, Matchmaker.com, and Amor.com in 2009. See http://entertainmentrundown.com/8573/top-celebrities-people-would-have-sex-with-if-they-had-a-pass (accessed April 19, 2011).
99 Raves a fan: www.youtube.com/user/laudepp/26x-1/15/10.
99 "mysterious—always": Quoted in Brian J. Robb, *Johnny Depp: A Modern Rebel* (London: Plexus, 2006), 196.
99 One costar, Missi Pyle: Quoted in "Johnny Depp, Sexiest Man Alive," *People*, November 30, 2009, 80. Missi Pyle was his costar in *Charlie and the Chocolate Factory*, and Leelee Sobieski, in the John Dillinger biopic *Public Enemies*.
99 "He was a": Chuck Berry, "Brown Eyed Handsome Man," Chess Records, 1956.

99 "disproportioned": Quoted in Simon Sebag Montefiore, *Potemkin: Catherine the Great's Imperial Partner* (New York: Vintage Books/Random House, 2000), 110.

100 Contrary to myth: See Jim Dryden's research at Washington University Medical School: "Erotic Images Elicit Strong Response from the Brain," Newsroom, Washington University in St. Louis, June 8, 2006, http://med news.wustl.edu/tips/page/normal/7319.html.

100 Their vision is: Helen Fisher, *The First Sex: The Natural Talents of Women and How They Are Changing the World* (New York: Ballantine, 1999), 90. For the eye and cervix dilation study, see Diane Ackerman, *A Natural History of the Senses* (New York: Vintage/Random House, 1990), 271.

100 Hooked up to a lie detector: See study in Judy Dutton, *Secrets from the Sex Lab* (New York: Broadway Books, 2009), 35.

100 Handsome has curb: See ibid., 41, 34–35.

100 hero, instructs: Leslie Wainger, *Writing a Romance Novel for Dummies* (Hoboken, NJ: Wiley, 2004), 65; and Sarah Wendell and Candy Tan, *Beyond Heaving Bosoms: The Smart Bitches' Guide to Romance Novels* (New York: Fireside Books/Simon & Schuster, 2009), 83. They itemize the requirements of male beauty, 83–95.

100 "Women do look": Nancy Friday, *My Secret Garden* (New York: Pocket Books, 1973), 214.

100 "The greatest provocations": Robert Burton, *The Anatomy of Melancholy*, ed. Floyd Dell and Paul Jordan-Smith (New York: Tudor, 1927), 687.

100 If you take a non-looker: For two costume experiment studies, see John Marshall Townsend, *What Women Want—What Men Want: Why the Sexes Still See Love and Commitment So Differently* (New York: Oxford University Press, 1998) 63 and 71.

100 Aware of women's: Women in one study rated how someone smells as the most important of the senses. Cindy M. Meston and David M. Buss, *Why Women Have Sex: Women Reveal the Truth about Their Sex Lives, from Adventure to Revenge (and Everything in Between)* (New York: St. Martin's Griffin, 2009), 5, 5–9.

101 Our Stone Age ancestors: Francois Boucher, *20,000 Years of Fashion* (New York: Harry N. Abrams, 1987), 22.

101 In most cultures: Geoffrey Miller, *The Mating Mind: How Sexual Choice Shaped the Evolution of Human Nature* (New York: Doubleday, 2000), 271.

101 She bathes him: *The Odyssey of Homer*, trans. E. V. Rieu (New York: Penguin, 1946), book 23, 345.

102 Decked in suits: Cliffe Howe, *Lovers and Libertines* (New York: Ace Books, 1958), 75.

102 His auburn curls: Benita Eisler, *Byron: Child of Passion, Fool of Fame* (New York: Vintage/Random House, 1999), 156.

102   "wild originality": Claire Clairmont quoted in John Clubbe, *Byron, Sully, and the Power of Portraiture* (Burlington, VT: Ashgate, 2005), 33.

102   plain-featured man: Julius Caesar was "slightly built and pale" with a face that was "too full." Adrian Goldsworth, *Caesar: Life of a Colossus* (New Haven, CT: Yale University Press, 2006), 61, 62.

102   "Romans, lock your wives": Quoted in Gaius Suetonius Tranquillus, *The Twelve Caesars*, trans. Robert Graves (Harmondsworth, UK: Penguin, 1960), 31.

103   During her four years: For the extent of Cleopatra's influence, see historian Michael Grant, *Cleopatra* (New York: Barnes and Noble, 1972), 88–91.

103   "rock cool threads": Paul Janka, Pick Up Artist guru, television celebrity and author of *Attraction Formula*, email, "Affects of a 'Rock Star Look,'" April 29, 2009, http://webmail.aol.com/42679/aol/en-us/mail/PrintMessage .aspx.

103   *New York Times* clothing maven: "On the Street," "Dash," Sunday Styles, *New York Times*, February 2, 2010.

103   "flood of memories": Nicholas Sparks, *The Notebook* (New York: Warner Books, 1996), 33.

104   "amorous space": Roland Barthes, *A Lover's Discourse: Fragments*, trans. Richard Howard (New York: Hill and Wang/Farrar, Straus and Giroux, 1978), 92.

104   "Passion": Jeff Turrentine, "The Pull of Place," review of Martha McPhee, *L'America*, *New York Times Book Review*, June 4, 2008, 8. The venues described refer to Herbert Beerbohm Tree's office, Casanova's assignation with Lucrezia on a stone bench in a garden maze, and Bob Evans's party mansion in Hollywood, quoted in Edward Douglas, *Jack: The Great Seducer* (New York: HarperEntertainment/HarperCollins, 2004), 248.

104   Passionate love sweeps: A location can work psychoactive effects on the brain and move us at unimaginable depths. See especially Gaston Bachelard, *The Poetics of Space*, trans. Maria Jolas (Boston: Beacon Press, 1964), 6.

104   "domestic bliss" strategy: Richard Dawkins, *The Selfish Gene* (New York: Oxford University Press, 1989), 153.

104   they also looked for beauty: Miller, *Mating Mind*, 271.

104   embellishment of place: See Andrew Trees, *Decoding Love* (New York: Avery/Penguin, 2009), 10. Studies have shown how the spell of place can actually halo someone with sex appeal, 12.

104   Watson tells of a patient: Cynthia Mervis Watson, *Love Potions: A Guide to Aphrodisiacs and Sexual Pleasures* (New York: Jeremy P. Tarcher/Perigee, 1993), 19.

105   In 4000 BC Sumer: Arthur Evans, *The God of Ecstasy: Sex Roles and the Madness of Dionysos* (New York: St. Martin's Press, 1988), 59.

105   the mythological Adonis and Psyche: Erich Neumann, *Amor and Psyche: The Psychic Development of the Feminine: A Commentary of the Tale by Apuleius*

(Bollingen Series vol. 54), trans. Ralph Manheim (Princeton, NJ: Princeton University Press, 1956), 9.

105   Eve beds Adam: John Milton, *Paradise Lost*, ed. Gordon Teskey (New York: W. W. Norton, 2005), book 4, lines 690, 693.

105   Emma Bovary: Gustave Flaubert, *Madame Bovary*, ed. Margaret Cohen and trans. Eleanor Marx Aveling and Paul de Man (New York: W. W. Norton, 2005), 208.

105   "Why was it": Patricia Gaffney, *To Love and To Cherish* (New York: New American Library, 1995), 215.

105   "born interior decorator": Philippe Jullian, *D'Annunzio*, trans. Stephen Hardman (New York: Viking, 1972), 63.

105   "love was nothing": Gabriele D'Annunzio, *The Child of Pleasure*, trans. Georgina Harding (Boston: Page, 1898), 193.

105   When asked why: Tom Antongini, *D'Annunzio* (Boston: Little, Brown, 1938), 71.

105   "excitation transfer": Dutton, *Secrets from the Sex Lab*, 46.

106   "from this earth": Quoted in Jullian, *D'Annunzio*, 243.

106   "alive and still": D. H. Lawrence, *Lady Chatterley's Lover and A Propos of "Lady Chatterley's Lover,"* ed. Michael Squires (1928; New York: Penguin 2006), 166.

106   "ever wanted to let him go": Meryle Secrest, *Frank Lloyd Wright: A Biography* (Chicago: University of Chicago Press, 1992), 314.

106   In his pioneering structures: Nancy Horan, *Loving Frank* (New York: Ballantine Books, 2007) 4.

106   His female clients: Ada Louise Huxtable, *Frank Lloyd Wright: A Life* (New York: Penguin, 2004), 66.

106   wilderness called Taliesin: Although Taliesin is not an officially recognized avatar, his death and rebirth by water, a classic motif of the fertility god, suggest his affinity with them.

107   "unprepossessing": Quoted in Secrest, *Frank Lloyd Wright*, 240.

107   "kissed his feet": Quoted in Huxley, *Frank Lloyd Wright*, 143.

107   Wright then married: Roger Friedland and Harold Zellman, *The Fellowship: The Untold Story of Frank Lloyd Wright and the Taliesin Fellowship* (New York: HarperCollins, 2006), 435.

107   "hideaway" or "blue lagoon": Richard Rodgers and Lorenz Hart, "My Romance," in *The Rodgers and Hart Songbook* (New York: Simon & Schuster, 1951), 151.

107   "space speaks": Quoted in David Givens, *Love Signals* (New York: St. Martin's Press, 2005), 175.

107   "A sweet voice": Burton, *Anatomy of Melancholy*, 699.

108   "the most ecstatic": Robert Jourdain, *Music, the Brain, and Ecstasy: How Music Captures Our Imagination* (New York: Avon Books, 1997), 328.

108   keener, more refined: For women's superior sense of hearing, see Fisher,

First Sex, 86–87. Louann Brizendine discusses women's ability to hear a broader range of emotional tones, in *The Female Brain* (New York: Broadway Books, 2006), 17.

108   In studies they rank: Cited in Givens, *Love Signals*, 175.

108   "the food of love": William Shakespeare, *Twelfth Night or What You Will*, ed. Charles T. Prouty (Baltimore: Penguin, 1958), act 1, scene 1.

108   "It's a matter of experience": *The Complete Kāma Sūtra*, trans. Alain Daniélou (Rochester, VT: Park Street Press, 1994), 11.

108   men must prepare themselves: Ibid., 48.

108   One medieval caliph: Wendy Buonaventura, *Serpent of the Nile: Women and Dance in the Arab World* (New York: Interlink Books, 1994), 183.

109   "rattle": Jourdain, *Music, the Brain, and Ecstasy*, xii.

109   "almost defenseless": Oliver Sacks, *Musicophilia: Tales of Music and the Brain* (New York: Vintage Books, 2007), 52.

109   One explanation: See Daniel J. Levitin, *This Is Your Brain on Music* (New York: Plume, 2006), 85–87, 248–249.

109   Darwin proposed: For Darwin's explanation, see ibid., 251.

109   Very likely, Pleistocene: Miller, *Mating Mind*, 276.

109   Music's erotic force: For the sacred origin of music, see Jourdain, *Music, the Brain, and Ecstasy*, 305, 307; and Geoffrey Miller, "Evolution of Human Music through Sexual Selection," in Nils L. Wallin, Björn Merker, and Steven Brown, eds., *The Origins of Music* (Cambridge, MA: MIT Press, 2000), 353.

109   opera's "diabolic" force: Doris Lessing, *Love, Again* (New York: HarperPerennial, 1997), 241.

109   Music can be just as ecstatic: See Joann Ellison Rodgers, *Sex: A Natural History* (New York: Times Books/Henry Holt, 2001), 245–247; and Ackerman, *Natural History of the Senses*, 179.

110   When Warren Beatty: See Suzanne Finstad, *Warren Beatty: A Private Man* (New York: Three Rivers Press, 2005), 209.

110   "Trembling like poor little larks": Quoted in Nigel Cawthorne, *Sex Lives of the Great Composers* (London: Prion, 2004), 93.

110   "perfectly crazy": Pianist Amy Fay quoted in ibid., 97.

111   toast of the music world: Kate Botting and Douglas Botting, *Sex Appeal: The Art and Science of Sexual Attraction* (New York: St. Martin's Press, 1996), 110.

111   electrified: She "felt the electricity going through [her] from head to toe." See Abram Chasins, *Leopold Stokowski: A Profile* (New York: Hawthorne Books, 1979), 255.

111   "glamorous to the end": Ibid., xiii.

111   "I am undone": Quoted in Burton, *Anatomy of Melancholy*, 699.

112   Maggie Tulliver: George Eliot, *The Mill on the Floss*, ed. Gordon S. Haight (1860; Boston: Houghton Mifflin, 1961), 365, 335.

112   "broads swarmed over him": Anthony Summers and Robbyn Swan, *Sinatra: The Life* (New York: Vintage Books, 2005), 52.

112 "wasn't the best singer": Kitty Kelley, *His Way: The Unauthorized Biography of Frank Sinatra* (New York: Bantam Books, 1986), 37.

112 "dick in [his] voice": John Lahr, *Sinatra: The Artist and the Man* (New York: Phoenix Paperback/Random House, 1997), 16.

112 "like a girl": Quoted in Summers and Swan, *Sinatra*, 33.

112 To seduce a woman: Ibid., 122.

112 "Oh god, it was magic": Quoted in Lahr, *Sinatra*, 38.

112 "Sing": Ovid, *The Art of Love*, trans. Rolfe Humphries (Bloomington: Indiana University Press, 1957), 123.

112 "Love": Burton, *Anatomy of Melancholy*, 757.

113 "You got to": Daddy DJ, "Let Your Body Talk," Radikal Records, 2003.

113 "Bodily movements may": Theodoor Hendrik van de Velde, *Ideal Marriage: Its Physiology and Technique*, trans. Stella Browne (New York: Random House, 1930), 39.

113 "Besides spoken language": *Complete Kāma Sūtra*, 114.

113 As well they should be: See Fisher, *First Sex*, xvii, 91–93; and Brizendine, *Female Brain*, 120–123. For more on the impact of nonverbal communication, see David B. Givens's classic "The Nonverbal Basis of Attraction: Flirtation, Courtship, and Seduction," *Psychiatry* 41 (November 1978), 346–359.

114 "You can say a lot": Ovid, *Art of Love*, 120.

114 In the first three: Martin Lloyd-Elliott, *Secrets of Sexual Body Language* (Berkeley, CA: Ulysses Press, 2005), 70. See Michael R. Cunningham et al., "What Do Women Want? Facial Metric Assessment of Multiple Motives in the Perception of Male Facial Physical Attractiveness," *Journal of Personality and Social Psychology* 59, no. 1 (July 1990), 61–72.

114 Women like features: See Lloyd-Elliott, *Secrets of Sexual Body Language*, 10.

114 Eyes are heavy artillery: Baudrillard, *Seduction*, 77.

114 Ancient cultures: See Hans Licht, *Sexual Life in Ancient Greece*, trans. J. H. Freese (London: Abbey Library, 1932), 309.

114 They create a "lustline": E. C. Sheedy, "Midnight Plane to Georgia," in *Bad Boys Southern Style* (New York: Brava Books/Kensington, 2006), 125. See Givens, *Love Signals*, 54, 82.

114 "eye sex": This means to stare at someone in "such a lustful way" that he or she "might as well be doing it." *Urban Dictionary*, ed. Aaron Peckam (Kansas City, MO: Andrews McMeel, 2005), 123.

114 rank men's eyes: Givens, *Love Signals*, 124.

114 watch men's mouths: Ibid., 26.

114 "vermillion lips": Quoted in Henry Dwight Sedgwick, *Alfred de Musset* (Indianapolis: Bobbs-Merrill, 1931), 51. Sarah Wendell and Candy Tan write that the hero's lips are invariably "Sensitive! Kissable! Full!" See discussion in *Beyond Heaving Bosoms*, 89.

114 Dallas Beaudine's: Susan Elizabeth Phillips, *Fancy Pants* (New York: Pocket Books/Simon & Schuster, 1989), 48, 121.

114   genuine "Duchenne" kind: Givens, *Love Signals*, 126.

115   instinctively: For the instinctive response to a smile, see Lloyd-Elliot, *Secrets of Sexual Body Language*, 89; and Gordon R. Wainwright, *Body Language* (New York: NTC/Contemporary, 1985), 31.

115   "the best smile": Quoted in Finstad, *Warren Beatty*, 164.

115   he was nothing to look at: Margaret Nicholas, ed., *The World's Greatest Lovers* (London: Octopus Books, 1985), 87.

115   "true artist": Quoted in Madeleine Bingham, *The Great Lover: The Life and Art of Herbert Beerbohm Tree* (New York: Atheneum, 1979), 93.

115   At close quarters: See psychologist Paul Ekman on this in *Emotions Revealed: Recognizing Faces and Feelings to Improve Communication and Emotional Life* (New York: Henry Holt, 2003), passim, 221–223.

115   Tree finessed this art: Bingham, *Great Lover*, 37.

116   In studies, women show: See Meston and Buss, *Why Women Have Sex*, 17–19.

116   "lithe, Indian-like": Margaret Mitchell, *Gone with the Wind* (1936; New York: Avon, 1973), 179.

116   "careless, lazy": Mikhail Lermontov, *A Hero of Our Time*, trans. Marian Schwartz (1839; New York: Modern Library, 2004), 49.

116   "I watched": Quoted in Botting and Botting, *Sex Appeal*, 104.

116   "primitive": Quoted in Shawn Levy, *The Last Playboy: The High Life of Porfirio Rubirosa* (New York: HarperCollins, 2005), 168.

116   "And then he danced": Lord Byron, *Don Juan* (London: Hamblin, 1828), vol. 2, canto 38, p. 279.

116   "I take them dancing": Quoted in Levy, *Last Playboy*, 224.

116   study after study has shown: Alok Jha, "It's True, Dancing Does Lead to Sex," *Sydney Morning Herald*, December 23, 2005; and Nic Fleming, "Good Dancers Make the Fittest Mates," *New Scientist*, July 2, 2009.

116   just because he dances well: See Meston and Buss, *Why Women Have Sex*, 17–18.

116   In one survey: Gail Arias, "Dance Survey: What Women Want from Men!" www.dancedancedance.com/whtwomen.htm (accessed January 1, 2010).

117   Ellis speculated: See Havelock Ellis, "Analysis of the Sexual Impulse," *Studies in the Psychology of Sex* (New York: Random House, 1936), 31, 32, 25.

117   Men whose feet smoke: See summary of the work at Rutgers University on the correlation between dancing skill and mate fitness: "Rutgers Researchers Scientifically Link Dancing Ability to Mate Quality," *Bio-Medicine*, http://news.bio-medicine.org/biology-news/Rutgers-researchers-scientifically-link-dancing-ability-to-mate-quality-1904-1/ (accessed March 30, 2009).

117   They also exhibit: Miller, *Mating Mind*, 407.

117   By miming intercourse: See Curt Sachs, *World History of the Dance*, trans. Bessie Schonberg (New York: W. W. Norton, 1963), 3.

117   Dionysus, "the leader": Quoted in Walter F. Otto, *Dionysus: Myth and Cult*, trans. Robert B. Palmer (Bloomington: Indiana University Press, 1965), 82.

117 Traditional cultures: Sachs, *World History of the Dance*, 96.

118 When Hardy Cates: Lisa Kleypas, *Sugar Daddy* (New York: St. Martin's Press, 2007), 135.

118 "honeys who can swing": Blogger "Susan," Romance Bandits, March 23, 2011, http://romancebandits.blogspot.com/2011/03/isnt-it-romantic.html.

118 "one of the best dancers": Quoted in H. Noel Williams, *The Fascinating duc de Richelieu: Louis Francois Armand du Plessis* (New York: Charles Scribner's, 1910), 1.

118 "Russian superstar Casanova": Review, Barbara Aria, *Misha! The Mikhail Baryshnikov Story, Publishers' Weekly*, March 1989.

118 Ballerina Gelsey Kirkland thought: "Biography for Mikhail Baryshnikov," IMDb.com, www.imdb.com/name/nm0000864/bio (accessed May 14, 2012).

118 "the greatest male dancer": Ibid.

118 "Baryshnikov leaps higher": Katha Politt, "Ballet Blanc," *New Yorker*, February 19, 1979.

119 "Dancing with a woman": Tony Clink, *Layguide* (New York: Citadel Press, 2004), 112.

119 "the dance floor" Tom Jackson, "Real Men Don't Dance," *The Yorker*, October 30, 2008, www.theyorker.co.uk/news/alphamale/2191.

119 "Love teaches even asses": Thinkexist.com, http://thinkexist.com/dommon/print.asp?id=176496&quote=love_teaches_even_asses_to (accessed June 21, 2011).

119 "Banging, nailing, and screwing": *The Secret Laughter of Women*, direc. Peter Schwabach, Paragon Entertainment, 1999.

120 landmark 1999 study: See study in Edward O. Laumann et al., "Sexual Dysfunction in the United States: Prevalence and Predictors," *Journal of the American Medical Association* 281 (February 10, 1999), 537–544.

120 more recent five-year survey: See Meston and Buss's five-year study of over 1,000 women in *Why Women Have Sex*, 78–210. For an overview, see Elizabeth Landau, "Love, Pleasure, Duty: Why Women Have Sex," CNN.com, September 30, 2009, edition.cnn.com; and Jessica Bennett, "The Pursuit of Sexual Happiness," *Newsweek*, September, 28, 2009.

120 several 2010 polls: See the sex study reported in the special issue of *Journal of Sexual Medicine* 7 (October 2010), 243–373, which polled 5,865 people, aged 14 to 94. For the study of married women, see the iVillage 2010 and 2011 online surveys summarized in "Sex in Marriage: Survey Reveals What Women Want," *Huffington Post*, February 7, 2012, www.huffingtonpost.com/2012/02/07/sex-in-marriage-study-rev_n_1260699.html?vie.

120 setup for hyperpleasure: For a summary, see Fisher, *First Sex*, 201–205.

120 It's a "whole": Natalie Angier, *Woman: An Intimate Geography* (New York: Anchor Books, 1999), 77, 78.

121 Classic male guides: For typical man-to-man advice, see Ian Kerner, *She Comes First: The Thinking Man's Guide to Pleasuring Women* (New York:

ReganBooks, 2004); Lou Paget, *The Great Lover Playbook* (New York: Gotham Books, 2005); and Paul Joannides, *Guide to Getting It On* (Oregon: Goofy Foot Press, 2000).

121   Therapists add intimacy: For a summary of the therapeutic view that "incubating intimacy leads to better sex," see Daniel Bergner, "What Do Women Want?" *New York Times Magazine*, January 25, 2009.

121   woman's optimal pleasure: For a discussion of this ultimate quest in sexual research, see Mary Roach, *Bonk: The Curious Coupling of Science and Sex* (New York: W. W. Norton, 2008), 302; and see Marta Meana on female narcissism in Bergner, "What Do Women Want?"

121   As studies have revealed: See Meston and Buss, *Why Women Have Sex*, 156, 166, 29.

121   Surprisingly, they're often: The most popular book genre, romance novels generated over 1.3 billion in 2010. See "Romance Literature Statistics: Overview," *About the Romance Genre*, www.rwa.org/cs/the_romance_genre/romance_literature_statistics (accessed May 14, 2012).

121   Jack Travis: Lisa Kleypas, *Smooth Talking Stranger* (New York: St. Martin's Paperbacks, 2009), 152.

121   "Murmuring words of love": Diane Wolkstein and Samuel Noah Kramer, eds., *Inanna, Queen of Heaven and Earth: Her Stories and Hymns from Sumer* (New York: Harper and Row, 1983), 108, 46, 108, 37, 38.

122   Taylor estimates: Timothy Taylor, *The Prehistory of Sex: Four Million Years of Human Sexual Culture* (New York: Bantam Books, 1996), 18.

122   Friedrich describes: Paul Friedrich, *The Meaning of Aphrodite* (Chicago: University of Chicago Press, 1978), 143–144.

122   To pass muster: *Complete Kāma Sūtra*, 179, 229.

122   If he does not succeed: Ibid., 113.

122   "complete harmony": Lydia Flem, *Casanova: The Man Who Really Loved Women*, trans. Catherine Temerson (New York: Farrar, Straus and Giroux, 1997), 74.

122   "three-fourths": Giacomo Casanova, *History of My Life*, trans. Willard R. Trask (Baltimore: Johns Hopkins University Press, 1997), vol. 2, chap. 2, p. 25.

122   he discovered the clitoris-climax link: See Judith Summers, *Casanova's Women* (London: Bloomsbury, 2006), 15.

122   He told her: Casanova, *History of My Life*, vol. 3, chap. 2, p. 36, and chap. 3, p. 39.

122   He conducted their love affair: Flem, *Casanova*, 112.

122   "never a thing to be hurried": Ovid, *Art of Love*, 151.

123   Rick is onto something: Givens, *Love Signals*, 111. Givens explains that women like super-gentle strokes that strum the tender C-fibers, which reach the "sensual centers of the emotional brain," 92–93.

123   Women have more sensitive skin: Ibid., 99, 111.

123   Skin is the largest organ: Ackerman, *Natural History of the Senses*, 80.

123   hero's ankle play: Jennifer Crusie, *Tell Me Lies* (New York: St. Martin's Paperbacks, 1998), 199.

123   kiss is turbocharged: See Meston and Buss, *Why Women Have Sex*, 68–69.

123   matter of timing: See Susan Quilliam, *Sexual Body Talk: Understanding the Body Language of Attraction from First Glance to Sexual Happiness* (New York: Carroll and Graf, 1992), 58–59.

123   Instead of rabid tonsil-hockey: See Givens, *Love Signals*, 104.

123   Michelangelo of oral pleasure: Jullian, *D'Annunzio*, 131, 243.

123   1950s lover Porfirio Rubirosa: Levy, *Last Playboy*, 225.

123   Like Aly Khan: Leonard Slater, *Aly: A Biography* (New York: Random House, 1964), 139.

124   Gray claims: John Gray, *Venus and Mars in the Bedroom: A Guide to Lasting Romance and Passion* (New York: HarperTorch, 1995), 116.

124   "This was all": Udana Powers, "The Private Life of Mrs. Herman," in Lonnie Barbach, ed., *Erotic Interludes* (New York: Harper Perennial, 1987), 29.

124   "Most sex is about nonfeeling": Quoted in Douglas, *Great Seducer*, 97.

124   "carried [her]": Quoted in ibid., 219.

124   "indefatigable": Quoted in ibid., 221.

124   "He satisfied me": Quoted in ibid., 246, 177.

125   "spiritual and talked": Quoted in ibid., 268.

125   "I felt in my heart": Quoted in Dennis McDougal, *Five Easy Decades: How Jack Nicholson Became the Biggest Movie Star in Modern Times* (Hoboken, NJ: John Wiley, 2008), 351.

125   *Kāma Sūtra* admits: Hugo Williams, "Some Kisses from the Kama Sutra," in Jon Stallworthy, ed., *The Penguin Book of Love Poetry* (New York: Penguin, 1973), 110. The *Kāma Sūtra* is emphatic about love canceling out the importance of technique: "when seized by passion, no particular order has to be followed." *Complete Kāma Sūtra*, 119.

125   "Gifts persuade even:" Euripides, *Medea*, in *The Hecuba, Medea, Phœnissæ and Orestes*, trans. G. Dindorf (London: Henry Washbourne, 1846), lines 968–969, 40.

126   recent poll: Cited in Hilary Black, "Introduction," in Hilary Black, ed., *The Secret Currency of Love* (New York: Harper, 2010), xvi.

126   another 2009 survey: "Bad Week, Good Week," *Week*, April 3, 2009, no. 4.

126   economic motive: For a summary of this, see Norman O. Brown, *Life against Death: The Psychoanalytical Meaning of History* (Middletown, CT: Wesleyan University Press, 1959), 238, 234–304.

126   "Wealth brings": Quoted in ibid., 254. Also see Georges Bataille: "Within the Dionysiac cult, money in principle played no part." Bataille, *The Tears of Eros*, trans. Peter Conner (San Francisco: City Lights Books, 1989), 64.

126   "Falling in love": Robert Louis Stevenson, "On Falling in Love," in James L. Malfetti and Elizabeth M. Eidlitz, eds., *Perspectives on Sexuality: A Literary Collection* (New York: Holt, Rinehart, and Winston, 1972), 238.

126   Romantic passion: Rollo May, *Love and Will* (New York: W. W. Norton, 1969), 122. Among one of the characteristics of love in the *Kāma Sūtra* is "indifference to money." Complete *Kāma Sūtra*, 417.

126   They're embedded: This is David Cheal's observation, cited in Helmuth Berking, *The Sociology of Giving*, trans. Patrick Camiller (London: SAGE, 1999), 13.

126   Women put stock: See Ellen Chrismer, "Researcher Examines Gender, Other Gift-Giving Trends," December 13, 2002, dateline.ucdavis.edu/121302/dl_rucker.html, in a review of Margaret Rucker's work on the science of gift-giving about women's "personal view" of gifts and preference for "a romantic gesture."

126   Receiving love tokens: Berking, *Sociology of Giving*, 11.

127   "The path" ibid., 12.

127   Zahavi's "handicap principle": See Miller's discussion of this in *Mating Mind*, 122–129, passim. This is the old principle popularized by Thorsten Veblen in *The Theory of the Leisure Class* that the best way to demonstrate wealth is by wasting it on luxuries.

127   Kristeva points out: Julia Kristeva, *Tales of Love*, trans. Leon S. Roudiez (New York: Columbia University Press, 1987), 196.

127   "quite an art": Ovid, *Art of Love*, 28.

127   Gifts must fulfill: See Marcel Mauss, *The Gift: The Form and Reason for Exchange in Archaic Societies*, trans. W. D. Halls (New York: W. W. Norton, 1990), 10, 24–25, 37–38, 74–75.

127   "At its finest": Quoted in J. D. Sunwolf, "The Shadow Side of Social Giving: Miscommunication and Failed Gifts," *Communication Research Trends*, September 1, 2006.

127   it's an object of beauty: See Miller's theory of this in *Mating Mind*, 258–291.

127   "emanation of Eros": Lewis Hyde, *The Gift* (New York: Vintage Books, 1979), 27.

127   Phallic deities embodied: Georges Bataille, *Eroticism: Death and Sensuality*, trans. Mary Dalwood (San Francisco: City Lights Books, 1986), 231.

128   Dionysus, the "giver of riches": Otto, *Dionysus*, 80.

128   Courtly love: See Andreas Capellanus, *The Art of Courtly Love*, trans. John Jay Parry (New York: Columbia University Press, 1960), 176–177.

128   Updike's "Hamlet" novel: John Updike, *Gertrude and Claudius* (New York: Ballantine Books, 2000), 62, 64.

128   presented one lover with a spaniel: Derek Parker, *Casanova* (Gloucestershire, UK: Sutton, 2002), 136.

128   "absolutely irresistible": Quoted in Charlotte Haldane, *Alfred: The Passionate Life of Alfred de Musset* (New York: Roy, 1960), 64.

129   "in her attic": Quoted in ibid., 67.

129   Riches raise the stakes: Berking, *Sociology of Giving*, 41.

129   "It was like": Quoted in Slater, *Aly*, 9.

129   Women were crazy: Judy Bachrach, "La Vita Agnelli," *Vanity Fair*, May 2003, 202.

129   He furnished total: Ibid., 214, 205.

129   "The loves of most people": Quoted in *A Thousand Flashes of French Wit, Wisdom, and Wickedness*, trans. J. De Finod (New York: D. Appleton, 1886), 142.

129   Sensual dishes follow: Guy de Maupassant, *Bel-Ami*, trans. Douglas Parmée (1885; New York: Penguin, 1975), 105, 108.

130   She hands him: Actually Duroy doesn't pay with his money but takes the bills from the hostess's purse at her request. The sexual symbolism is patent.

130   "After a perfect meal": Quoted in Botting and Botting, *Sex Appeal*, 168.

130   Taste is the multisensory sense: For a summary, see Kate Hilpern, "Taste the Difference: How Our Genes, Gender and Even Hormones Affect the Way We Eat, *Independent* (UK), November 11, 2010.

130   Although men have: See "Male vs. Female: The Brain Difference," www .columbia.edu/itc/anthropology/v1007/jakabovics/mf2.html (accessed May 14, 2011); and "Girls Have Superior Sense of Taste to Boys," *Science Daily*, December 18, 2008, www.sciencedaily.com/releases/2008/12/081216104035 .htm.

130   Just as animal species: See Miller, *Mating Mind*, 209.

130   "gift of wine": Quoted in Arthur Evans, *The God of Ecstasy: Sex-Roles and the Madness of Dionysos* (New York: St. Martin's Press, 1988), 58.

130   "rich cream": Wolkstein and Kromer, eds., *Inanna*, 33.

130   In rural Peru: Botting and Botting, *Sex Appeal*, 81.

131   "Definitely rich, creamy": Janelle Dension, *Wilde Thing* (New York: Brava Books/Kensington, 2003), 101.

131   "highly seasoned dishes": Casanova, *History of My Life*, vol. 7, Introduction, p. 32.

131   He set the table: Flem, *Casanova*, 18.

131   "was never inclined to drink": Peter Biskin, *Star: How Warren Beatty Seduced America* (New York: Simon & Schuster, 2010), 18.

131   His fabulous fêtes: Simon Sebag Montefiore, *Potemkin: Catherine the Great's Imperial Partner* (New York: Vintage Books, 2005), quoted in 339, 341.

132   Food researchers point: See Eleanor Glover, "Rise of the 'Gastrosexual' as Men Take Up Cooking in a Bid to Seduce Women," Mail Online, July 21, 2008, www.dailymail.co.uk/femail/article-1036921/Rise-gastrosexual -men-cooking-bid-seduce-women.html.

132   Allende argues: Isabel Allende, *Aphrodite: A Memoir of the Senses* (New York: HarperFlamingo, 1998), 40.

132   Money, says book: Kate Ashford, "Women, Men & Money—How It Can Muck Up True Love," HerTwoCents.com, February 15, 2010, interview with Hilary Black, ed., *The Secret Currency of Love*, www.lemondrop.com/2010/ 02/15/the-secret-currency-of-love-truth-about-men-women-and-money/.

132   "hedonic treadmill": The notion of the "hedonic treadmill," coined by
      Brickman and Campbell in 1971, argued that increased wealth does not
      bring a permanent gain in happiness. Instead, we adapt and experience both
      decreased pleasure and increased desire for more goods. See P. Brickman
      and D. T. Campbell, "Hedonic Relativism and Planning the Good Society,"
      in *Adaption Level Theory: A Symposium* (New York: Academic Press, 1971),
      287–302.

CHAPTER 4: LASSOING LOVE: THE MIND

134   "Love looks not": William Shakespeare, *A Midsummer Night's Dream*, in
      Complete Works, ed. Stanley Wells and Gary Taylor (Oxford: Clarendon
      Press/Oxford University Press, 1988), act 1, scene 1, line 234.

135   "be fully explained": Irving Singer, *Sex: A Philosophical Primer* (New York:
      Rowman and Littlefield, 2001), 32.

135   Meredith Chivers: See Daniel Bergner, "What Do Women Want?" *New York
      Times Magazine*, January 25, 2009.

136   conscious part of the female mind: See cognitive neuroscientists Ogi Ogas
      and Sai Gaddam, *A Billion Wicked Thoughts: What the World's Largest Exper-
      iment Reveals about Human Desire* (New York: Dutton/Penguin Group,
      2011), 76–83, where they discuss this complex neural female operation.

136   "The powers of seduction": *Juliet of the Spirits*, direc. Frederico Fellini, Riz-
      zoli Film, Francoriz Production, 1965.

136   "Who loves, raves": Baron George Gordon Byron Byron, *Childe Harold's
      Pilgrimage: A Romaunt* (London: G. S. Appleton, 1851), canto 4, stanza 123,
      182.

137   "The important thing": Email, May 30, 2009.

137   Romantic love, by nature: Robert Burton, *The Anatomy of Melancholy*, ed.
      Floyd Dell and Paul Jordan-Smith (New York: Tudor, 1927), 840.

137   "switch on a woman's libido": Quoted in Bergner, "What Do Women
      Want?" 51.

137   Over half of female fantasies: See B. J. Ellis and D. Symons, "Sex-Differences
      in Sexual Fantasy—An Evolutionary Psychological Approach," *Journal of
      Sex Research* 27, no. 4 (1990), 527–555; and Bergner, "What Do Women
      Want?"

137   What a woman craves: Quoted in Bergner, "What Do Women Want?" 51.

138   ardent advance: Stephen Kern, *The Culture of Love: Victorians to Moderns*
      (Cambridge, MA: Harvard University Press, 1992), 307.

138   "Let the man": Ovid, *The Art of Love*, trans. Rolfe Humphries (Blooming-
      ton: Indiana University Press, 1957), 127.

138   Hindu author: *The Complete Kāma Sūtra*, trans. Alain Daniélou (Rochester,
      VT: Park Street Press, 1994), 252.

138   "the door of love's palace": Andreas Capellanus, *The Art of Courtly Love*, trans. John Jay Parry (New York: Columbia University Press, 1960), 83.

138   "anaemic and tailorish": Robert Louis Stevenson, "On Falling in Love," in Jeremy Treglown, ed., *The Lantern-Bearers and Other Essays* (New York: First Cooper Square Press, 1999), 44, 45.

138   feel only aversion: Henry T. Finck quoted in Elaine Walster, "Passionate Love," in Bernard I. Murstein, ed., *Theories of Attraction and Love* (New York: Springer, 1971), 91.

138   males are the seducers: Matt Ridley, *The Red Queen: Sex and the Evolution of Human Nature* (New York: HarperCollins, 1993), 178.

138   Fisher traces: Helen Fisher, *Why We Love: The Nature and Chemistry of Romantic Love* (New York: Henry Holt, 2004), 111.

138   Evolutionary psychologists see: See David M. Buss, who writes that "one strong signal of commitment is a man's persistence in courtship," in *The Evolution of Desire: Strategies of Human Mating* (New York: Basic Books/ HarperCollins, 1994), 102–103.

138   Whatever the motive: Louann Brizendine, *The Female Brain* (New York: Broadway Books, 2006), 59.

138   "I am here for you": Ovid, *Art of Love*, 122.

138   when Freyr: www.hurstwic.org/history/articles/mythology/myths/text/ freyr.htm (accessed July 7, 2011).

139   "For pity's sake": Chretien de Troyes, "The Knight of the Cart (Lancelot)," in *Arthurian Romances*, trans. William W. Kibler (New York: Penguin, 1991), 214.

139   "violent, unbridled": Choderlos de Laclos, *Dangerous Liaisons*, trans. P. W. K. Stone (New York: Penguin, 1961), 190.

139   "I shall on no condition": Ibid., 147.

139   His love is earth-shaking: Madame de Lafayette, *The Princesse de Clèves*, trans. Nancy Mitford (London: Penguin, 1950), 60.

139   "Let's get some tea": Mary Wesley, *Not That Sort of Girl* (New York: Penguin Books, 1987), 66.

140   In the first chapter: Maureen Child, *Turn My World Upside Down* (New York: St. Martin's Paperbacks, 2005), 1.

140   "The man": Ibid.

140   She crumbles: Mary Jo Putney, *The Rake* (New York: Topaz Books/ Penguin, 1998), 172.

140   "intense and aggressive": Mary Jo Putney, "Welcome to the Dark Side," in Jayne Ann Krentz, ed., *Dangerous Men and Adventurous Women: Romance Writers on the Appeal of the Romance* (Philadelphia: University of Pennsylvania Press, 1992), 110.

140   Filippo Strozzi: Georgina Masson, *The Courtesans of the Italian Renaissance* (New York: St. Martin's Press, 1975), 95.

140   "That is nonsense": Giacomo Casanova, *History of My Life*, trans. Wil-

lard R. Trask (Baltimore: Johns Hopkins University Press, 1966), vol. 7, chap. 10, pp. 216, 217.

141 "doubts, qualms": Dan Hofstadter, *The Love Affair as a Work of Art* (New York: Farrar, Straus and Giroux, 1996), 6.

141 "My whole life": Benjamin Constant, *Adolphe*, trans. Leonard Tancock (New York: Penguin, 1964), 54, 55.

141 abstract painter fastened on: Ruth Kligman, *Love Affair: A Memoir of Jackson Pollock* (New York: Cooper Square Press, 1974), 31.

141 "I want you": Quoted in ibid., 41, 44.

142 To nail "targets": Neil Strauss, *The Game: Penetrating the Secret Society of Pickup Artists* (New York: HarperCollins, 2005), 21.

142 "will do almost anything": David DeAngelo, email, June 2, 2007; and *The Tao of Steve*, direc. Jenniphr Goodman, Good Machine, Thunderhead Productions, 2000.

142 According to *Maxim*: Lisa Lombardi, "Conquer Her," *Maxim*, November 2001, 50.

142 To enamor women: Tom Terell, "Ten Ways to Be a Lover: A Man Looks at Romance Novels," *Salon*, August 12, 2004, salon.com; and Why Your Wife Won't Have Sex with You, Julia Grey Blog, http://juliagrey.word press.com/contributors-stories/ten-ways-to-be-a-lover-a-man-looks-at -romance-novels/ (accessed April 24, 2012).

142 "*do* appreciate men": Quoted in Joann Ellison Rodgers, *Sex: A Natural History* (New York: W. H. Freeman Books/Times Books/Henry Holt, 2001), 221.

142 Charleen, a character: *Sherman's March*, direc. Ross McElwee, First Run Features, 1986.

143 "O flatter me": William Shakespeare, *Two Gentlemen of Verona* in *Complete Works*, ed. Stanley Wells and Gary Taylor (Oxford: Clarendon Press/ Oxford University Press, 1988), act 2, scene 4, line 146.

143 Rolf possesses: Bernard Schlink, "The Other Man," in *Flights of Love*, trans. John E. Woods (New York: Pantheon, 2001), 138.

143 "I was made": Ibid., 145, 121.

143 According to erotic theorists: See Robert C. Solomon, *About Love: Reinventing Romance for Our Times* (New York: Touchstone Books/Simon & Schuster, 1988), 40–41, 199, 148, passim; and see Ethel S. Person, *Dreams of Love and Fateful Encounters: The Power of Romantic Passion* (New York: Penguin, 1988), 29, 30, 259, passim, where she points out that a defining premise of romantic love is to be "the most important person in someone else's life."

143 "maximizes self-esteem": Solomon, *About Love*, 199.

143 Some extremists: See Theodor Reik, *Psychology of Sex Relations* (New York: Farrar and Rinehart, 1945), 91, 243.

144 They accord higher importance: See study in Anne M. Doohan and Valerie Mausov, "The Communication of Compliments in Romantic Relationships:

An Investigation of Relational Satisfaction and Sex Differences and Similarities in Compliment Behavior," *Western Journal of Communications* (Salt Lake City) 68, no. 2 (Spring 2004), 170–195.

144 may be flattery-operated: For a summary of the erotic effect of praise on women see Tracy Clark-Flory, "Narcissism: The Secret to Women's Sexuality!" *Salon*, January 24, 2009, www.salon.com/2009/01/24/female_desire/.

144 "the object of erotic admiration": Quoted in Bergner, "What Do Women Want?"

144 Beauvoir made the same point: See Simone de Beauvoir, "The Narcissist," in *The Second Sex*, trans. H. M. Parshley (1952; New York: Vintage Books/ Random House, 1988), 629–644.

144 "devil's gateway": Church Father Tertullian quoted in Susan Groag Bell, ed., *Women: From the Greeks to the French Revolution* (Stanford, CA: Stanford University Press, 1973), 85.

144 Fifty-five to eighty percent of women: For the 55 percent figure, see Cindy M. Meston and David M. Buss, *Why Women Have Sex: Women Reveal the Truth about Their Sex Lives, from Adventure to Revenge (and Everything in Between)* (New York: St. Martin's Press, 2009), 193. On low female self-esteem, see Ulrich Orth, Kali H. Trzesniewski, and Richard W. Robins, "Self-Esteem Development from Young Adulthood to Old Age: A Cohort-Sequential Longitudinal Study," *Journal of Personality and Social Psychology* 98, no. 4 (2010), 645–658.

144 Women are biologically primed: See discussion in Louann Brizendine, *Female Brain*, 40–41. For summary, see Aimee Lee Ball, "Women and the Negativity Receptor," *O, The Oprah Magazine*, August 2008.

144 "A man can win us": Geoffrey Chaucer, *The Canterbury Tales*, trans. Nevill Coghill (New York: Penguin, 1958), 283.

144 "applause response": See Michael R. Liebowitz, *The Chemistry of Love* (Boston: Little, Brown, 1983), 102.

145 We feel exhilarated: Ibid., 91.

145 "Flattery works on the mind": Ovid, *Art of Love*, 124.

145 "as much as possible": Quoted in Richard Stengel, *You're Too Kind* (New York: Simon & Schuster, 2002), 155.

145 "What if our strongest wish": Adam Phillips, *Monogamy* (New York: Vintage Books/Random House, 1996), 43.

145 He's seconded by many theorists: See, for example, Jean Baudrillard, *Seduction*, trans. Brian Singer (New York: St. Martin's Press, 1990), 68; Solomon, *About Love*, 239; Roland Barthes, *A Lover's Discourse*, trans. Richard Howard (New York: Hill and Wang, 1978), 19, 28, 158; and Ronald de Sousa, "Love as Theater," in Robert C. Solomon and Kathleen M. Higgins, eds., *The Philosophy of (Erotic) Love* (Lawrence: University Press of Kansas, 1991), 477.

145 worst gaffe: See discussion of the "Above-Average Effect" in 2010 *Scientific American* reported in "Health & Science," *Week*, January 29, 2010, 23.

146   "I marvel at you": *The Odyssey of Homer*, trans. Allen Mandelbaum (New York: Bantam Classic, 1990), book 6, line 121.

146   The Eve that Milton portrays: For a summary of women's position in Milton's England, see Antonia Fraser, *The Weaker Vessel* (New York: Alfred A. Knopf, 1984).

146   She will be an "Empress": John Milton, *Paradise Lost*, ed. Gordon Teskey (New York: W. W. Norton, 2005), 212, 213.

146   He admires her "difference": Edith Wharton, *Summer* (New York: Harper and Row, 1979), 67.

146   "He was praising her": Ibid

147   Sukie the town reporter: John Updike, *The Witches of Eastwick* (New York: Ballantine, 1984), 46.

147   They assure her: Gael Greene, *Blue Skies, No Candy* (New York: William Morrow, 1976), 20, 43.

147   She's "Remarkable": Ibid. 33.

147   to be a man's deity: See Denis de Rougemont, *Love in the Western World*, trans. Montgomery Belgion (Princeton, NJ: Princeton University Press, 1983), 260, where he notes that at bottom, "passion requires that the self shall become greater than all things, as solitary and powerful as God."

147   The "good," authentic heroes: Sarah Wendell and Candy Tan, *Beyond Heaving Bosoms: The Smart Bitches' Guide to Romance Novels* (New York: Simon & Schuster, 2009), 233.

147   "Rick had been exposed": Carly Phillips, *The Playboy* (New York: Grand Central, 2003), 13.

147   sailor, meanwhile, is even more: Jill Shalvis, *The Sweetest Thing* (New York: Forever, 2011), 228.

148   Excusing his ardor: Casanova, *History of My Life*, vol. 1, chap. 9, p. 276.

148   "Darling of the English Cleopatra": Robert Lacey, *Sir Walter Ralegh* (London: Phoenix Press, 1973), 51.

148   The lady was: Gabriele D'Annunzio, *L'Innocente*, trans. Georgina Harding (1892; New York: Hippocrene Books, 1991), 12.

148   "To hear oneself": Isadora Duncan, *Isadora* (1927 as *My Life*; New York: Award Books, 1968), "Introductory," 11.

148   Lady Diana Manners: Philip Ziegler, *Diana Cooper* (New York: Alfred A. Knopf, 1982), 94.

149   "the brightest color": Quoted in ibid., 97.

149   "Two lily hands": Quoted in John Julius Norwich, ed., *The Duff Cooper Diaries: 1915–1951* (London: Weidenfeld and Nicolson, 2005), 154.

149   "empress of seduction": Quoted in Jean Bothorel, *Louise ou la vie de Louise de Vilmorin* (Paris: Gernard Gasset, 1993), 290.

149   "returned [his] kisses": Norwich, ed., *Duff Cooper Diaries*, 332.

149   "You are a treasure": Quoted in Botherel, *Louise ou la vie de Louise de Vilmorin*, 160.

150   With his usual panache: Norwich, ed., *Duff Cooper Diaries*, 436.

150   "Cad" Cooper: Quoted in Selina Hastings, "A Dedicated Hedonist Duff Cooper Was the Consummate Diplomat—Except in His Love Life, Says Selina Hastings," *Sunday Telegraph* (London), October 2, 2005.

150   Hip dating instructors: Mystery, *Mystery Method*, 97, 96.

150   "love is a form of flattery": William Gass, "Throw the Emptiness out of Your Arms: Rilke's Doctrine of Nonpossessive Love," in Solomon and Higgins, eds., *Philosophy of (Erotic) Love*, 453.

150   "Thy other self ": John Milton, *Paradise Lost* (London: Bensley, 1802), vol. 2, book 8, lines 450–451, 55.

151   When Lucy arrives: Megan Chance, *An Inconvenient Wife* (New York: Grand Central, 2005), 64.

151   course of her treatment: Ibid., 109.

151   "I understand you": Ibid., 156.

151   Desperate to be: Ibid., 233.

151   say erotic philosophers: Barthes, *Lover's Discourse*, 228, 226; Solomon, *About Love*, 24, passim., especially the "Intimacy" chapter, 272–283; Robert Sternberg, for whom "intimacy" is one of the three essential components of love, "Triangulating Love," in Robert J. Sternberg and Michael L. Barnes, eds., *The Psychology of Love* (New Haven, CT: Yale University Press, 1988), 120; and John R. Haule, *Divine Madness: Archetypes of Romantic Love* (Boston: Shambhala, 1990), 42–61.

151   While both sexes crave ego fusion: Hormonally, desire generates the release of vasopressin in men and oxytocin, "the love hormone," in women, which triggers intimacy and connection. See Liebowitz, *Chemistry of Love*, 116.

152   complain of inadequate intimacy: Meston and Buss, *Why Women Have Sex*, 51. Surveys continually document this. Women's rise in infidelity, according to a *Newsweek* study, is caused in part by parallel lives "instead of intersecting ones." Lorraine Ali and Lisa Miller, "The Secret Lives of Wives," *Newsweek*, July 12, 2004. See, too, Nancy Friday, *Women on Top: How Real Life Has Changed Women's Sexual Fantasies* (New York: Pocket Books, 1991), 50.

152   Diamond believes: Cited in Bergner, "What Do Women Want?"

152   Even in the womb: See Brizendine, *Female Brain*, 37, 67–70, passim; and Natalie Angier, *Woman: An Intimate Geography* (New York: Anchor Books, 1999), 330–348.

152   man who acknowledges that need: Rafford Pyke, "What Women Like in Men (1901)," in Susan Ostrov Weisser, ed., *Women and Romance* (New York: New York University Press, 2001), 48.

152   Egyptian myth: "Isis and Osiris," in Diane Wolkstein, ed., *The First Love Stories: From Isis and Osiris to Tristan and Iseult* (New York: HarperPerennial, 1991), 14.

152   Kali, the Hindu energy: "Shiva and Sati" in ibid., 79.

152   Becoming "one": Walter F. Otto, *Dionysus: Myth and Cult*, trans. Robert B. Palmer (Bloomington: Indiana University Press, 1965), 123.

152   women of fairy tales and myth: Haule, *Divine Madness*, 51.

152   "red, bald, and short-sighted": Quoted in "Frederick II," GluedIdeas .com, http://gluedideas.com/Encyclopedia-Britannica-Volume-9-Part-2 -Extraction-Gambrinus/Frederick-Ii.html (accessed August 21, 2011).

153   "They were one person": Johann Wolfgang von Goethe, *Elective Affinities*, trans. R. J. Hollingale (1809; New York: Penguin, 1971), 286.

153   "Nelly, I am Heathcliffe": Emily Brontë, *Wuthering Heights*, ed. Pauline Nestor (1847; New York: Penguin, 1995), 82.

153   "or the impression of it": Claire Messud, *The Emperor's Children* (New York: Vintage, 2006), 10.

153   "into the heads of women": James Collins, *Beginners' Greek* (New York: Little, Brown, 2008), 64.

153   "The human heart": Ibid., 111.

153   "can read her mind!": Christie Ridgway, *Unravel Me* (New York: Berkley, 2008), 221.

153   Botts argues: Amber Botts, "Cavewoman Impulses: The Jungian Shadow Archetype in Popular Romance Fiction," in Anne K. Kaler and Rosemary E. Johnson-Kurek, eds., *Romantic Conventions* (Bowling Green, OH: Bowling Green State University Popular Press, 1999), 62–74.

153   "You're not really": Jane Green, *Mr. Maybe* (New York: Broadway Books, 1999), 19.

154   "you've got your other half": Ibid., 298.

154   "I would do anything": Paul to Meg, TV Megasite, "As the World Turns Transcript 3/27/08," http://tvmegasite.net/transcripts/atwt/main/2008 transcripts.html (accessed May 15, 2012).

154   "The desire for intimacy": Martha Nochimson, *No End to Her: Soap Opera and the Female Subject* (Berkeley: University of California Press, 1992), 127.

154   "like two wheels": *Complete Kāma Sūtra*, 76.

154   advocate of up-close seduction: Ovid, *Art of Love*, 140.

154   Stendhal adjured men: Stendhal, *Love*, trans. Gilbert Sale and Suzanne Sale (New York: Penguin, 1975), 104–108.

154   concept of spiritual union: For a summary of this yearning, see Norman O. Brown, *Life against Death: The Psychoanalytical Meaning of History* (Middleton, CT: Wesleyan University Press, 1959), 43, 40–53.

154   unrelieved togetherness can also depress: See Esther Perel, *Mating in Captivity: Reconciling the Erotic and the Domestic* (New York: HarperCollins, 2006), 24, where she concludes from her work that "emotional intimacy is often accompanied by decreased sexual desire."

155   engineers of intimacy: John Lahr describes Frank Sinatra as an "engineer of intimacy" in *Sinatra: The Artist and Man* (New York: Random House, 1997), 22.

155 "the kiss that unites": Judith Summers, *Casanova's Women: The Great Seducer and the Women He Loved* (New York: Bloomsbury, 2006), 14.

155 With the castrato Bellino: Lydia Flem, *Casanova: The Man Who Really Loved Women*, trans. Catherine Temerson (New York: Farrar, Straus and Giroux, 1997), 101.

155 "absolutely loved him": Quoted in Nick Salvatore, *Singing in a Strange Land: C. L. Franklin: The Black Church and the Transformation of America* (New York: Little, Brown, 2005), 205.

155 "his uncanny ability": Quoted in ibid., 157, 209.

155 "old guy": Quoted in John D. Gartner, *In Search of Bill Clinton: A Psychological Biography* (New York: St. Martin's Press, 2008), 308.

155 Sheehy observes: Gail Sheehy, *Hillary's Choice* (New York: Ballantine Books, 2000), 99.

155 "he makes you feel": Quoted in Gartner, *In Search of Bill Clinton*, 304.

155 "crawl into your soul": Quoted in ibid., 99.

156 Many inamoratas have stayed close: See ibid., 44; Sheehy, *Hillary's Choice*, 186–188; and Joe Klein, *The Natural: The Misunderstood Presidency of Bill Clinton* (New York: Broadway Books, 2002), 115.

156 But he made the exploration: Dr. C. George Boeree, "Personality Theories: Carl Jung: 1875–1961," webspace.ship.edu/cgboer/jung.html (accessed May 29, 2009). See Sara Corbett, who asserts that "Carl Jung founded the field of analytical psychology," in "The Holy Grail of the Unconscious," *New York Times Magazine*, September 16, 2009.

156 "a great lover": Quoted in Ronald Hayman, *A Life of Jung* (New York: W. W. Norton, 1999), 147.

156 In therapy, patients projected: C. G. Jung, *The Psychology of Transference* (Bollingen Series, vol. 16), trans. R. F. C. Hull (Princeton, NJ: Princeton University Press, 1966), 14.

156 Jung's manner invited intimacy: Irving Wallace et al., *The Intimate Sex Lives of Famous People* (New York: Delacorte Press, 1981), 428.

156 Through a revolutionary regimen: Person, *Dreams of Love*, 251.

157 "Jungfrauen": This is a comic pun on the German word for "virgin."

157 "What would you expect": Quoted in Deidre Bair, *Jung: A Biography* (New York: Little, Brown, 2003), 248.

157 "like the two poles": Boeree, "Personality Theories: Carl Jung."

157 "story of [his] life": "Jung on Freud," excerpt from *Memories, Dreams, Reflections* by C. G. Jung, ed. Aniela Jaffe, in *Atlantic Monthly*, November 1962, 47, 48.

157 coaches caution men: Paul Janka, ebook, "Attraction Formula—Step-by-Step Secrets to Meeting Women," 2008, 30; and Paul Janka, email, "Lose My Number," March 18, 2009.

CHAPTER 5: LOCKING IN LOVE

159   "Love consists almost": Honoré de Balzac, *The Physiology of Marriage: Petty Troubles of Married Life*, ed. J. Walker McSpadden (Philadelphia: Avil, 1901), 195.

160   "Give me ten minutes": Attributed, perhaps apocryphally, to Voltaire, en.wikiquote.org/wiki/Talk:Voltaire (accessed July 22, 2010).

160   "Women": Wilkie Collins, *The Woman in White* (New York: New American Library, 1985), 259.

161   Women have a larger communication center: See Louann Brizendine, *The Female Brain* (New York: Broadway Books, 2006), 36, 131.

161   emotional-linguistic parts: See ibid., 127–128, 38.

161   When women connect: Ibid., 37.

161   In poll after poll: Laurence Roy Stains and Stefan Bechtel, *What Women Want: What Every Man Needs to Know about Sex, Romance, Passion, and Pleasure* (New York: Ballantine, 2000), 149; Fiona M. Wilson, *Organizational Behaviour and Gender* (Hants, UK: Ashgate, 2003), 179; John Townsend, *What Women Want—What Men Want* (New York: Oxford University Press, 1998), 11–13; and Cindy M. Meston and David M. Buss, *Why Women Have Sex: Women Reveal the Truth about Their Sex Lives, from Adventure to Revenge (and Everything in Between)* (New York: St. Martin's Griffin, 2009), 134.

161   Silence is the number-one gripe: Stains and Bechtel, *What Women Want*, 149; and Deborah Tannen, *You Just Don't Understand: Women and Men in Conversation* (New York: Ballantine Books, 1990), 81.

161   Studies suggest: For a sample, see Deborah Tannen, "Sex, Lies, and Conversation; Why Is It So Hard for Men and Women to Talk to Each Other?" *Washington Post*, June 24, 1990, www9.georgetown.edu/faculty/tannend/sexlies.htm (accessed November 19, 2011); and Lorraine Ali and Lisa Miller, "The Secret Lives of Wives," *Newsweek*, July 12, 2004. See especially John Gottman, *Why Marriages Succeed or Fail . . . And How You Can Make Yours Last* (New York: Fireside Books/Simon & Schuster, 1994), where he predicts with 91 percent accuracy who will get divorced based on problematic communication.

161   Sociolinguists attribute the problem: See Tannen's seminal *You Just Don't Understand*, 42, passim. Professor of developmental psychopathology Simon Baron-Cohen contends that the male brain is hardwired for tunnel vision—building systems and negotiating status via conversation—not for empathy and intimacy. See the discussion in Sabine Durant, "Are Men Boring?" *Intelligent Life*, June 11, 2008, www.moreintelligentlife.com/story/are-men-boring.

161   "to be in a relationship": Maureen Dowd, *Are Men Necessary? When Sexes Collide* (New York: Berkley Books/Penguin, 2006), 47.

161 In and out of bed: Lionel Shriver, *The Post-Birthday World* (New York: HarperPerennial, 2007), 6.

162 In Elin Hilderbrand's: Elin Hilderbrand, *A Summer Affair* (New York: Little, Brown, 2008), 233, 177, 234.

162 The Irish Ogma: Gertrude Jobes, *Dictionary of Mythology, Folklore and Symbols* (New York: Scarecrow Press, 1961), 1,200, 761.

162 "clever speech": Quoted in Euripides, *The Bacchae, Classical Myths*, trans. Herbert M. Howe, ed. Barry B. Powell (Englewood, NJ: Prentice Hall, 1995), 263.

162 "sweet and persuasive": Quoted in Adam, "Gorgias + Derrida = Seductive Communication," New Media and the Futures of Writing, March 21, 2011, http://fow.jamesjbrownjr.net/2011/03/gorgias-derrida-seductive -communication//.

162 "Verbal courtship": Geoffrey Miller, *The Mating Mind: How Sexual Choice Shaped the Evolution of Human Nature* (New York: Anchor Books/Random House, 2001), 351.

162 Language itself: Norman O. Brown, *Life against Death: The Psychoanalytic Meaning of History* (Middletown, CT: Wesleyan University Press, 1959), 69. See Dr. C. George Boeree, "The Origins of Language," http://webspace .ship.edu/cgboer/langorigins.html (accessed May 15, 2012); Jean Baudrillard, who analyzes the "primitive seduction of language," in *Seduction*, trans. Brian Singer (New York: St. Martin's Press, 1990), 54; and Timothy Taylor, *The Prehistory of Sex* (New York: Bantam, 1996), 48–49.

163 mark of "mating intelligence": Glenn Geher, Geoffrey Miller, and Jeremy Murphy, "Mating Intelligence: Toward an Evolutionarily Informed Construct," in Glenn Geher and Geoffrey Miller, eds., *Mating Intelligence: Sex, Relationships, and the Mind's Reproductive System* (New York: Psychology Press, Taylor and Frances Group, 2007), 20.

163 "Women are conquered": Ovid, *The Art of Love*, trans. Rolfe Humphries (Bloomington: Indiana University Press, 1957), 119.

163 European, Arabic, and Indian love literature: Andreas Capellanus, *The Art of Courtly Love*, trans. John Jay Parry (New York: Columbia University Press, 1960), 195. The Arabian *Perfumed Garden* places a large emphasis on verbal courtship, maintaining that "a woman can always be made rampant by words of love." Shaykh Nefzawi, *The Perfumed Garden*, trans. Sir Richard F. Burton (New York: Putnam, 1964), 85. The Indian *Kāma Sūtra* is still more emphatic on the need for men to master seductive speech: a man who even suffers "a certain contempt, has success with women if he is a good talker." *The Complete Kāma Sūtra*, trans. Alain Daniélou (Rochester, VT: Park Street Press, 1994), 56.

163 "no man": William Shakespeare, *Two Gentlemen of Verona*, in *Complete Works*, ed. Stanley Wells and Gary Taylor (Oxford: Clarendon Press/ Oxford University Press, 1988), act 3, scene 1, lines 104–105.

163   From Balzac to the present: Honoré de Balzac stated that "love consist[ed] almost always in conversation." Balzac, *Physiology of Marriage*, 69. Over time, dozens of guides in the "language of love" came to men's aid, instructing them in "eloquence," or as the Italians called it, *bel parlare* (fascinating speech). Quoted in Nina Epton, *Love and the French* (New York: World, 1959), 123, 122. See, for example, André Maurois, "The Art of Loving," in *The Art of Living*, trans. James Whitall (New York: Harper and Row, 1959); Roland Barthes, *A Lover's Discourse*, trans. Richard Howard (New York: Hill and Wang/Farrar, Straus and Giroux, 1978), 73, 167, 192; Theodore Zeldin, *Conversation* (London: Harvill Press, 1998), 32; John Chandos, *A Guide to Seduction* (London: Frederick Muller, 1957); and Erich Fromm, *The Art of Loving* (New York: Harper and Row, 1956), 102–104.

163   "Speech is the true realm": Quoted in Sarah Wright, *Tales of Seduction: The Figure of Don Juan in Spanish Culture* (London: Tauris Academic Studies, 2007), 3.

163   "zone of magic": Quoted in Vera John-Steiner, *Creative Collaboration* (New York: Oxford University Press, 2000), 191.

164   "There was speech": William Shakespeare, *A Winter's Tale*, in *Complete Works*, ed. Wells and Taylor, act 5, scene 2, lines 13–14.

165   Women read this: For women as superior body readers, see Helen Fisher, *The First Sex: The Natural Talents of Women and How They Are Changing the World* (New York: Ballantine Books, 1999), 91–94.

165   Harvard University study: Study reported in Barbara Pease and Allan Pease, *The Definitive Book of Body Language* (New York: Bantam Books, 2004), 13.

165   woman is on high alert: When women perceive incongruence between words and movements, they rely on the nonverbal message and discard the verbal, write the Peases in ibid., 23.

165   "Sexual Olympian" Corcoran: T. Coraghessan Boyle, *The Inner Circle* (New York: Penguin Books, 2004), 197.

165   say body-language students: Barbara and Allan Pease claim that men make fewer than a third of the facial expressions that women make, and that if a man reflects a woman's expression during conversation, she will describe him as "caring, intelligent, interesting, and attractive." Pease and Pease, *Definitive Book of Body Language*, 255. For further discussion, see 254, 175, 185.

165   inclined, asymmetric posture: For the significance of the "forward lean" in courtship, see David Givens, *Love Signals: A Practical Field Guide to the Body Language of Courtship* (New York: St. Martin's Press, 2005), 61–62, 139–140; and Gordon R. Wainright, *Body Language* (Lincolnwood, IL: NTC/Contemporary, 1999), 125. For the significance of a head duck or bow, see Pease and Pease, *Definitive Book of Body Language*, 230–232; for foot-pointing, ibid., 210 and 284; and for open positions, ibid., 289.

166   Expressive hands: Women, claims anthropologist David Givens, find men's hands and wrists especially sexy. Given, *Love Signals*, 5, 6.

166   Actress Madame Simone: Philippe Julian, *D'Annunzio*, trans. Stephen Hardman (New York: Viking, 1971), 125.

166   woman tends to stand closer: Pease and Pease, *Definitive Book of Body Language*, 196. Some tests indicate that a light brush of the fingers can carry surprisingly erotic weight, tripling one's chances of success. The authors cite many tests here. See 104–106.

166   "almost carnal": Joe Klein, *The Natural: The Misunderstood Presidency of Bill Clinton* (New York: Broadway Books, 2002), 40.

166   Along with his way with words: Lydia Flem, *Casanova: The Man Who Really Loved Women*, trans. Catherine Temerson (New York: Farrar, Straus and Giroux, 1997), 84.

166   "can be hypnotized": *Complete Kāma Sūtra*, 211.

166   female weakness for vocal seduction: Kate Botting and Douglas Botting, *Sex Appeal: The Art and Science of Sexual Attraction* (New York: St. Martin's Press, 1996), 113.

166   Even as babies: Fisher, *First Sex*, 60; and Brizendine, *Female Brain*, 14.

166   Vocally expressive themselves: The fact that deep, soft voices appeal to women has been well documented. See, for example, Sindya N. Bhanoo, "A Magnet for Women? Try a Deep Male Voice," *New York Times*, September 19, 2011; and for the "sing-songy" reference, see "Attuned to Feelings," *Scientific American Mind*, July/August 2010, 9.

167   "A voice": Quoted in Elaine Scolino, *La Seduction: How the French Play the Game of Life* (New York: Times Books/Henry Holt, 2011), 49.

167   Hermes, the Greek: Norman O. Brown, *Hermes the Thief: The Evolution of a Myth* (Madison: University of Wisconsin Press, 1947), 15.

167   Vronsky accosts Anna: Leo Tolstoy, *Anna Karenina*, trans. Richard Pevear and Larissa Volokhonsky (New York: Penguin Books, 2000), 76.

167   ladykiller Lorcan: Marian Keyes, *Last Chance Saloon* (New York: Avon Books/HarperCollins, 1999), 20.

167   "bedroom voices": Carly Phillips, *The Playboy* (New York: Grand Central, 2003), 18, 20.

167   "his voice and accent": Quoted in Derek Parker, *Byron and His World* (New York: Studio Books/Viking, 1968), 103.

167   "an instrument of music": Quoted in Nicholas Murray, *Aldous Huxley: A Biography* (New York: Thomas Dunne Books/St. Martin's Press, 2002), 6, 7.

167   "an extraordinary range": Quoted in John Edward Hasse, *Beyond Category: The Life and Genius of Duke Ellington* (New York: Da Capo Press, 1993), 347.

167   "You're a low-talker": Mika Brezinski, *Morning Joe*, MSNBC, September 23, 2011.

168 "[Love's] first task": Paul Tillich, *Love, Power, and Justice: Ontological Analysis and Ethical Applications* (New York: Oxford University Press, 1980), 84.

168 Nearly every relationship study: See, for example, Stains and Bechtel, *What Women Want*, 151–156; Helen Fisher, *Anatomy of Love: The Mysteries of Mating, Marriage, and Why We Stray* (New York: Fawcett Columbine, 1992), 27, 191; Townsend, *What Women Want—What Men Want*, 11; and Alon Gratch, *If Men Could Talk: Unlocking the Secret Language of Men* (New York: Little, Brown, 2001), 132.

168 "Love is listening": Ann Lamott, *Blue Shoe* (New York: Riverhead Books, 2002), 78.

168 a way of saying, "I love you": Quoted in Stains and Bechtel, *What Women Want*, 158.

168 If so, legions of women: Deborah Tannen, *That's Not What I Meant: How Conversational Style Makes or Breaks Relationships* (New York: Ballantine Books, 1986), 133; and Tannen, "Sex, Lies, and Conversation."

168 "It's very important": Quoted in Ali and Miller, "Secret Life of Wives," 53.

168 traditional guides underscore: See, for example, Andreas Capellanus, *The Art of Courtly Love*, trans. John Jay Parry (New York: Columbia University Press, 1960), 61; and *Complete Kāma Sūtra*, 246.

168 claim several philosophers: See José Ortega y Gasset, *On Love*, trans. Toby Talbot (New York: New American Library, 1952), 47; Robert C. Solomon, *About Love: Reinventing Romance for Our Times* (New York: Touchstone/Simon & Schuster, 1989), 334; Eric Fromm, *The Art of Listening* (New York: Continuum, 1994), 193; and Theodor Reik, *Psychology of Sex Relations* (New York: Farrar and Rinehart, 1945), 210.

168 Fromm Compares: Fromm, *Art of Listening*, 197.

169 hint of insincerity: See Pease and Pease, *Definitive Book of Body Language*, 178, 254.

169 must supply spirited feedback: See Deborah Tannen, *That's Not What I Meant*, 137; and Barbara Pease and Allan Pease, *Why Men Don't Listen and Women Can't Read Maps: How We're Different and What to Do about It* (New York: Three Rivers Press, 2001), 87–95.

169 "beyond ordinary perception": "Lord Shiva," Hindu Deities, Kashmiri Overseas Association, www.koausa.org/Gods/God9.html (accessed September 29, 2011).

169 The Greeks considered him: See "Pan & Satyrs," Carnaval.com, www.carnaval.com./pan (accessed September 29, 2011). For Pan as the deity of theatrical criticism, see Alfred Wagner, *Das historische Drama der Griechen Münster* (1878), cited in "Pan (God)," Wikipedia, http://en.wikipedia.org/wiki/Pan(god) (accessed September 29, 2011).

169 "So," Griffin says: Laura Dave, *The First Husband* (New York: Viking, 2011), 32.

169 "slow, silent interest": JoAnn Ross, *One Summer* (New York: Signet/ Penguin Group, 2011), 147.

170 "Thank you for listening": Ibid., 199.

170 "King of Conversation": Quoted in David Lawday, *Napoleon's Master: A Life of Prince Talleyrand* (New York: Thomas Dunne Books/St. Martin's Press, 2006), 36.

170 "fascinated by": Quoted in ibid., 35.

170 "in the presence": Quoted in John C. Maxwell, "Charismatic Leadership," *Mindful Network*, May 22, 2008, www.themeetupprofessor.com/readings .html.

170 "is the mother": Benjamin Disraeli, *Wit and Wisdom of Benjamin Disraeli, Earl of Beaconsfield* (London: Longmans, Green, 1881), 320.

170 "was a great listener": Quoted in Jeffrey Meyers, *Gary Cooper, American Hero* (New York: William Morrow, 1998), 38.

170 "It's like he": Quoted in Suzanne Finstad, *Warren Beatty: A Private Man* (New York: Three Rivers Press, 2005), 293.

171 "Soft is the roucoulade": Ovid, *Art of Love*, 144.

171 Unlike men, say linguists: See Tannen, *You Just Don't Understand*, 42 and 100; and Brizendine, *Female Brain*, 21.

171 They're really singing: J. B. Priestley, *Talking: An Essay* (New York: Harper and Brothers, 1925), 5.

171 they derive a neural payoff: See Brizendine, *Female Brain*, 36.

171 In contrast to a man's: Natalie Angier, *Woman: An Intimate Geography* (New York: Anchor/Random House, 1999), 77 and see 78–79. Also see Brizendine's section on "Sex, Stress, and the Female Brain," in *Female Brain*, 72–82. Anxiety, she writes, is four times more common in women, 132.

172 "If you're not relaxed": Brizendine, *Female Brain*, 78.

172 Few sexual sedatives: Fisher, *First Sex*, 198.

172 "voluptuous sleepiness": Barthes, *Lover's Discourse*, 104.

172 Baby talk between lovers: See Jena Pincott, "What Can Singles Learn from Baby Talk?" *Psychology Today*, March 28, 2011.

172 "My Lumps": Quoted in Sam Kashner and Nancy Schoenberger, *Furious Love: Elizabeth Taylor and Richard Burton and the Marriage of the Century* (New York: HarperCollins, 2010), 360, 312, 301.

172 "Relaxing the Girl": *Complete Kāma Sūtra*, 229.

172 *Kāma Sūtra* devoted: ibid., 229–238.

172 Ovid directed men: Ovid, *Art of Love*, 144.

172 Others counseled: Ortega y Gasset, *On Love*, 71, 73; Jean Baudrillard, *Seduction*, 75; Reik, *Psychology of Sex Relations*, 207; and Joseph O'Connor and John Seymour, *Introducing Neuro-Linguistic Programming* (London: Element/HarperCollins, 1990).

172 Dumuzi uses this device: Diane Wolkstein and Samuel Noah Kramer, eds.,

Inanna, Queen of Heaven and Earth: Her Stories and Hymns from Sumer (New York: Harper and Row, 1983), 40.

172 Mann's "god of love": Frederick A. Lubich, "The Confessions of Felix Krull, Confidence Man," in Ritchie Robertson, ed., *The Cambridge Companion to Thomas Mann* (Cambridge, UK: Cambridge University Press, 2002), 208; and Thomas Mann, *Confessions of Felix Krull Confidence Man*, trans. Denver Lindlay (New York: Vintage Books/Random House, 1969), 20.

172 "softly": Mann, *Confessions*, 203.

173 "but I mean": A. S. Byatt, *The Children's Book* (New York: Alfred A. Knopf, 2009), 249.

173 "Aw baby girl": Sandra Jackson-Opoku, *Hot Johnny (And the Women Who Loved Him)* (New York: Ballantine Books, 2001), 7.

173 "Enchanter": André Maurois, *Chateaubriand: Poet, Statesman, Lover*, trans. Vera Frasier (New York: Harper and Brothers, 1938), 131.

173 "rich and sympathetic": Francis Gribble, *Chateaubriand and His Court of Women* (New York: Charles Scribner's, 1909), 78.

173 "*suddenly* and *forever*": Ortega y Gasset, *On Love*, 26.

173 "disagreeable": Ibid., 29.

173 "hump-back": Quoted in ibid., 244.

174 "came to him": Maurois, *Chateaubriand*, 67.

174 "He was prepared": Quoted in ibid., 115–116.

174 "the loveliest woman": Ibid., 101.

174 "How have you": Quoted in *Memoirs and Correspondence of Madame Récamier*, trans. Isaphene M. Luyster (1867; Honolulu: University Press of the Pacific, 2002), 135.

175 "the single most effective tactic": Meston and Buss, *Why Women Have Sex*, 21.

175 If a woman laughs: See study of speed dating in Robert R. Provine, *Laughter: A Scientific Investigation* (New York: Penguin, 2000), 34; and Meston and Buss, *Why Women Have Sex*, 21.

175 "Make her laugh": Capellanus, *Art of Courtly Love*, 37; and Baldesar Castiglione, *The Book of the Courtier*, trans. Charles S. Singleton (Garden City, NY: Anchor Books/Doubleday, 1959), 167.

175 Stanford University study of humor: Eleanor Hayes, "The Science of Humour: Allan Reiss," *Science in School*, December 6, 2010, www.science inschool.org/2010/issue17/allenreiss.

175 witty conversationalist exhibits: See "Fast Forces of Attraction," *Psychology Today*, December 28, 2007.

175 "What is more seductive": Baudrillard, *Seduction*, 102.

175 "linguistic zaniness": This is Steven Pinker's catchall phrase for all forms used by "entertainer language mavens." Pinker, *The Language Instinct* (New York: HarperPerennial/HarperCollins, 1994), 386.

176 Comedy, by nature: Susanne K. Langer, *Feeling and Form: A Theory of Art* (New York: Scribner's, 1953), 84, 85.

176   "tricked the mind": Brown, *Hermes the Thief*, 14.

176   They're members of: See Stephen Nachmanovitch, *Free Play: Improvisation in Life and Art* (New York: Jeremy P. Tarcher/Putnam, 1990), 46–47.

176   "limp with laughter": Derek Walcott, *The Joker of Seville and O Babylon: Two Plays* (London: Jonathan Cape, 1928), 30.

176   "merriment": George Eliot, *Middlemarch*, ed. Bert G. Hornback (1873; New York: W. W. Norton, 2000), 131.

176   "hero should make": Leslie Wainger, *Writing a Romance Novel for Dummies* (New York: Wiley, 2004), 66.

177   "one of nature's": Mary Jo Putney, *The Rake* (New York: Topaz/Penguin Group, 1998), 135.

177   "how intimate": Ibid.

177   He ribs her: Susan Elizabeth Phillips, *Fancy Pants* (New York: Pocket Books/Simon & Schuster, 1989), 185, 186.

177   "It is because the slave": Giacomo Casanova, *History of My Life*, trans. Willard R. Trask (Baltimore: Johns Hopkins University Press, 1966), vol. 1, chap. 2, p. 62.

177   Seated alone once: Ibid., 100.

178   "crazy for him": Quoted in Donald Sturrock, *Storyteller: The Authorized Biography of Roald Dahl* (New York: Simon & Schuster, 2010), 182, 230.

178   "like a parish magazine": Roald Dahl, "The Visitor," in *The Best of Roald Dahl*, intro. James Cameron (New York: Vintage Books, 1978), 287.

178   "more wittily": Ibid., 289.

179   "chucklefucker": Mandy Stadtmiller, "New York Comedians Score with Ha-Ha Hottie Groupies," *New York Post*, January 12, 2010.

179   "My weight": Quoted in Fiona MacCrae, "Who Gets the Girl? Funny Men Have the Last Laugh . . . ," *Mail Online*, April 2, 2009, www.dailymail.co.uk/femail/article-1166610/who-gets-girl-funny-men-laugh-.html.

179   "Finding someone funny": Tad Safran and Molly Watson, "Tad & Molly: Do Women Prefer Rich or Funny Men?" *Times*, July 17, 2008.

180   female preference: Ewen Callaway, "Nerds Rejoice: Braininess Boosts Likelihood of Sex," ABC News, October 6, 2008, abcnews.go.com/Technology/story?id=595197&page=1#T5_vRYvgE.

180   "always a turn-on": Ceri Marsh and Kim Izzo, "A Fine Romance," *Globe and Mail*, February 9, 2002.

180   "ornamental brain" theory: Miller, *Mating Mind*, 386.

180   "All that information": Francine Prose, *Blue Angel* (New York: HarperCollins, 2006), 22.

180   "intellectual brilliance": Guy Sircello, "Beauty and Sex," in Alan Soble, ed., *The Philosophy of Sex* (Savage, MD: Rowan and Littlefield, 1991), 132.

180   "discourse[s] of desire": Lawrence D. Kritzman, "Roland Barthes: The Discourse of Desire and the Question of Gender," *MLN: Modern Language Notes* 103, no. 4 (French issue, September 1988), 848–864.

180   Ovid believed: Ovid, *Art of Love*, 133.

181   In one exemplum: *Complete Kāma Sūtra*, 200.

181   "destitute of mental vigor": Balzac, *Physiology of Marriage*, 104.

181   "the gods in Olympus": George du Maurier, *Trilby* (1894; New York: Penguin Books, 1994), 58.

181   "to insert his penis": Jonathan Franzen, "Breakup Stories," *New Yorker*, November 8, 2004.

181   "preeminent philosopher": "Peter Abelard," *Stanford Encyclopedia of Philosophy*, November 9, 2010, http://plato.stanford.edu/entries/abelard/.

182   "place in [his bed]": Quoted in James Burge, *Heloise and Abelard* (San Francisco: HarperSanFrancisco, 2003), 30.

182   "I feared," he: Quoted in ibid., 90.

182   "remained absolutely": M. T. Clanchy, *Abelard: A Medieval Life* (Oxford, UK: Blackwell, 1997), 5.

182   "greatest talent": Flem, *Casanova*, 84.

182   "most entertaining man": Derek Parker, *Casanova* (Gloucestershire, UK: Sutton, 2002), 36.

182   "Without words": Casanova, *History of My Life*, vol. 6, chap. 5, p. 106.

182   "beautiful faculty of talk": Henry James, "Ivan Turgenev," 1903, www.eldritch.press.org/list/hj2.htm (accessed May 15, 2012).

183   At a house party: Ivan Turgenev, *Rudin*, trans. Richard Freeborn (New York: Penguin Books, 1974), 52.

183   "possessed what is almost": Ibid., 63.

183   Their affair: V. S. Pritchett, *The Gentle Barbarian: The Work and Life of Turgenev* (New York: Ecco Press, 1977), 168.

183   "erotic in its urgency": William Deresiewicz, "Love on Campus," *American Scholar*, June 1, 2007.

183   "the quintessential ladies' man": Michel Serres, *Hermes: Literature, Science, Philosophy*, ed. Josué V. Harari and David F. Bell (Baltimore: Johns Hopkins University Press, 1982), 3.

183   "smart and ardent": Louis Menand, "Stand by Your Man," *New Yorker*, September 26, 2005.

183   "Seduction": Jean-Paul Sartre, *Being and Nothingness*, trans. Hazel E. Barnes (New York: Washington Square Press, 1984), 486.

183   "golden tongue": Quoted in Arthur M. Wilson, *Diderot* (New York: Oxford University Press, 1957), 39.

184   "a fresh and limpid river": Quoted in "Chattering Classes," *Economist*, December 23, 2006.

184   "loquacious [and] expansive": Leslie Gilbert Crocker, *The Embattled Philosopher: A Biography of Denis Diderot* (East Lansing: Michigan State College Press, 1954), 20.

184   "ravishingly beautiful": R. N. Furbank, *Diderot: A Critical Biography* (New York: Alfred A. Knopf, 1992), 17.

184 "were standing beside her": Quoted in Wilson, *Diderot*, 449.

184 "fruits of the mind": Deresiewicz, "Love on Campus."

184 "in love with him": Wilson, *Diderot*, 295.

184 "Diderot among the most": Ibid., 639.

185 "love's best weapon": Michel de Montaigne, "On Some Verses of Virgil," in *The Complete Essays of Montaigne*, trans. Donald M. Frame (Garden City, NY: Anchor Books/Doubleday, 1960), vol. 3, pp. 66, 67.

185 Cyrano de Bergerac: Edmond Rostand, *Cyrano de Bergerac*, trans. Lowell Bair (New York: Signet Classic, 2003,) act I, scene 4, line 39.

185 At last, fatally wounded: Ibid., act 3, scene 7, line 130.

185 "Lavish fine words": Ovid, *The Amores*, in Peter Green, ed., *The Erotic Poems* (New York: Penguin Books, 1982), book 2, p. 111.

185 One suggestion: See Jon Stallworthy, "Introduction" in Jon Stallworthy, ed., *The New Penguin Book of Love Poetry* (New York: Penguin Books, 2003), xxiv; and J. B. Broadbent, *Poetic Love* (London: Chatto and Windus, 1964).

185 "I know it's poetry": Quoted in Thomas H. Johnson, ed., *The Letters of Emily Dickinson* (Cambridge, MA: Belknap Press/Harvard University Press, 1958), letter 342 to Colonel T. W. Higginson, August 1870; and www.wisdom portal.com/Poems/DickinsonDefinitionPoetry.html (accessed October 28, 2010).

185 "parched tongue": Carl Yapp and Andrew Marvell quoted in "Love Poetry's 'Fevered Brow' Test," BBC News, February 9, 2010, http://news.bbc.co .uk/2/hi/uk_news/wales/mid_/8504616.stm.

185 "an exaltation": Stallworthy, "Introduction," xxiv.

185 "the universal sources": Mircea Eliade, *Shamanism: Archaic Techniques of Ecstasy* (Bollingen Series vol. 76), trans. Willard R. Trask (Princeton, NJ: Princeton University Press, 1964), 510; and Joseph Campbell, *The Masks of God: Primitive Mythology* (New York: Arkana/Penguin, 1969), 4.

186 Miller argues: See Miller, *Mating Mind*, 380.

186 One woman in a survey: See Stains and Bechtel, *What Women Want*, 147.

186 professor Richard Wiseman: "What Women Want: Top Ten Romantic Gestures," *Telegraph* (UK), July 15, 2009.

186 Women agree: See, for example, Barbara De Angelis, *What Women Want Men to Know: The Ultimate Book about Love, Sex, and Relationships for You—And the Man You Love* (New York: Hyperion, 2001), 305–306; Felicity Huffman and Patricia Wolff, *A Practical Handbook for the Boyfriend* (New York: Hyperion, 2007), 90; Lucy Sanna with Kathy Miller, *How to Romance the Woman You Love* (New York: Three Rivers Press, 1995), 93–109; and "Why Do Women Love Poems?" Yahoo! Answer, http://answers.yahoo .com/question/index?qid=20110728093928AAKJ9VW (accessed October 20, 2011).

186 "luscious love note": Eve Salinger, *Pleasing Your Woman: Complete Idiot's Guide* (New York: Alpha/Penguin Group, 2005), 35; and online female

forum, "Sex Tips for Geeks: How to Be Sexy," September 25, 2000, catb
.org/~esr/writings/sextips/sexy.html.

186   poets report twice as many: This is from a study by Dr. Daniel Nettle, lec-
turer in psychology at Newcastle University's School of Biology, reported
in the *Proceedings of the Royal Society*, November 29, 2005. See also "Creative Spark Fuels Active Sex Life," *HealthDay News*, November 30, 2005,
sexualhealth.e-healthsource.com/?p=news1&id=529379.

186   Women are more verbal: On language and emotionality, see Larry Cahill,
"His Brain, Her Brain," *Scientific American*, May 2005, 41, 46. That poetry
uses both sides of the brain, see Kenn Nesbitt, "Left Brain, Right Brain, and
the Power of Poetry," Kenn Nesbitt's Poetry4kids.com, October 11, 2011,
www.poetry4kids.com/modules.php?name=News&file=article&sid=249.

186   "spur a love bond": See Ilana Simons, "You Look Nasty in That Dress,"
Psychology Today, March 25, 2009.

186   "bewitchment of magical speech": Baudrillard, *Seduction*, 75. Observes *Science Daily*: "The effect [of poetry] on the brain is a bit like a magic trick; we
know what the trick means but not how it happened." It "surprises the brain."
"Reading Shakespeare Has Dramatic Effect on Human Brain," *Science Daily*,
December 16, 2006, www.sciencedaily.com/releases/2006/12/061218122613
.htm. T. S. Eliot wrote that a poem is like a burglar throwing meat to a dog
in the house, the better to enter the unconscious. T. S. Eliot, *The Use of
Poetry and the Use of Criticism: Studies in Relation to Criticism to Poetry in
England* (Charles Eliot Norton Lectures for 1932–33) (London: Faber and
Faber, 1939), 151.

186   "skill in composing": Paul Friedrich, *The Meaning of Aphrodite* (Chicago:
University of Chicago Press, 1978), 144.

187   "The first device": Ibn Hazm (994–1064), *The Ring of the Dove*, trans.
A. J. Arberry (London: Luzac Oriental, 1994), 65.

187   "quote a verse": Ibid., 65.

187   With courtly love: In Shakespeare's time "skill at rhyming was the indispensable accomplishment of a gallant." See E. S. Turner, *A History of Courting* (New York: E. P. Dutton, 1955), 54, 134.

187   "poet's talking": J. M. Synge, *The Playboy of the Western World*, in Ann Sad-
dlemyer, ed., *The Playboy of the Western World and Other Plays* (New York:
Oxford University Press, 1995), act 3, line 137.

187   In the movie: See two other examples in film: Elliott (Michael Caine), who
quotes E. E. Cummings's "somewhere I have never traveled, gladly beyond"
to seduce Lee in *Hannah and Her Sisters*, and Mr. Big, who wins back Carrie
with poetry emails in the movie version of *Sex and the City*.

187   "dancing cloud of words": Marge Piercy, *Small Changes* (New York: Fawcett Crest, 1972), 101.

187   "She had": Ibid., 463.

187   "music of the soul": Quoted in Danielle Hollister, "Top 20 Poetry Quo-

tations," http://ezinearticles.com/?Top-20-Poetry-Quotations&id=5061 (accessed February 17, 2012).

188   Or pen lyrics: Annabella Milbank, Byron's wife, first gained his attention through her poems. See Fiona MacCarthy, *Byron: Life and Legend* (New York: Farrar, Straus and Giroux, 2002), 172. And see the mutual poetic courtship of poets Robert Browning and Elizabeth Barrett Browning; and the relationship (probably platonic) between Restoration rake and poet John Wilmot, Second Earl of Rochester, and playwright/poet Aphra Behn, who called him the "great, the godlike Rochester." Quoted in Graham Greene, *Lord Rochester's Monkey* (New York: Penguin, 1974), 220.

188   Niccolò Martelli: Georgina Masson, *Courtesans of the Italian Renaissance* (New York: St. Martin's Press, 1975), 113.

188   modern poetic "lothario": Andrew Mullins and Patrick McDonagh, "A Poet's Life," *McGill News: Alumni Quarterly*, Winter 1997. Among Leonard Cohen's songs written for particular women are "So Long," "Marianne," "Suzanne," and "Sisters of Mercy."

188   "poetic love": Quoted in Michael Munn, *Richard Burton: Prince of Players* (New York: Herman Graf Books/Skyhorse, 2008), 74.

188   "I had a tried": Quoted in ibid., 74.

188   "lyricism of spirit": Kashner and Schoenberger, *Furious Love*, 102.

188   "wonderful poetry": Quoted in Munn, *Richard Burton*, 74.

188   "late into the night": Quoted in Kashner and Schoenberger, *Furious Love*, 121.

188   "the only man": Quoted in ibid., 122.

188   "death," and "liquor": Quoted in ibid., 383.

188   "marriage of the century": Book subtitle, ibid.

188   "Imagine having Richard Burton's": Quoted in ibid., 48, 391.

189   "tongue-enchanted": Quoted in Hugh and Mirabel Cecil, *Clever Hearts: Desmond and Molly MacCarthy: A Biography* (London: Victor Gollancz, 1991), 202.

189   "delectable Desmond": Quoted in ibid., 173, 180, 192.

189   "the most gifted": Quoted in ibid., 188.

189   "smallish genitals": Ibid., 239.

189   "the company of pretty women": Ibid., 173.

189   "dancing on a floor": Quoted in ibid., 180.

189   "bewildered people": Quoted in ibid., 273.

190   "inarticulate": David Denby, "Just the Sex," review of *Crazy, Stupid, Love* and *Friends with Benefits*, *New Yorker*, August 1, 2011.

190   "seven-minute seduction": Tom Wolfe, *I Am Charlotte Simmons* (New York: Farrar, Straus and Giroux, 2004), 195.

190   "like rival mesmerists": Robert Louis Stevenson, "Talk and Talkers," Literature Network, www.online-literature.com/stevenson/essays-of-stevenson/4/, 1 (accessed September 11, 2011).

190   "talkable man": Ibid., 3, 9.
190   "Talk to her first": *Sade*, direc. by Benoît Jacquot Alicéléo, Canal+ et al., 2000.

CHAPTER 6: TORCHING UP LOVE

191   "none of Medea's herbs": Ovid, *The Art of Love*, trans. Rolfe Humphries (Bloomington: Indiana University Press, 1957), 133.
192   They burn out: For the burnout studies, see Ayala Malach Pines, *Couple Burnout: Causes and Cures* (New York: Routledge, 1995), 112. They're responsible for 60 to 75 percent of split-ups as well. See Scott Haltzman, *The Secrets of Happily Married Men* (San Francisco: Jossey-Bass/Wiley, 2006), 1.

According to some theorists, such as Sarah Blaffer Hrdy and Natalie Angier, females are more prone to straying. See Natalie Angier, *Woman: An Intimate Geography* (New York: Anchor Books/Random House, 1999), 73–74; Sarah Blaffer Hrdy, *The Woman That Never Evolved* (Cambridge, MA: Harvard University Press, 1981); Mary Jane Sherfey, *The Nature and Evolution of Female Sexuality* (New York: Vintage Books/Random House, 1966), 136–140; and Barbara Ehrenreich, "The Real Truth about the Female Body," *Time*, March 8, 1999.
192   viewed their brains: For these studies, see Adoree Durayappah, "Brain Study Reveals Secrets of Staying Madly in Love," *Psychology Today*, February 3, 2011.
193   "frustratingly elusive": Quoted in Emily Sohn, "How Love Lasts," *Discovery News*, February 10, 2011, http://news.discovery.com/human/valentine's-day-love-first-sight-110210.html?print=true.
193   "bewitchment techniques": *The Complete Kāma Sūtra*, trans. Alain Daniélou (Rochester, VT: Park Street Press, 1994), 505.
193   "The art of love": Havelock Ellis, "The Art of Love," in *Studies in the Psychology of Sex* (New York: Random House, 1936), vol. 2, 561.
193   It requires dedication: Ibid., 544.
193   They're obligated, stress amorists: Helen Fisher, *Why We Love: The Nature and Chemistry of Romantic Love* (New York: Henry Holt, 2004), 112. See, for example, Ellis, "Art of Love," 530, 548–549; Bertrand Russell, *Marriage and Morals* (New York: Bantam, 1959), 93; Honoré de Balzac, *The Physiology of Marriage: Petty Troubles of Married Life*, ed. J. Walker McSpadden (Philadelphia: Avil, 1901), 58, passim; and Theodor Reik, *Psychology of Sex Relations* (New York: Farrar and Rinehart, 1945), 95.
194   "How much fun": Dr. Phil, *Relationship/Sex*, "Roles in Marriage," http://drphil.com/articles/arcticle/322 (accessed April 25, 2012).
195   Howard Markman, a psychologist: See University of Denver Department of Psychology entry on Dr. Markman's PREP (Prevention and Relationship Enhancement Program) at www.du.edu/psychology/people/markman.htm (accessed February 21, 2012).

195 flair for gaiety: Simon Blackburn, *Lust* (New York: Oxford University Press, 2004), 81; and Ellis, "Prostitution," in *Studies in the Psychology of Sex*, vol. 2, 222.

195 "Perfect Man": Erica Jong, "The Perfect Man," in *What Do Women Want?* (New York: Jeremy P. Tarcher/Penguin, 2007), 171.

195 In studies, women report: See B. J. Gallagher, "America's Working Women: Stress, Health and Wellbeing," *Huffington Post*, March 8, 2011, www .huffingtonpost.com/bj-gallagher/international-women's-day_b_831811 .html. Stress as a key source of sexual disinterest can be found in Esther Perel, *Mating in Captivity: Unlocking Erotic Intelligence* (New York: Harper, 2007), 88.

196 Kipnis speculates: Laura Kipnis, *Against Love: A Polemic* (New York: Vintage Books/Random House, 2003), 135.

196 Joyous revelry provides: See Kay Redfield Jamison, *Exuberance: The Passion for Life* (New York: Random House, 2004), 147.

196 Playfulness: Geoffrey Miller, *The Mating Mind: How Sexual Choice Shaped the Evolution of Human Nature* (New York: Doubleday, 2000), 408, passim; and Jamison, *Exuberance*, 53–63.

196 Prehistoric men were prone: See Hara Estroff Marano, "The Power of Play," *Psychology Today*, July/August 1999, 39.

196 "affinitive display": Jamison, *Exuberance*, 144.

196 Sex gods were "liberators": Walter F. Otto, *Dionysus: Myth and Cult*, trans. Robert B. Palmer (Bloomington: Indiana University Press, 1965), 97.

196 Dionysus: Ibid., 113, 65.

196 Scholars of eros: Ovid, *Art of Love*, 135.

196 "magnificent banquets": Baldesar Castiglione, *The Book of the Courtier*, trans. Charles S. Singleton (Garden City, NY: Anchor Books, 1959), 320.

197 Modern thinkers agree: Ethel S. Person, *Dreams of Love and Fateful Encounters: The Power of Romantic Passion* (New York: Penguin Books, 1988), 336; and Adam Phillips, *Monogamy* (New York: Vintage Books, 1996), 43.

197 "Why cry out": Gustave Flaubert, *Madame Bovary*, ed. Margaret Cohen (New York: W. W. Norton, 2005), 117.

197 "You were good": Carol Edgarian, *Three Stages of Amazement* (New York: Scribner, 2011), 233.

197 He appears in jeans: Emily March, *Hummingbird Lake* (New York: Ballantine Books, 2011), 307.

198 "gigantic adolescent": Ernle Bradford, *Cleopatra* (New York: Harcourt Brace Jovanovich, 1972), 151.

198 His looks helped: Stacy Schiff, *Cleopatra: A Life* (New York: Back Bay Books/Little, Brown, 2010), 129.

199 That evening, they say: Ibid., 340.

199 "crazy about him": Quoted in Graham Lord, *Niv: The Authorized Biography of David Niven* (London: Orion, 2003), 1.

199 "total fun": Quoted in ibid., 248, 90.

199 "as if it was God": Quoted in ibid., 157.

199 "joyful one": Otto, *Dionysus*, 103.

200 "seemed to have": Zachary Leader, *The Life of Kingsley Amis* (London: Jonathan Cape, 2006), 421.

200 "yellow and snarly": Ibid., 166.

200 "made everyone laugh": Quoted in ibid., 228.

200 "the most powerful seduction": Quoted in ibid., 420, 421.

200 "his weaknesses": Clive James, "Kingsley without the Women," review of Zachary Leader, *The Life of Kingsley Amis*, *Times Literary Supplement*, February 2, 2007, www.clivejames.com/kingsleyamis.

200 "melancholy marriages": Pamela Haag, *Marriage Confidential: The Post-Romantic Age of Workhorse Wives, Royal Children, Undersexed Spouses, and Rebel Couples Who Are Rewriting the Rules* (New York: Harper/HarperCollins, 2011), 4.

200 "drab and joyless": Barbara Ehrenreich, *Dancing in the Streets: A History of Collective Joy* (New York: Holt Paperback/Metropolitan Books/Henry Holt, 2006), 249.

202 unexpected, say scientists: See Eric Nagourney, "Vital Signs," *New York Times*, April 17, 2001; and Helen Fisher interview, Judy Dutton, "Love Explained," chemistry.com, www.chemistry.com/Help/Advice/Love Explained (accessed December 14, 2011).

202 New and exciting things: Helen Fisher, *Why We Love: The Nature and Chemistry of Romantic Love* (New York: Owl Books/Henry Holt, 2004), 206; and Michael R. Liebowitz, *The Chemistry of Love* (Boston: Little, Brown, 1983), 131.

202 unforeseen can make: A person's desire for novelty, however, is quite variable. See Natalie Angier, "Variant Gene Tied to a Love of New Thrills," *New York Times*, January 2, 1996; and Anil K. Malhorta and David Goldman, "The Dopamine D4 Receptor Gene and Novelty Seeking," *American Journal of Psychiatry* 157, no. 11 (November 1, 2000).

202 Meston and David Buss found: Cindy M. Meston and David M. Buss, *Why Women Have Sex: Women Reveal the Truth about Their Sex Lives, from Adventure to Revenge (and Everything in Between)* (New York: St. Martin's Griffin, 2009), 152, 161–165.

202 "change for the sake": Quoted in Miller, *Mating Mind*, 411.

202 This prompted men: See ibid., 411–425.

202 "If one just knows": Søren Kierkegaard, *The Seducer's Diary*, ed. Howard Vincent Hong and Edna Hatlestad Hong (Princeton, NJ: Princeton University Press, 1997), 90.

202 "equivalent to love": Roland Barthes, *A Lover's Discourse*, trans. Richard Howard (New York: Hill and Wang/Farrar, Straus and Giroux, 1978), 199, 135.

203 "arrayed in all the graces": Honoré de Balzac, *The Physiology of Marriage:*

Petty Troubles of Married Life, ed. J. Walker McSpadden (Philadelphia: Avil, 1901), 64, 106.

203   "old boyfriend syndrome": Liebowitz, *Chemistry of Love*, 131.

203   amorist thinkers caution: André Maurois, "The Art of Loving," in *The Art of Living*, trans. James Whitall (New York: Harper and Row, 1959), 25. The tradition that women are changeable in their affections is a long one. See, for instance, William Shakespeare, *As You Like It*, act 3, scene 2; Robert Burton, *The Anatomy of Melancholy*, ed. Floyd Dell and Paul Jordan-Smith (1651; New York: Tudor 1927), 791; and Michel de Montaigne, "On Some Verses of Virgil," in *The Complete Essays of Montaigne*, trans. Donald M. Frame (Garden City, NY: Anchor Books/Doubleday, 1960), vol. 3, 109.

203   "mysterious and paradoxical": Otto, *Dionysus*, 65.

203   Norse fertility god: For more on Odin as a fertility deity, see Folke Ström, excerpt "Odin and the Dísir: Dísir, Norns, and Valkyrias—Fertility Cult and Sacred Kingship in the North," Odin and the dísir/The Old Norse Ritual of Initiation, http://mardallar.wordpress.com/odin-and-the-disir/ (accessed December 16, 2011).

203   "Pajama Playboy": Marisha Pessl, *Special Topics in Calamity Physics* (New York: Penguin Books, 2006), 101.

203   "Having a secret": Ibid., 82.

204   "unexpected or unknown": Lonnie Barbach, *Erotic Interludes: Tales Told by Women* (New York: HarperPerennial/HarperCollins, 1986), 6.

204   "mysterious hero": Baroness Orczy, *The Scarlet Pimpernel* (New York: Signet/Penguin Group, 1974), 155.

204   "How could anyone": Lisa Kleypas, *Mine Till Midnight* (New York: St. Martin's Paperbacks, 2007), 311.

204   "three quarters curiosity": Quoted in Reik, *Psychology of Sex Relations*, 165.

204   While "ever-available" to: Lydia Flem, *Casanova: The Man Who Loved Women*, trans. Catherine Temerson (New York: Farrar, Straus and Giroux, 1997), 68.

204   "*Coups de théâtre* are": Quoted in ibid., 16. In Willard Trask's translation this reads, "I want to enjoy the beauty of your surprise. Bolts from the blue are my passion." Giacomo Casanova, *History of My Life*, trans. Willard R. Trask (Baltimore: Johns Hopkins University Press, 1966), vol. 8, chap. 8, p. 200.

204   "fantastic renown": H. Noel Williams, *The Fascinating duc de Richelieu: Louis Francois Armand du Plessis (1696–1788)* (New York: Charles Scribner's, 1910), vii.

205   "dashing little duke": Title of a nineteenth-century British musical about Richelieu, cited in ibid., viii, note 1.

205   One day the duke returned: Quotes from Cliff Howe, "Duc de Richelieu," in *Lovers and Libertines* (New York: Ace Books, 1958), 12.

205   Each day she repaired: Andrew C. P. Haggard, *The Regent of the Roués* (1905; London: Elibron Classics, 2006), 165.

206   She was the mystery lady: On Klimt's preliminary sketch for "The Kiss," he wrote "Emil[i]e." See Susanna Partsch, *Gustav Klimt: Painter of Women* (New York: Prestel, 1994), 87.

206   Remembering her obsession with Klimt: See account of this in ibid., 73.

206   "not a particularly": Nina Kränsel, *Gustav Klimt* (New York: Prestel, 2007), 48.

207   "a refined and delicate form": Colin Scott quoted in Havelock Ellis, "Love and Pain," in *Studies in the Psychology of Sex* (New York: Random House, 1933), vol. 1, 67.

208   Aggression, fear, and power: See Reik, *Psychology of Sex Relations*, 96, 94–95, where he says that without challenge and negative emotions to overcome there can be no passionate love. Many scholars have weighed in on this controversial issue. See especially Elaine Walster, "Passionate Love," in Bernard I. Murstein, ed., *Theories of Attraction and Love* (New York: Springer, 1971), 87; Robert J. Stoller, *Sexual Excitement: Dynamics of Erotic Life* (New York: Simon & Schuster, 1979), 6, passim; and Konrad Lorenz's theories discussed in Irenaus Eibl-Eibesfeldt, *Love and Hate: The Natural History of Behavior Patterns* (New York: Schocken Books, 1978), 126, 127, 128.

208   "aversion to conflict": Louann Brizendine, *The Female Brain* (New York: Broadway Books, 2006), 130.

208   women seem strangely partial: See a new study from Massachusetts General Hospital in which researchers found from videotapes of 156 couples that "women tend to want to engage around conflict" because the intensity of their partners' response showed they were invested in the relationship. Psychologist Shiri Cohen, quoted in "Health & Science," *Week*, March 23, 2012, 21.

208   "Conflict": Quoted in Jane Shilling, review of *Let's Call the Whole Thing Off: Love Quarrels from Anton Chekov to ZZ Packer*, ed. Kasia Boddy, Ali Smith, and Sarah Wood, *Telegraph* (London), February 14, 2009.

208   confirmed this proclivity: See Meston and Buss, *Why Women Have Sex*, 245, 241, 249–250. For the aphrodisiac of jealousy, see ibid., 100–106; and David M. Buss, *The Dangerous Passion: Why Jealousy Is Necessary as Love and Sex* (New York: Free Press, 2000), 217.

208   Women, they also found: See Meston and Buss, *Why Women Have Sex*, 134; and Fisher, *Why We Love*, 195.

208   "feel like an intellectual equal": Quoted in Michael Munn, *Richard Burton: Prince of Players* (New York: Herman Graf Books/Skyhorse, 2008), 151.

208   "are a sign of strength": Robert C. Solomon, *About Love: Reinventing Romance for Our Times* (New York: Touchstone Books/Simon & Schuster, 1988), 312.

208   periodic bacchanals: This is a paraphrase from psychiatrist Ethel Person that the release of a quarrel often feels like "a periodic Bacchanalia or Carnival," and "allows passion to continue." Person, *Dreams of Love*, 65.

208 Like opposition, jealousy: Jealousy is a classic aphrodisiac. Theorist René Girard believes the "triangle" is the prime mover of desire, arguing with Buss and others that jealousy both sparks and rekindles sexual passion in relationships. See Montaigne, "On Some Verses of Virgil," 72; René Girard, *A Theatre of Envy: William Shakespeare* (New York: Oxford University Press, 1991); and Buss, *Dangerous Passion.*

209 Great lovers read: Havelock Ellis, "Love and Pain," in *Studies in the Psychology of Sex*, vol. 1, 185.

209 "the right amount": Phillips, *Monogamy*, 84, 28.

209 "Queen of the Palace": Diane Wolkstein and Samuel Noah Kramer, eds., *Inanna, Queen of Heaven and Earth: Her Stories and Hymns from Sumer* (New York: Harper and Row, 1983), 34.

210 "Look how aroused": Sylvia Day, *The Stranger I Married* (New York: Brava/Kensington, 2007), 44.

210 "I have just enough": Ibid., 70.

210 "sad and deeply distressed": Derek Watson, *Liszt* (New York: Schirmer Books/Macmillan, 1989), 70.

210 "prodigy of love": Tom Antongini, *D'Annunzio* (Boston: Little, Brown, 1938), 59.

210 "Even if all the women": Quoted in Philippe Jullian, *D'Annunzio*, trans. Stephen Hardman (New York: Viking, 1971), 92.

210 After this "game": Quoted in ibid., 121.

210 "I hate D'Annunzio:" Quoted in ibid., 112.

211 "gentle man": Linda H. Davis, *Charles Addams: A Cartoonist's Life* (New York: Random House, 2006), 127.

211 Barbara Skelton: Ibid., 168.

211 "It was impossible": Quoted in ibid., 306.

211 "all the ladies": Ibid., 312.

211 "God's own mad lover": Irving Wallace et al., *The Intimate Sex Lives of Famous People* (New York: Delacourt Press, 1981), 156.

211 "his fate": Quoted in James L. Haley, *Wolf: The Lives of Jack London* (New York: Basic Books, 2010), 163.

212 His adventures began: Clarice Stasz, *Jack London's Women* (Amherst: University of Massachusetts Press, 2001), 62.

212 When star-struck candidates: Haley, *Wolf*, 190.

212 first time she beat him: Clarice Stasz, *American Dreamers: Charmian and Jack London* (Lincoln, NE: iUniverse, 1988), 101.

212 He hailed her: Ibid., 166.

212 "Dearest love woman": Quoted in Haley, *Wolf*, 279.

213 "When self-improvement stops": Solomon, *About Love*, 156.

213 forever-interesting type: Christiane Bird, "Almost Homeless," in Harriet Brown, ed., *Mr. Wrong: Real Life Stories about the Men We Used to Love* (New York: Ballantine Books, 2007), 71.

213 "Someone who will enlarge": Ibid., 77.

213 "There is no end": Roberto Mangabeira Unger, *Passion: An Essay on Personality* (New York: Free Press/Macmillan, 1984), 95.

213 "like a mine": Quoted in Helen Handley, ed., *The Lover's Quotation Book: A Literary Companion* (New York: Barnes and Noble, 2000), 67.

214 growth-fueled, polysided mate: See Miller, *Mating Mind*, 151–157; David Schnarch, *Passionate Marriage: Love, Sex, and Intimacy in Emotionally Committed Relationships* (New York: Owl Books/Henry Holt, 1997), 73; and Solomon, *About Love*, 341.

214 No wonder women in surveys: See John Marshall Townsend, *What Women Want—What Men Want: Why the Sexes Still See Love and Commitment So Differently* (New York: Oxford University Press, 1998), 150–151; Laurence Roy Stains and Stefan Bechtel, *What Women Want: What Every Man Needs to Know about Sex, Romance, Passion, and Pleasure* (New York: Ballantine Books, 2000), 507; and Dalma Heyn, *The Erotic Silence of the American Wife* (New York: Plume/Penguin Books, 1997), 146–147, 258, passim.

214 "I mean my husband": Ibid., 147.

214 Love at its best: See Rollo May, *Love and Will* (New York: W. W. Norton, 1969), 81.

214 Maslow distinguished: Abraham H. Maslow, *Toward a Psychology of Being* (New York: Van Nostrand Reinhold, 1968), 43, 55.

214 "always in a state": Jong, "Perfect Man," 179.

215 Rather than a misogynistic rake: Jan Kjærstad, *The Seducer*, trans. Barbara J. Haveland (London: Arcadia Books, 2003), 4.

215 As all twenty-three women: Ibid., 144, 99.

215 His inspiration is reciprocal: Ibid., 148.

215 "No simple Lothario": Tim O'Brien, *Tomcat in Love* (New York: Broadway Books, 1998), 173, 181.

215 "attractive beyond words": Ibid., 27.

215 "Omega Man": This use of "Omega Man" as the all-powerful, sexy individualist comes from Stephanie Burkhart, "Genre Tuesday—Types of Romantic Men," Romance under the Moonlight (blog), April 13, 2010, http://sgcardin.blogspot.com/2010/04/genre-tuesday-types-of-romantic-å-men.html. There are, however, variant meanings for "omega male," but here it is used as meaning number two in the *Urban Dictionary*: "The highest possible status a man can achieve. Eats alpha men for breakfast. When an Omega male is born its game over. The end." www.urbandictionary.com/define.pht?term=omega%20male (accessed February 27, 2012).

215 "You make me": Laura Kinsale, *Flowers from the Storm* (New York: Avon Books/HarperCollins, 1992), 526.

216 "Big-bellied": Robert M. Myers, *Reluctant Expatriate: The Life of Harold Frederic* (Westport, CT: Greenwood Press, 1995), 86; and Bridget Bennett,

The Damnation of Harold Frederic (Syracuse, NY: Syracuse University Press, 1997), 39.

217   While drifting apart: Quoted in Myers, *Reluctant Expatriate*, 87.

217   "a man of power": Quoted in ibid., 87.

217   He was not, however: Ibid., 44.

217   "sex at every pore": Quoted in ibid., 93.

218   "the frankest man": Scott Donaldson, "Introduction," in Stanton Garner and Scott Donaldson, eds., *The Damnation of Theron Ware: Or the Illumination* (New York: Penguin, 1986), ix.

218   "great amorist": From H. G. Wells, *Experiment in Autobiography*, 1934, cited in Prose & Poetry—H.G. Wells, firstworldwar.com, www.firstworldwar .com/poetsandprose/wells.htm (accessed May 16, 2012).

218   "sexual system": Quoted in Michael Sherborne, *H. G. Wells: Another Kind of Life* (London: Peter Owen, 2010), 170.

218   He sought "lover-shadows": See H. G. Wells, *H. G. Wells in Love: Postscript to an Experiment in Autobiography*, ed. G. P. Wells (London: Faber and Faber, 2008), 51–57.

219   "seeing Nureyev dance": Quoted in Sherborne, *H. G. Wells*, 261.

219   Beside him was always: Ibid., 298.

219   Wells thought: See Wells, *H. G. Wells in Love*, 53.

219   "To be equal to his": Quoted in Sherborne, *H. G. Wells*, 256.

220   "about giving you": *The Wedding Date*, direct. Clare Kilner, Gold Circle Films, 26 Films and Visionview Production, 2005.

CHAPTER 7: THE GREAT SEDUCER NOW

221   "I say to you": William Makepeace Thackeray, *Sketches and Travels*, in *Miscellanies* (1847; London: Wildside Press, 2009), vol. 3, 111.

221   "If men knew": Quoted in Peter Haining, ed., *The Essential Seducer* (London: Robert Hale, 1994), 54.

223   none on the dating scene: Maryanne Fisher, "Romance Is Dead: Reflections on Today's Dating Scene," *Psychology Today*, June 2, 2010. Also see Anahad O'Connor, "Has Romance Gone? Was It the Drug?" *New York Times*, May 4, 2004.

223   "The love experience": Feona Attwood, "Sexed Up: Theorizing the Sexualization of Culture," *Communication and Computing Research Centre Papers*, Sheffield Hallam University, 2006, 13, http://digitalcommons.shu.ac.uk/ ccrc_papers/22 (accessed September 11, 2011).

223   Rather than grand amours: Stephen Holden, "Trailblazers, but Selling a Romantic Kind of Love," *New York Times*, May 13, 2008.

224   "Sexual boredom": Quoted in Laura Kipnis, *Against Love: A Polemic* (New York: Vintage/Random House, 2003), 191.

224   Love is "liquid": See Zygmunt Bauman, *Liquid Love: On the Frailty of Human Bonds* (Malden, MA: Polity Press, 2003).

224   "dissatisfaction with": Hal Arkowitz and Scott O. Lilienfield, "Sex in Bits and Bytes," *Scientific American Mind*, July/August 2010, 64.

224   Desire has insidiously: Jonathan Franzen, "Anti-Climax: No Sex Please, We're Readers," *New Yorker*, April 21, 1997.

224   "a sexual malaise": Camille Paglia, "No Sex Please, We're Middle Class," *New York Times*, June 26, 2010.

224   Nothing is sexy: See Erica Jong, "Is Sex Passe?" *New York Times*, July 9, 2011.

224   note cultural commentators: See Maureen Dowd, "What a Girl Wants . . . ," *New York Times*, May 24, 2000; Maureen Dowd, "Liberties; Pretty Mean Women," *New York Times*, August 1, 1999; and Maureen Dowd, *Are Men Necessary? When the Sexes Collide* (New York: Berkley Books, 2005), 178, passim. See, for example, Pamela Haag, *Marriage Confidential: The Post-Romantic Age of Workhorse Wives, Royal Children, Undersexed Spouses and Rebel Couples Who Are Rewriting the Rules* (New York: Harper/Harper-Collins, 2011); and Alessandra Stanley, "Say, Darling, Is It Frigid in Here?" *New York Times*, August 19, 2007.

225   unprecedented cultural shift: See Hanna Rosin, "The End of Men," *Atlantic*, July/August 2010; and "Female Power," *Economist*, January 2, 2010.

225   Feeling increasingly demoralized: See Joe Macfarlane, "Men Aged 18 to 30 on Viagra to Keep Up with Sex and the City Generation," *Mail Online*, June 14, 2008, www.dailymail.co.uk/health/article-1026523/men-aged-18-30-viagra-Sex-And-The.

225   "The men of my generation": Quoted in Allison Glock, "The Man Show," Review of Charlie LeDuff, *The True and Twisted Mind of the American Man*, *New York Times*, February 11, 2007.

225   recent retrosexist outbreak: For the Yale incident, see "Title IX Complaint Press Release," *Yale Herald*, March 31, 2011.

225   "sexual politics are going backward": Anthony Lane, "Big Men," Review of *This Means War* and *Bullhead*, *New Yorker*, February 27, 2012.

226   The biggest surprise: Laurence Roy Stains and Stefan Bechtel, *What Women Want: What Every Man Needs to Know about Sex, Romance, Passion, and Pleasure* (New York: Ballantine Books, 2000), 15.

226   For every misogynistic Tucker Max: Jeffrey Zaslow, "Girl Power as Boy Bashing: Evaluating the Latest Twist in the War of the Sexes," *Wall Street Journal*, April 21, 2005.

226   Two scholarly books: See Paul Nathanson and Katherine K. Young, *The Teaching of Contempt for Men in Popular Culture* (Montreal: McGill-Queens University Press, 2003); and Paul Nathanson and Katherine K. Young, *Legalizing Misandry: From Public Shame to Systematic Discrimination against Men* (Montreal: McGill-Queens University Press, 2007).

226   "What is that": See Bashing Men Jokes, November 8, 1997, http://ifag.wap
      .org/sex/bashingmenjokes.html (accessed November 20, 2011).

226   Two-thirds of women: Kim I. Hartman, "Study: Two-Thirds of Married
      Women Opt for Anything but Sex," *Digital Journal*, May 21, 2010, www
      .digitaljournal.com/print/article/292307. See Jessica Bennett, "The Pur-
      suit of Sexual Happiness," *Newsweek*, September 28, 2009; and Rohi Caryn
      Rabin, "Condom Use Is Highest for Young, Study Finds," *New York Times*,
      October 4, 2010.

226   "Women's sex lives": Quoted in Duff Wilson, "Push Market Pill Stirs
      Debate on Sexual Desire," *New York Times*, June 16, 2010.

227   several 2009 studies: For the seminal studies, see Betsey Stevenson and Jus-
      tin Wolfers, "The Paradox of Declining Female Happiness," *American Eco-
      nomic Journal: Economic Policy, American Economic Association*, no. 2 (August
      2009), 190–225; and Maria Shriver and the Center for American Progress,
      "The Shriver Report: A Woman's Nation Changes Everything," ed. Heather
      Boushey and Ann O'Leary, Center for American Progress, October 2009.

227   trend caused in part: Lisa Solod Warren, "Who Is Kidding Whom? The
      Shriver Report on Women," *Huffington Post*, October 22, 2009, www.huffing
      tonpost.com/lisa-solod-warren/who-is-kidding-whom-the-s_b_330060
      .html.

227   Spouses and boyfriends: Warren, "Who Is Kidding Whom?"

227   Women's infidelity is rising: A conservative estimate is 40 to 50 percent,
      and pollsters say it's on the upswing, rapidly gaining on, perhaps surpass-
      ing, the number of male dalliances. See cover story, Lorrain Ali and Lisa
      Miller, "The Secret Lives of Wives," *Newsweek*, July 12, 2004. Also see Jag-
      preet Kaur, "The Anatomy of Extramarital Affairs, Part II," from *Consumer
      Electronics*, November 27, 2007, available at http://articles.maxabout.com/
      marriage-divorce/the-anatomy-of-extramarital-affairs-part-ii/article-6411,
      which notes the dramatic rise in the number of female extramarital affairs,
      equating them with women's entry into the workplace.

227   "Women," said one: Mike Torchia quoted in Ali and Miller, "Secret Lives of
      Wives."

227   Straus and others document: Jillian Straus, *Unhooked Generation* (New York:
      Hyperion, 2006), 36–39, passim; and Laura Sessions Stepp, *Unhooked: How
      Young Women Pursue Sex, Delay Love and Lose at Both* (New York: River-
      head/Penguin Group, 2007), 251, passim.

227   Women with options: Monique Honaman, "I Just Wish He Would Have an
      Affair," *Huffington Post*, March 8, 2012, www.huffingtonpost.com/monique
      -honaman/i-just-wish-he-would-have_b_129799.html. See, too, Stepp,
      Unhooked, 37, where she found that settled companionship "didn't rank very
      high on the desire scale" with young women; and Justin Wolfers, "How
      Marriage Survives," *New York Times*, October 12, 2010.

227   2012 survey of romantic values: "Harlequin's 2012 Romance Report Findings

Indicate Romance + Technology = #ITSCOMPLICATED," *PRNewswire*, February 9, 2012, www.prnewswire.com/news-releases/harlequins-2012 -romance-report-findings-indicate-romance-technology-itscomplicated -13900.html.

228 "Too needy": Ibid.

228 The brighter the woman: "Money Ain't a Thing," *Psychology Today*, July/ August 2008; and see Ginia Bellafante, "A Romance Novelist's Heroines Prefer Lover over Money," *New York Times*, August 23, 2006. For the University of Louisville study, see Michael R. Cunningham, *New York Times*, September 23, 2007.

228 "female gaze": See discussions of the "female gaze" in romance novels by scholars Catherine Asaro and Kay Mussell in Linda Ledford-Miller, "Gender and Genre Bending: The Futuristic Detective Fiction of J. D. Robb," *Reconstruction: Studies in Contemporary Culture* 11, no. 3 (2011), http:// recon struction.eserver.irg/113/Ledford-Miller_Linda.shtml (accessed December 11, 2011).

228 Women notice beautiful men: See Paul Hollander, *Extravagant Expectations: New Ways to Find Romantic Love in America* (Chicago: Ivan R. Dee, 2011), 7; and Cindy M. Meston and David M. Buss, *Why Women Have Sex: Women Reveal the Truth about Their Sex Lives, from Adventure to Revenge (and Everything in Between)* (New York: St. Martin's Griffin, 2009), 12–16.

228 *Psychology Today* feature: Jill Neimark, "The Beefcaking of America," *Psychology Today*, November 1, 1994.

228 "it's really to do": Quoted in Matt Rudd, "Ripped: Man's Cosmetic Pursuit of Perfection," *Sunday Times* (London), October 23, 2011, 12, 11–13. Barbara Thau reports that the number of cosmetic procedures among men rose 2 percent in 2010 from 2009. That's 1.1 million procedures, with the ten fastest-growing ones being surgical. Thau, "Plastic Surgery Procedures Rise . . . and Men Are Fueling the Trend," DailyFinance, March 23, 2011, www.daily finance.com/2011/03/23/plastic-surgery-procedures-rise-and-men-are -fueling-the-tren/.

228 Pertschuk discovered: Cited in Neimark, "Beefcaking of America."

229 studied the "orgasm gap": Shelby Martin, "Stanford Sociology Professor Details Gender 'Orgasm Gap,'" *Stanford Daily*, November 6, 2007, http:// archive.stanforddaily.com/?p=1025749. See, too, Laura Kipnis, *The Female Thing: Dirt, Sex, Envy, Vulnerability* (New York: Pantheon Books, 2006), 57. Gynecologist Monica Peacocke told me that the problem is two parts: women don't know their own anatomy well enough, and "men are lazy."

229 "inner vixen is coming out": Gail Konop Baker, "Do Women Now Want Sex More Than Men?" *Huffington Post*, October 25, 2011, www.huffingtonpost .com/gail-konop-baker/women-want-sex-more-than-men_b_977416.html.

229 "women want": Norman Rush, *Mortals* (New York: Vintage, 2003), 213.

229   their 2011 investigation: Ogi Ogs and Sai Gaddam, *A Billion Wicked Thoughts: What the World's Largest Experiment Reveals about Human Desire* (New York: Dutton/Penguin, 2011), 109.

229   same finding: See Stepp, *Unhooked*, 14, 57, 126–137.

229   Weary of putting the make: E. L. James, *Fifty Shades of Grey* (Waxahachie, TX: Writer's Coffeeshop, 2011), 52.

229   sexual psychologist Marta Meana: Cited in Daniel Bergner, "What Do Women Want?" *New York Times Magazine*, January 25, 2009.

229   "Strike one": *A Lot Like Love*, direc. Nigel Cole, Walt Disney Studios, 2005.

230   Seventy-five percent of women: "Harlequin's 2012 Romance Report."

230   "the most unexpected": Hollander, *Extravagant Expectations*, 191.

230   "macho": "Quotes about Men," *QuotationsBook.com*, Google, 2011, 7.

230   swing toward "M-ness": Marian Salzman, Ira Matathia, and Ann O'Reilly, *The Future of Men* (New York: Palgrave/Macmillan, 2005), 213.

230   Such "M" heroes: Abby Zidle, "From Bodice-Ripper to Baby-Sitter: The New Hero in Mass-Market Romance," in Anne K. Kaler and Rosemary E. Johnson-Kurek, eds., *Romantic Conventions* (Bowling Green, OH: Bowling Green University Press, 1999), 28. See "Gender-Bending," *Economist*, October 25, 2008, 97; Lois Rogers, "Feminine Face Is Key to a Woman's Heart," *Sunday Times* (London), December 8, 2002; and Ayala Malach Pines, *Falling in Love: Why We Choose the Lovers We Choose* (New York: Routledge, 1999), 114–115.

230   "worthy sparring partner": Stepp, *Unhooked*, 61.

230   Female medical students: John Marshall Townsend, *What Women Want— What Men Want: Why the Sexes Still See Love and Commitment So Differently* (New York: Oxford University Press, 1998), 150.

231   In personals and polls: Hollander, *Extravagant Expectations*, 156, 190; and for conversation, see chap. 13 of Stains and Bechtel, *What Women Want*, 148–171.

231   "Renaissance characters abound": Hollander, *Extravagant Expectations*, 111.

231   "grow at the same rate": Townsend, *What Women Want*, 151.

231   "growing type of man": Salzman et al., *Future of Men*, 207.

232   major female grievance: See "Harlequin's 2012 Romance Report."

232   "Falling in love": José Ortega y Gasset, *On Love: Aspects of a Single Theme*, trans. Toby Talbot (New York: New American Library, 1957), 44.

232   Every romance hero: Rosemary E. Johnson-Kurek, "Leading Us into Temptation: The Language of Sex and the Power of Love," in Kaler and Johnson-Kurek, eds., *Romantic Conventions*, 130.

232   Attention is the food of love: See Meston and Buss, *Why Women Have Sex*, 201; and James V. Cordova, "Attention Is the Most Basic Form of Love," *Psychology Today*, May 6, 2011.

232   "The snap of the ladies' man": Molly Peacock, email, February 28, 2012.

232   "In our post-feminist age": Glenda Cooper, "May the Worst Man Win: A

New Study Has Proved beyond Doubt That Women Love Cads and Bounders. Of Course They Do, Says Glenda Cooper," *Daily Telegraph* (UK), September 28, 2007.

232   "God's gift": Marina Warner, "Valmont—or the Marquise Unmasked," in Jonathan Miller, ed., *Don Giovanni: Myths of Seduction and Betrayal* (New York: Schocken Books, 1990), 99, 98.

232   "I've met a few": "Sienna's Casanova Hopes," *Mail Online*, September 3, 2005, www.dailymail.co.uk/tvshowbiz/article-361175/Sienna's-Casanova-hopes.html.

233   "If Liszt": Quoted in Nigel Cawthorne, "Lisztomania," in *Sex Lives of the Great Composers* (London: Prion, 2004), 93.

233   "Some men are so delightful": Jane Smiley, "Why Do We Marry?" *Utne Reader*, September/October 2000, 51.

233   Recent research: Tara Parker-Pope reports that "the people with the highest expectations for marriage usually end up with the highest quality marriages." Tara Parker-Pope, "Can Eye-Rolling Ruin a Marriage? Researchers Study Divorce Risk," *Wall Street Journal*, August 6, 2002.

233   "never succeed": Ortega y Gasset, *On Love*, 28.

233   "an orang-outang": Honoré de Balzac, *The Physiology of Marriage: Petty Troubles of Married Life*, ed. J. Walker McSpadden (Philadelphia: Avil, 1901), 70.

235   new research: See Helen Fisher on the study "Single in America," in "The Forgotten Sex," match.com, blog.match.com/2011/04/the-forgotten-sex-men (accessed February 5, 2012); and Nancy Kalish, "Are Men Romantic?" *Psychology Today*, June 1, 2009. For results of a Wake Forest study, see Robin Simon, "Nonmarital Romantic Relationships and Mental Health in Early Adulthood: Does the Association Differ for Women and Men?" *Journal of Health and Social Behaviors* 51 (June 2010), 168–182.

235   Eighty-four percent of men: Fisher, "Forgotten Sex."

235   "is the mainspring": Garrison Keillor, "The Heart of the Matter," *New York Times*, op-ed, February 14, 1989.

235   "we need a new myth": Michael Vincent Miller, *Intimate Terrorism: The Crisis of Love in an Age of Disillusion* (New York: W. W. Norton, 1995), 224. See also Rollo May, *The Cry for Myth* (New York: W. W. Norton, 1991), 15–21, passim.

235   "Sexual behavior": Willard Gaylin, *The Male Ego* (New York: Viking, 1992), 117.

235   "hazardous business": Stephen A. Mitchell, *Can Love Last? The Fate of Romance over Time* (New York: W. W. Norton, 2002), 139.

236   "strong warrior energy": Robert Bly, *Iron John: A Book about Men* (New York: Addison-Wesley, 1990), 151.

236   "Archetypes": Robert Moore and Douglas Gillette, *King, Warrior, Magi-*

cian, Lover: Rediscovering the Archetypes of the Mature Masculine (New York: Harper One/HarperCollins, 1991), 127.

236 "from seed to flower": Bly, *Iron John*, 133.

236 Her teaching: Madeleine M. Henry, *Prisoner of History: Aspasia of Miletus and Her Biographical Tradition* (New York: Oxford University Press, 1995), 47.

236 "It takes": Quoted in Edgar H. Cohen, *Mademoiselle Libertine: A Portrait of Ninon de Lenclos* (Boston: Houghton Mifflin, 1970), 92.

236 Schooled in "Special Techniques": Aldous Huxley, *Island* (New York: Perennial Classics/Harper and Row, 1962), 63, 126, 158.

237 Men are freed: Ibid., 241.

237 educators unanimously plead: See Glenn Geher and Geoffrey Miller, eds., *Mating Intelligence: Sex, Relationships, and the Mind's Reproductive System* (New York: Psychology Press/Taylor and Francis, 2007). See D. F. Jansen on the absence of sexual education in general: "Sex Training: The Neglected Fourth Dimension in Erotagogical Ideologies," *Growing Up Sexually: The Sexual Curriculum* 3 (October 2002), www.2.huberlin.de./sexology/ GESUND/ARCHIV/GUS/GUSVOLllCH7.HTM (accessed May 10, 2011). Also, on the gap in love education in America, see John Money, *Love and Love Sickness: The Science of Sex, Gender Difference, and Pair Bonding* (Baltimore: Johns Hopkins University Press, 1980), 63.

237 If men would spend: I paraphrased Robert Haas quoted in Theodoor Hendrik van de Velde, *Ideal Marriage: Its Physiology and Technique*, trans. Stella Browne (New York: Random House, 1926), 125.

237 majority of men: Perper's study discussed in Andrew Trees, *Decoding Love: Why It Takes Twelve Frogs to Find a Prince and Other Revelations from the Science of Attraction* (New York: Avery/Penguin, 2009), 175.

237 series of tests: ibid.

237 "Tell me what you want!": *Blue Valentine*, direc. Derek Cianfrance, Incentive Filmed Entertainment, 2010.

238 "The gentlemen": Stephen Jeffreys, *The Libertine* (London: Nick Hern Books, 1994), 3.

238 Favorites of women: Lucy Hughes-Hallet, *Heroes: A History of Hero Worship* (New York: Anchor Books/Random House, 2004), 9; and Ruth Karrass, *Sexuality in Medieval Europe: Doing unto Others* (New York: Routledge, 2005), 129.

238 "foppish dreamers": Anthony Giddens, *The Transformation of Intimacy: Sexuality, Love and Eroticism in Modern Society* (Stanford, CA: Stanford University Press, 1992), 59.

238 "have generally been scorned": Irving Singer, *Sex: A Philosophic Primer* (New York: Rowman and Littlefield, 2001), 47.

238 How other men regard: "Jackman, Hugh: Someone Like You," *urban*

cinefile, December 13, 2011, www.urbancinefile.comau/home/view.asp ?ArticleID=5040.

238 Women love him: Ben Brantley, "Hugh Jackman Keeps His Pants On," *New York Times*, December 8, 2011.

238 "puddle[s] of desire": Film critic Carrie Rickey of the *Philadelphia Inquirer*, quoted in Glenn Whipp, "Ladies' Man," *Los Angeles Daily News*, January 1, 2002.

239 He looks and moves: Tim Struby, "Hugh Jackman: Hollywood's Baddest Good Guy," *Men's Fitness*, October 2011.

239 During his preparations: "Jackman, Hugh."

239 Etiquette, she writes: Professor Marlene Powell, email, January 29, 2011.

239 Japanese folktale: See story in Stephen Nachmanovitch, *Free Play: Improvisation in Life and Art* (New York: Jeremy P. Tarcher/Penguin Putnam, 1990), 2, 1–3.

239 Can we *teach*: *Sexy Beast*, direc. Jonathan Glazer, Recorded Picture Company, 2001.

240 "Erotic charisma": Powell, email, January 26, 2011.

240 recalls Joseph Campbell's hero's journey: See Joseph Campbell, *The Hero with a Thousand Faces* (Bollingen Series vol. 17) (1949; Princeton, NJ: Princeton University Press, 1972).

240 "psychological voltage": Quoted in Len Oakes, *Prophetic Charisma: The Psychology of Revolutionary Religious Personalities* (Syracuse, NY: Syracuse University Press, 1997), 26.

241 "ineffable specialness": Sara Wheeler, *Too Close to the Sun: The Life and Times of Denys Finch Hatton* (London: Jonathan Cape, 2006), 10.

241 "Just leave it alone": Roland Barthes, *A Lover's Discourse: Fragments*, trans. Richard Howard (New York: Hill and Wang/Farrar, Straus and Giroux, 1978), 137.

241 Batten explains: Mary Batten, *Sexual Strategies: How Females Choose Their Mates* (New York: Jeremy P. Tarcher/Putnam's, 1992), 97; and Miller, *Mating Mind*, 39–45.

241 "When women start": Quoted in William F. Allman, "The Mating Game," *U.S. News and World Report*, July 19, 1993.

242 "deliver the greatest rapture": Miller, *Mating Mind*, 156.

242 "almost indecent magnetism": Quoted in Paul Chutcow, *Depardieu: A Biography* (New York: Alfred A. Knopf, 1994), 251.

243 "joie de vivre": Quoted in ibid., 187.

243 "Gérard knows": Quoted in ibid., 87.

243 "lovable": Quoted in Glenn Collins, "The Mystery of Depardieu: A Gentle Heart in a Boxer's Body," *New York Times*, June 4, 1990.

243 Although so timid: Chutcow, *Depardieu*, 107.

244 Under an inspired teacher: Ibid., 130.

244 "whole new language": Ibid., 148.

244 "guided him": Ibid., 173.

244 "I always turned": Quoted in ibid., 173.

244 "He was all there": Quoted in ibid., 266.

244 "Eros the masterpiece": Quoted in Roy Porter, "Libertinism and Promiscuity," in Jonathan Miller, ed., *Don Giovanni: Myths of Seduction and Betrayal* (New York: Shocken Books, 1990), 8.

245 "The power to charm": Charles Darwin, *The Descent of Man*, ed. Michael T. Ghiselin (1871; New York: Dover, 2010), 172.

245 "the interesting man": Ortega y Gasset, *On Love*, 167–190.

245 "Don Juan to his wife": Van de Velde, *Ideal Marriage*, 10.

245 "the adulterer's art": Havelock Ellis, *Studies in the Psychology of Sex* (New York: Random House, 1936), vol. 2, 547.

246 "the culmination of life": Ortega y Gasset, *On Love*, 142.

246 "the supreme thing": Quoted in Havelock Ellis, "The Valuation of Sexual Love," in *Studies in the Psychology of Sex*, vol. 2, 141.

246 "sing with rapture": *Meet Joe Black*, direc. Martin Brest, City Light Films, Universal Pictures, 1998.

246 "Expect the lightning": Ibid.

246 "The seductive": Georges Bataille, *Eroticism: Death and Sensuality*, trans. Mary Dalwood (San Francisco: City Lights Books, 1986), 236.

246 "If you know": *What Women Want*, direc. Nancy Meyers, Paramount Pictures, 2000.

Text Credits

Illustration Credits

Giacomo Casanova (1725–1798) (engraving), Ismael Mengs (1688–1764) (after) Private Collection / Archives Charmet / The Bridgeman Art Library.

Lord Shiva Dancing on Apasmar. Courtesy of Exotic India at www.exoticindiaart. com.

Guido Reni, *Bacchus and Ariadne*, ca. 1619–1620 (oil on canvas), Gift of the Ahmanson Foundation, Digital Image at Museum Associates / LAMA. Courtesy of Los Angeles Museum of Art.

Bust of Alcibiades (ca. 450–404 BCE), Galleria degli Uffizi, Florence, Italy / The Bridgeman Art Library.

Louis François Armand de Vignerot du Plessis (1696–1788), Duke of Richelieu (oil on canvas), Louis M. Tocque (1696–1772) / Musée des Beaux-Arts, Tours, France / Giraudon / The Bridgeman Art Library.

Gabriele D'Annunzio (1863–1938) (b/w photo) / Private Collection / Ken Welsh / The Bridgeman Art Library.

Lord Byron, Thomas Phillips, National Portrait Gallery, London, Great Britain, Photo Snark / Art Resource, NY.

Photo shot on the Hollywood lot of RKO Pictures of Duke Ellington pursued by a group of women. Courtesy of Frank Driggs Collection of Duke Ellington Photographic Reference Prints, Archives Center, National Museum of American History, Smithsonian Institution.

Robert Louis Stevenson (b/w photo), English photographer (nineteenth century)/ Private Collection / Courtesy of Swann Auction Galleries / The Bridgeman Art Library.

Livanos & Rubirosa Slow Dance, photographer Express Newspapers, Hulton Archive, Getty Images.

Photo of Sam Cooke, photographer Michael Ochs, Michael Ochs Archives, Getty Images.

Former President Bill Clinton signing books at Books and Books, photographer Vallery Jean, Getty Images Entertainment, Getty Images.

Clemens Lothar Wenzel, Prince Metternich, 1815 (oil on canvas), Sir Thomas Lawrence (1769–1830) / The Royal Collection © 2011 Her Majesty Queen Elizabeth II / The Bridgeman Art Library.

Denis Diderot, 1767, Louis Michel van Loo (1707–1771), Louvre, Paris, France, photographer Erich Lessing/Art Resource, NY.

Aldous Huxley, photographer Edward Gooch, Hulton Archive, Getty Images.

Portrait of Sir Walter Raleigh, 1598 (oil on panel), William Segar (fl. 1585–d. 1633) (attributed to) / National Gallery of Ireland, Dublin, Ireland / The Bridgeman Art Library.

Johann-Baptist I. Lampi, *Portrait of Prince Grigory Potyomkim-Tavrichesky* (oil on canvas)/ The State Hermitage Museum, St. Petersburg. Photograph © The State Hermitage Museum/photo by Vladimir Terebenin, Leonard Kheifets, Yuri Molodkovets.

Portrait of Franz Liszt, 1811–1886, Hungarian Composer, Musée Carnavalet, Paris, Photo Alfredo Dagli Orti / The Art Archive at Art Resource, NY.

Portrait of François-René, viscount of Chateaubriand (1768–1848), Meditating in the Roman Ruins with a View of the Colosseum, Anne Louis Girodet de Roussy-Trioson, 1811 (oil on canvas), Photo Gérard Blot, Châteaux de Versailles et de Trianon, Versailles, France. Réunion des Musées Nationaux / Art Resource, NY.

Portrait of Carl Gustav Jung (1875–1961) (b/w photo), Swiss School (twentieth century), Archives Larousse, Paris, France / Giraudon / The Bridgeman Art Library.

Roald Dahl, (1916–1990), ca. 1970, photographer Paul Popper / Popperfoto / Contributor, Popperfoto Collection, Popperfoto/Getty Images.

Mick Jagger, 53rd Annual Grammy Awards Show, photographer Kevin Winter/ Staff, Getty Images Entertainment, Getty Images.

Warren Beatty on the set of *Splendor in the Grass*. Courtesy of Wesleyan University Cinema Archives.

Photo of Jack London in a bathing suit. This image is reproduced by permission of The Huntington Library, San Marino, California.

Francoise Dorleac and David Niven, photo Time Life Pictures / Contributor, Time & Life Pictures Collection, Time & Life Pictures/Getty Images.

Photo of Gérard Depardieu, Courtesy of Thomson Reuters.

Index